CUT
CORDS

of

*Heal Yourself and Others
with Energy Spirituality*

Attachment

ROSE
ROSETREE

 Women's Intuition Worldwide
STERLING

This book was manufactured in the U.S.A. 10 9 8 7 6 5 4 3 2 1

Cover: Melanie Matheson, Rolling Rhino Communications, Winnipeg, MB, www.rollingrhino.com. **Editors:** Catharine Rambeau, Mitch Weber

Publisher's Cataloging-In-Publication Data
(Prepared by The Donohue Group, Inc.)

Rosetree, Rose.
    Cut cords of attachment : heal yourself and others with energy spirituality / by Rose Rosetree.

    p. ; cm.

    Includes bibliographical references and index.

    ISBN-13: 978-0-9752538-2-3
    ISBN-10: 0-9752538-2-4

1. Energy—Therapeutic use. 2. Vital force—Therapeutic use. 3. Spiritual healing. 4. Mind and body. 5. Interpersonal relations. 6. Self-help techniques. I. Title.

RZ999 .R67 2007
615.8/51   2007932021

Website for this book: www.cutcordsofattachment.com
Author's website and blog: www.rose-rosetree.com

Dedication

To those who have been bruised by life
and those who feel called to heal:
Each release of a cord allows
a new start, an opening into peace.

As you are strengthened, help others.
Use the unique gifts of your soul
to awaken a deeper version of truth
with wisdom that you, distinctively, bring.

Cutting cords of attachment is sacred work
that already has changed many lives for the better.
Join with our group of spiritual healers.
Serve humanity as a transformer,
releasing the heart's hidden causes of suffering.
May we transmute pain into freedom.

Contents

An Online Supplement is available to
enrich your experience of this book.
Find it here:
www.cutcordsofattachment.com

Acknowledgments

At this time of writing, I can't acknowledge how much I owe to previous books about cutting cords of attachment. I'd love to praise their proven procedures and gush over the theory base. Only problem—to my knowledge, there hasn't been any such book.

And much as I'd love to acknowledge the prestigious graduate program where I got my degree in cord cutting, alas, no such program exists either. Actually, I hope this book can help one to become established, but it would be tad anachronistic (not to mention inaccurate) for me to brag about all I learned from it.

So how did I write this book? In the first chapter, I acknowledge the generous teachers who helped me develop the method now known as 12 Steps to Cut Cords of Attachment™ Yet most of my knowledge about cutting cords has come from the "teachers" who were my clients and students. Knowledge flows through service, so 20 years of experience have taken me through a succession of initiations into healing.

Quick yet profound, powerful and permanent: For me, these qualities are the essence of cutting cords of attachment. Often, I am amazed by the information within a cord. Gathering insights at depth when doing the 12 Steps brings experiences like awe and humility. I am grateful for all I have learned from the cords themselves, especially acknowledging how much they have taught me about being human.

Finally, I am grateful for the help of Divine Beings in this method for cutting cords of attachment. Their presence is essential for all forms of Energy Spirituality. No matter how disturbing the contents of a cord, a Divine Being will bring an underlying feeling of safety, even joy. Above all, I am grateful for the privilege of being present for this.

The Need for Skill

A **cord of attachment** is an energy structure between two people that causes patterns from the past to continue into the present. Cords distort thinking and feeling, moving people around like marionettes.

If you can't see these invisible strings, how much do they matter? Cords of attachment may be the most significant, treatable cause of problems in your life, keeping you stuck in old patterns. This is the first book to teach a comprehensive method for removing them.

Cutting a cord does not mean ending a relationship. It means releasing problems that repeat endlessly on the level of energy.

Considering a tough relationship in your life now, you might wonder, "Am I better off with him or without him?" To decide most wisely, first remove the energy patterns that pull and tug at you, throwing you out of balance.

At least you never need ask, "Am I better off with or without my cord of attachment?" The answer will always be "Yes." Removing a toxic cord of attachment can only improve any relationship.

Sometimes those new to this form of healing worry, "But am I ready to let him go?"

Let go of what? Don't confuse spiritual ties with cords of attachment. Relationships generate both.

Frankly, you'll never be ready to release **spiritual ties.** Why would you? These are beautiful energy exchanges between yourself and those you love. To picture spiritual ties, think ribbons of beautiful light, not puppet strings.

Spiritual ties shine with caring, compassion, wisdom and other heart-melting qualities. We couldn't remove spiritual ties even if we tried. Here at Earth School, all our spiritual learning is cumulative, including the evolutionary power of spiritual ties.

Cords of attachment are another story. Even for the sake of healing a present relationship, it would be wise to remove its cord of attachment. Cords contain patterns of energy that are annoying at best, highly disruptive at worst. The negative effects of a cord of attachment are ongoing and chronic, repeating 24/7 at the level of the subconscious mind.

These energy-based attachments keep old history alive, inwardly repeating events or energies that you would just as soon forget.

When you got up this morning, chances are that you didn't consciously choose to rehash all the painful incidents of your childhood, then relive every trauma from school and work and then, just for fun, remember every time anyone hurt your feelings significantly.

Plus, if you've had any kind of love life at all, surely it has included disappointments and break-ups. Perhaps there have been unpleasant surprises, betrayals, maybe even divorce.

Did you consciously think about all those past influences before you got out of bed? I sure hope not! Still, every one of these memories lives on—vividly—in cords of attachment.

Negative energy from your past is whooshing in and out of your aura right now, moving through cords of attachment. Expect this patterning to continue until the day you die... unless you can release the cords.

So you can see why I'm so excited to be able to teach you this skill. We'll be using the method called **12 Steps to Cut Cords of Attachment™**. You can use it for yourself and also, if you wish, to help others.

What makes this particular method so effective for healing at depth? It contains a set of easy-to-learn techniques that wake up your **Deeper Perception,** which means noticing things at the level of auras and angels, the very deepest human secrets. From birth, you have had a complete gift set for this kind of perception.

Picture using it, if you will, as learning to swim underwater with eyes wide open. Deeper Perception has a different quality from ordinary perception, yet feels completely natural and effortless once you learn how to use it.

Reading the human energy field in depth and detail, trusting your intuition, paying attention to what really is happening in the here and now—being able to do this is your birthright. Actually, you might also consider it a survival skill for the 21st century. All of us receive far too much information every day, complete with advertising and spin galore. How can you choose what really matters? Use Deeper Perception.

And what else works better with Deeper Perception? **Energy Spirituality.** This is my term for techniques that use direct awareness of the human energy field as a point of entry for holistic healing. Your success as a practitioner of Energy Spirituality is directly proportional to the clarity of your inner experience.

If you're new to Energy Spirituality, cutting cords of attachment is a fine place to begin. And speaking of preparation, any work you do that depends upon being perceptive has prepared you as well. *Emotional healers,* like psychotherapists, counselors and life coaches, are natural candidates for learning Energy Spirituality. So are practitioners of Energy Psychology.

What if, rather than specializing in emotions, you're already a *physical healer?* The 12 Steps to Cut Cords will add depth to your practice. So I extend a special welcome to every reader who already is a physician, chiropractor, Reiki healer, Healing Touch practitioner, massage therapist, physical therapist, or other health care provider. Doing yoga, Tai Chi and other forms of self-care can also qualify you as a physical healer, you know. All forms of Energy Medicine (including, and especially, Donna Eden's system of Energy Medicine) count as an excellent preparation for Energy Spirituality.

Finally, although you hardly need be a psychic or medium in order to cut cords of attachment (I'm neither), techniques in this book can help you to supplement any services you provide for clients as a *psychic-level healer.*

Whatever your professional training or belief system, all you really need bring to this work is an open mind and a willingness to open your heart. Plus, like the mainstream 12-step programs, the 12 Steps to Cut Cords of Attachment do require your being willing to connect to a Higher Power.

Otherwise, what you read here is very different from the original 12-step programs. For instance, you don't begin each cord-cutting with an announcement like, "I'm Bobby and I have a really bad cord to my Mom." Your opening statement will likely sound way more cheerful. At this point in our journey together, *my* opening statement goes like this:

"I feel so grateful to everyone who has prepared me to learn and teach this method."

HOW MY 12-STEP METHOD EVOLVED

The story began in 1985. A friend recommended that I go see a healer named Joanna Lester for "amazing" personal sessions that involved cutting cords of attachment. I wondered if this might be important for my spiritual quest. For 17 years, my life had centered around teaching Transcendental Meditation. While helping students, I did well enough. But my personal life was a mess. So I couldn't wait to find out if this cord-cutting stuff would help.

When Joanna opened the door to her house in Takoma Park, Maryland, I become more curious than ever. She was a slender, exotically beautiful woman with enormously kind dark eyes, an expressive voice, and a professional manner that immediately won my trust. Together, we entered a back room that she had fitted out nicely with a massage table. A sweet silence filled the atmosphere.

Thus we began the enormous task of upgrading my sanity by selecting one cord of attachment to cut. Joanna's work flowed like a graceful dance.

By the end, I felt dazed but happy. Joanna's insights were extraordinary, but aside from that I felt somehow different, helped beyond any healing method I had encountered before.

Later I would understand why. Her work belonged to the general category of Energy Spirituality, not psychological healing. At Step 10, I'll clarify this distinction. The important point for now is that, although both are important, these complementary types of healing are apples-and-oranges different from each other. Joanna's healing session had permanently changed my aura.

Back home, my usual skepticism returned. I thought, "Let's find out if all this happy talk actually makes any difference to my *life*."

Within a week, my life did change... significantly. So I scheduled many more sessions with Joanna, cutting a total of 14 cords. I overcame sexual addiction to a very unappreciative man. I released an eating disorder with a 10-year history. And I even made a start on loosening my slavish dependence upon the guru I had followed for most of my adult life, Maharishi Mahesh Yogi.

Nothing had ever helped me so much, not meditation, not psychotherapy, not crystal healing, not Reiki, nothing. Within six months, most of my significant cords of attachment were gone. Still, I nearly burst into tears at the end of one session, when Joanna told me she would soon move to Montana.

Numbly, I went home. Then I started thinking, and the very next day, I picked up my phone to make Joanna an uncharacteristically bold proposition:

"I've been watching how you do our sessions. I think that maybe I could do this kind of work."

Imagine—she didn't laugh. She listened.

And then Joanna did something unlike any spiritual authority figure I had ever known before. She offered to help me.

What a shock! Joanna cared more about helping people than protecting her turf. She sounded open and interested. Without making a big deal about it, she was introducing me to one of the great principles of New Age spirituality: Everyone has wisdom, not just some authority figure on high.

But at this point I knew nothing about New Age. I was used to the role of a spiritual ignoramus whose only hope was to diligently follow my guru's path. Now Joanna was treating me like a peer whose ideas deserved respectful consideration. I was flabbergasted, and all the more so when she added, "How about this? What if I come over to your apartment and you show me what you can do?"

"Show you what I can do?" I repeated lamely.

"Sure. You can try to cut a cord of attachment on me. Then I'll give you my honest opinion of your work. We'll find out if you really can do this thing."

We set a date. Immediately, my stage fright began. Of all the fears blazing around the back of my head like a miniature forest fire, the worst one involved clairvoyance. Joanna could easily see cords of attachment and everything else about auras. Not me.

In this respect, I was more like most people. I had an equally valuable but different gift set for Deeper Perception, something I'll be explaining at Step 3 in this book but didn't begin to understand in 1985.

At this point, I believed clairvoyants to be far superior to everyone else. So I figured my big audition would play out like The Emperor's New Clothes, where even a small child could spot the deluded fool—who in this case would be me.

When cutting my first cord of attachment, I would have been absolutely terrified if Joanna hadn't been such a sweet person. But she was, so I wasn't, and therefore the cord cutting actually went quite well. I enjoyed giving something back to the person whose work had helped me so much.

Afterwards Joanna praised what I had done. Deep down, I knew she was simply being honest, as she had promised to be. Despite my lack of clairvoyance, I had located the cord perfectly and done the whole job just fine.

I asked, "Do you think I could do this kind of work?"

Her answer was a resounding "Yes." Generously, she even said that she would refer clients to me.

So I was on my way. One session at a time, I begin cutting cords of attachment for friends and, later, paying clients. Within a year, I quit my day job and turned pro. Credentialed as a minister, I hung out my shingle, becoming a practitioner of what I would eventually call Energy Spirituality.

DEVELOPING MY 12-STEP METHOD

Over the years, I learned from experience. Being technique-oriented, I experimented with refining the basic skills I had learned from Joanna.

My next important resource became a group that teaches something called "Inner Sensitivity" (www.teachingoftheinner-Christ.com). Rev. Rich Bell and Rev. AlixSandra Parness taught me how to detect and remove various kinds of astral debris that can clutter up an aura. I also learned how easily I could connect directly with Divine Beings and yet remain myself.

Technically, this is called "**conscious channeling**," in contrast to the **trance channeling** during which people connect with spirits of astral beings and sometimes are taken over by them, speaking in a different voice and, personally, being disconnected from the experience. (These days, my preferred term for conscious channeling is "co-creating with spiritual Source.")

Back in 1986, I was finishing my second course in Inner Sensitivity when my teacher, Rev. Sandi, pulled me aside.

"You're really good at this," she said. "Please start to teach it. You don't need to take the official ministerial training. People need this knowledge. Consider yourself a Lay Minister, effective right now."

She then, of course, proceeded to knock me over with a feather— or could have.

But Sandi was quite correct that, thanks to her superb teaching, I had learned to consciously connect with Divine Beings. In years to come, I would write book after book by co-creating with one Ascended Master or another.

Other inspiring teachers who come my way were Tantra Maat (www.metapoints.com) and Bill Bauman (www.billbaumann.net). Inspired by their support, I refined my skill at developing The 12 Steps to Cut Cords of Attachment.

By 2001, I had cut so many cords of attachment that I could do it over the phone just as easily as in person, so 95 percent of my sessions became phoners. Next, Japan's seminar company, VOICE, began to sponsor me, starting in 2003. I discovered that, with the help of a good interpreter, cord cutting could be done in any language.

Clients and healers from different parts of the world began asking me to teach them so they could do this kind of work themselves. For a spiritual teacher, there can be no sweeter call to action. In 2004, I started training students in my 12 Steps. Since then, several have turned pro, making me feel like a delighted grandparent.

This book was written as a teaching tool for those who don't have the chance to study with me personally. *Cut Cords of Attachment* is for do-it-yourselfers aiming to cut their own cords, as well as for healing professionals who wish to learn a new skill set.

I feel confident that this book will give you all you need to know about this leading-edge technology. You will learn exactly the same method I use.

Eventually, if you wish, you can use this method to do professional-level paid work as a practitioner of Energy Spirituality. Or you can cut cords as a volunteer. Perhaps you may always prefer to cut only your own cords of attachment. Are these great possibilities or what? Now, let me give you a clearer picture of what, exactly, is involved in cutting cords of attachment.

THE PROMISE

You meet John at work. Charming! Smart, too. He makes such a great first impression, by the end of the day you're thinking, "That John could definitely be friend material."

All it takes is one quick thought: "I'm interested." Instantly, the two of you forge a spiritual tie, all sweetness and light, just wonderful for teaching you both about *unconditional* love.

But something else is installed, as well. Faster than you could say "Abracadabra," you and John have been connected by an energy structure about *conditional* love. It becomes as real as the rest of your aura, this cord of attachment.

Cords carry very human emotions, like fear, pain, and worry. Regarding their consequences, they are not unlike puppet strings. And how quickly do they appear? Instantly.

In everyday life, most things take longer. Ever move to a new home where you must wait for days to get a land line? On the level of auras, no problem! Service is instant. Faster than any phone company, the Home Office will automatically install your cable or cord.

Well, congratulations… sort of. You and John are connected by a cord of attachment whose energy will distort your aura's normal functioning. John may become your best friend, a helpful colleague —or your worst nightmare. Whichever energy pattern between you becomes the most toxic, that will dominate your cord of attachment.

How long will the two of you remain connected in this way? Usually you will be stuck with that cord for the rest of your life.

No, I don't mean to depress you. But even after John drops his physical body (becoming what, in earth-speak, passes for "dead"), your cord to him will keep repeating its most toxic pattern, relentlessly repeating 24/7 right until the day you die.

Unless, of course, you can find someone with enough skill to help you to sever that connection.

Soon, of course, that someone will be you.

Physically, what is a cord of attachment? It is made of electromagnetic energy, the same frequencies found in other part of the human energy field, or aura. Later we'll go into more detail about auras. For now, does this help? You could consider the substance in question to be completely real and physical… for something metaphysical.

That cord reaches from part of your body to part of the other person's body.

"How big?" you may be wondering, starting to feel queasy.

When a cord is first formed, the circumference could be as small as a bite of rigatoni. But later, depending on what happens as your relationship develops, your cord to John could grow as wide as a decent-sized pizza. That size depends upon how much energy flows through the cord.

Unfortunately, bigger is not necessarily better. That's because a cord of attachment never contains positive energy. You know how people talk about giving with no strings attached? That would be spiritual ties, that other kind of connection I mentioned earlier.

Spiritual ties don't bind. Actually, a big part of our learning here at Earth School comes from those wonderful, super-evolutionary, positive relationships. Through them, we discover loving kindness, compassion, inspiration, and more. It is the stuff that makes angels weep for joy.

Cords of attachment, on the other hand, set off a different kind of weeping, the kind for which tissues were invented.

Admittedly, learning is involved, but it's a messier kind than the evolution we receive courtesy of spiritual ties.

Have you noticed? One of your biggest assignments at Earth School is to be yourself. For that, you may have to smash through a thousand illusions.

Energetically, socially, physically, sexually, psychologically, spiritually, etc., who are you? One worthy goal for human life is to serenely remain yourself, whatever the give-and-take between yourself and anybody else.

Cords of attachment make this harder. Cutting those cords makes it easier. Here are a few examples of the differences cutting a cord of attachment can make:

- Liam spent three years in psychoanalysis dealing with issues about his father. After cutting their cord of attachment, Liam stopped dealing and started living.

- Valerie's blood pressure would go sky high whenever she spent time with her sister-in-law. The reaction made no sense whatsoever, not until Valerie cut the cord and learned what she had been receiving through it: The equivalent of a ton of rage each day. Afterwards, the reaction stopped permanently.

- Rape, like any trauma, creates its own cord of attachment. Meg did all she could to get beyond the memory, but for more than 30 years she reacted to that rape every day of her life... until the cord of attachment was cut and, finally, she could go free.

- Brian wanted to stay married to Anne, but it was a struggle to deal with her mood swings. Having cut their cord of attachment, he found he could love his wife without taking on her problems, and because of the way the cord was cut, Anne wasn't hurt in any way when Brian regained his peace of mind.

- After realizing that she was in a cult, Sherry did what she could to exit, but this was as hard as leaving behind any other kind of addiction. Cords of attachment increase the challenge of disconnecting from bad influences. Sherry couldn't find the strength to start her new life until that cord was cut.

Yes, cords of attachment are energy structures that keep a person stuck in old patterns. Whether you want to release a relationship or continue it, you'll do better if you can release the corresponding cord of attachment.

For generations, cords of attachment were permanent. But living when we do, at a time of transition into the Age of Aquarius, techniques have become available to remove old obstacles. With skill, cord removal brings freedom to release energetic ties to the past, a freedom that comes cleanly and permanently, quickly and insightfully. That, of course, is what you can experience with the 12 Steps to Cut Cords of Attachment.

Cutting cords is an important set of skills for Energy Spirituality, a 21st century approach for breathing new life into the perennial search for spiritual connection. Humanity is evolving rapidly now, making Deeper Perception available to anyone who seeks it. Using this perception, reading the human energy field, it becomes possible to remove blockages to spiritual clarity. These are forms of astral debris, physical structures that exist at a metaphysical level.

Cords of attachment are especially important to remove. Whether you seek more intimacy in love relationships or a clearer connection to Spiritual Source, cutting cords can help bring the results that you seek.

In this book, I will teach you how to cut cords with professional-level skill, resulting in enormous gains for your emotional freedom, physical healing and spiritual awakening. Other benefits come just from opening up your inner circuits to make what I call an "Energy

Sandwich," and not the least of these benefits is avoiding the problem I'll discuss next.

THE PROBLEM

There's one huge problem with cutting cords of attachment: Quality control. I don't pretend that one and only one method will work.
But many attempts to cut cords of attachment aren't very effective.

Some people have heard only vague rumors about cords and how
to remove them. And, bluntly, some practitioners have such limited
technical skill at cord cutting—well, they'd do better wishing on
dandelions.

Unfortunately, most people don't yet know enough to be able to
evaluate what's being offered in the marketplace. Hey, it's a cutting
edge skill!

So how can consumers choose wisely? That big abstract problem
with quality control gives rise to many smaller, tangible problems.
Sometimes they're sad, sometimes funny. Here are samples.

*"I have a weekly appointment to see my healer. We have to keep re-cutting
the cord of attachment to my mother."*

Hold on: We're not talking manicures here. Cutting cords is supposed to change your aura for good.

Yes, with skill, a cord of attachment is cut *permanently*. Once
should do it. The method you're about to learn will do the job right.

*"My healer tried to cut the cord to my ex, Joe. But Joe was way too powerful,
so he re-corded."*

Puhleeze! Nobody is that powerful. That's like having a dentist say,
"Sorry, I couldn't pull that particular tooth. It was just too scary."

When you have learned how to do the job properly, *nobody on
earth will have the power to stop you* from cutting a cord of attachment. It's a matter of technique, not which of you is bigger and
badder, the healer or that scary person at end of a cord of attachment.

One story of questionable cord cutting was touching:

"It was a beautiful thing. My therapist asked if I was ready to cut the cord to my brother. I decided I was. After she cut the cord, it reattached instantly, only now it was a beautiful shade of blue. I guess that's because I still love him."

Look, I think love is beautiful, too. And I'm delighted to hear about a therapist cutting cords, because this can be such a powerful adjunct to more traditional forms of therapy. But *a properly cut cord won't pop back up, like spam on the Internet.*

It's great that this client put a positive spin on what happened, plus she has enjoyed a memorable experience of clairvoyance. But if she (or the therapist) think that they cut a cord of attachment, they could be fooling themselves.

Sometimes cord stories turn sinister, like this one:

"When my healer cut some cords of attachment for me, I know it really worked because two of the people had car accidents right afterwards. Isn't that great?"

Not to me. Cord cutting, as you'll learn it here, doesn't involve black magic. "First, do no harm" is a time-hallowed goal of healers. The procedure you're about to learn includes the principle of Divine Homeostasis, a term I will explain later. Meanwhile, know that nobody—and I mean nobody—is going to be hurt when you learn these 12 Steps to Cut Cords of Attachment. What I teach you will lead to *less drama in life, not more.*

After I facilitate a session of Energy Spirituality, a client might, perhaps, receive a phone call from the cordee, despite their having been out of touch for years. But car crashes? Never.

Hey, notice that? Did I just refer to the "cordee"?

Yes, **cordee** is my shorthand expression for "The person at the other end of a cord of attachment."

Plenty of horror stories come, not from cordees, but from people who tried and failed to remove their own cords. The mildest version sounds like this:

"I cut all my cords of attachment, but so what? It did nothing."
Of course it did nothing. Sure, I know that some people claim, "Anyone can cut cords of attachment. It takes two minutes." In what fantasy world does that happen? And how long does brain surgery take there, half an hour?

Most of us have learned not to believe everything we hear, or all that we read on the Net, but some myths about cord cutting are spread by credible sources. For instance, the first person I ever heard discuss cords of attachment was a magnificent spiritual teacher (whose real name I won't mention for a reason that will soon become obvious).

"Gloria" gave me a past-life regression that changed this life forever. She introduced me to Ascended Masters and Archangels. And her character was as much an inspiration as her knowledge. Talk about sweet! Add hard working, compassionate, brilliantly smart.

Gloria's talents included highly developed clairvoyance. So, of course I believed her when she said, "Any time you have a difficult relationship, call on Archangel Michael to cut your cord of attachment, and he'll do it instantly."

No doubt, Gloria could see him doing this, too. But she hadn't studied cord cutting in depth, so I'm guessing she never checked back again the next day. Then she might have seen him replace that very same cord of attachment right where it had been before.

Now, if you've ever enlisted the help of Archangel Michael, you know that he does good work. But he won't simply follow your instructions if asked to do something that would, ultimately, hurt you.

As you'll soon understand more fully, the information in a cord of attachment is precious for spiritual and emotional evolution. We're not talking garbage here, where your highest aspiration would be to demand that some cosmic garbage collector takes the smelly stuff down to the dump. What happens if you don't actively use the information from a cut cord? You'll have to re-create that cord, or the equivalent, in order to learn the intended life lesson.

Nobody likes quick 'n' easy better than I. But some things in life take time. The 12 Steps to Cut Cords of Attachment are as quick 'n' easy as can be... while still getting the job done right.

And, in case you, too, have heard some famous teacher say something like the wishful thinking from Gloria, use your common sense. Just because a psychic can do certain things brilliantly doesn't mean she knows everything. That's God's job. So take the good from any healer or psychic, therapist or teacher, and leave the rest.

Okay, on to a comical story of no quality control, the woman who cheerfully told me:

"I cut my cords every day. It takes me hours to keep cutting them back."

And this is supposed to be a good thing? Is there soon going to be a pop culture version of cutting cords, like spending two hours a day perfecting your hairstyle? My goal is not to add yet another chore to your grooming regimen.

When you cut cords properly, the job takes minutes, not hours. *And every session of cord cutting brings about a powerful, permanent healing.* Lacking quality control, you could be doing the equivalent of trying to mow your lawn with nail scissors.

And speaking of problems with trimming, one client told me:

"I know all about cutting cords. I've been working at it for years. One cord was especially hard. It started bleeding and then it got infected."

Never, ever, in more than 20 years have clients of mine had reactions like this.

So, please, use method, not madness. You can certainly learn how to do these 12 Steps to Cut Cords of Attachment. Just keep reading.

How to Get the Most from Cutting Cords

Have you thought yet about your personal goals for reading this book? Below I have listed six important motivations. Which one matches you best?

Choose your favorite match-up. Then read my suggestions to help you to get the most from this book.

Opening up possibilities: Count yourself in this category if you aren't sure yet why, exactly, you're reading. Maybe you will decide to cut cords, maybe not. You could be reading out of pure curiosity. Sure, Rose thinks that cutting cords could transform your life, but how about you? This book will help you to make an informed decision. See page 19.

Consumer smarts: Are you interested in having some cords of attachment removed? Who says you must already have made up your mind?

Keep that mind open and go surfing this book. Though slower than the Internet and costing a bit more, at least you know this information comes from a trustworthy source.

That source also happens to care a lot about consumerism herself, so she made sure her book would answer questions like these: What, exactly, is reasonable to expect from this form of healing? How can you tell a good practitioner from a wishful thinker? For you, this book could be where *Consumer Reports* meets *Chicken Soup for the Soul*. Turn next to page 19.

Cutting cords for yourself only: Does the potential excite you? Personally, I can't think of a more effective and easy way to make life better. Owning this skill set is a great way to overcome childhood limitations, adult disappointments. Also, you can think of this knowledge as a kind of psychic-level accident insurance. Whatever life brings in the future, when you know how to cut cords you can cope way better. Besides, for a do-it-yourselfer, what a plus: Between these covers are all the how-to's you will need to do professional caliber work. See page 20.

Branching out from therapy: As a therapist yourself or as a veteran of many years of counseling, you are uniquely qualified to evaluate these 12 Steps to Cut Cords of Attachment. What a notion, that cord structures between people could keep sending toxic patterns of energy! How counter-culture, that attachment, the magnificent concept defined by John Bowlby, could be a bad thing! What chutzpah, that Rose says therapy sometimes is limited to providing ways to re-package energy patterns that, instead, could be ended for good! Keep reading and I'll let you in on a secret related to this. See page 21. (Read more about Bowlby and Attachment Theory in the Online Supplement to this book.)

To supplement your other mind-body-spirit services: Millions of Americans already do energy healing, angelic readings, or other holistic services. Are you one of these Lightworkers? Professional or amateur, you can love the work but still feel stuck. Clients may not be growing as fast as you wish, ditto the number of people helped by your services. Alternatively, clients may be delighted with what you offer yet secretly you feel a wee bit stuck as a healer. Do you wonder if cutting cords could move you forward professionally? What is the potential of Energy Spirituality? Move your mind-body-spirit down some paragraphs to learn more at page 22.

Becoming a spiritual healer for the first time: Fundamentalists don't own the field, you know. In order to serve humanity with Energy Spirituality, you need not belong to any organized religion.

Maybe you're cheerfully involved in *disorganized* religion. Or maybe, like many of my students, you are a person of faith who has a church home. Either way, surely you've heard that cleanliness is next to Godliness. What is the spiritual benefit of cleaning out cords of attachment? See page 23.

OPENING UP POSSIBILITIES

To get a simple overview of possibilities, I recommend this: Read about TECHNIQUE BOXES at page 24. Then skip to the end of this chapter for "12 Steps in Action." Now you're prepared to leap-frog at will through the rest of the book.

Another point about those technique boxes: They reveal the heart of what I have to offer. The 12 Steps to Cut Cords of Attachment are really like one big box with lots of smaller boxes inside.

You'll find more than 12 of these boxes in this book, actually. Altogether, this book contains some 60 different techniques. (And I doubt you'll find a single one of them described by other authors, at least not until this book has been out for a while.)

Each box is brimming with possibilities. Can you remember being a kid on your birthday or Christmas, a bunch of well wrapped presents before you? Who didn't want to tear open the paper on every box before doing anything else? Once you know what the toys are, you can decide how to play.

CONSUMER SMARTS

Since you're already a savvy consumer, you don't need me to tell you how to read between the lines of a book. But I can alert you to two useful things about the design of this particular book. If you scan through the pages, stop to **read all the words in bold type.** These are key concepts being introduced for the first time, language that could be indispensable for your personal growth, not to mention your further exploits as a consumer.

Most strong consumer advocates are iconoclasts at heart. You (we) like to sort out truth from fiction. If this applies to you, I especially recommend that you read the following myth-smashing sections:

- At Step 2, learn what is involved in making an Energy Sandwich.
- At Step 3, check out "What is an aura?" and then the explanation about gift sets.
- At Step 4, distinguish "Minor vs. major cords of attachment." Also, be sure to read about ego hooks.
- Step 9 is the book's ultimate consumer chapter. Read it all and you'll appreciate at depth why cutting cords of attachment can change people's lives.
- If you come to this book with skepticism, I also recommend strongly that you read Steps 10 and 11. Then you can appreciate the full scope of this method for cutting cords.

When and if you're ready to actually *learn* how to cut cords, go to the part about Technique Boxes on page 24, and read on from there.

CUTTING CORDS FOR YOURSELF

Take your time, learning to cut cords of attachment. I don't mean to scare you, but this is a form of psychic-level surgery, done to a person's subtle body. You can definitely succeed at this, even if you'd never dream of going to med. school. But mastering the skills takes doing, not skimming.

Please, don't think that just because you are "only" doing the work on yourself that you can afford to skim over the technique boxes. Don't be cheap with yourself. As the client, you deserve better.

In this book, I take the approach of calling the person whose cord is cut **"Your client."** Why? I want you to give yourself full credit as a healer, even if the only client you ever plan to help is yourself.

Also I want you to be able to work objectively, especially important if you're cutting a cord for yourself that carries a big emotional charge.

Besides, it's no harder to learn how to cut cords for others as well as yourself. And some day, that skill set might come in handy for helping someone you love.

Turn next to the part about Technique Boxes on page 24, and read on from there.

HOW THERAPISTS CAN BRANCH OUT

Psychotherapy works so much better when augmented by Energy Spirituality. The same goes for life coaching, grief counseling, hypnotherapy and other forms of counseling. If you're involved in any form of therapy, whether as a practitioner or client, this book was written for you.

Certainly it was influenced by the years I spent in a part-time graduate program, working towards a Master's in Social Work. In 1986, I dropped out of that program to pursue my healing work full-time. Since then, many of my clients and students have been therapists. So the apple isn't falling far from my favorite tree.

As a therapist, you can appreciate the big secret (oops, now former secret) about how I present the 12 Steps to Cut Cords of Attachment. It's all about empowerment. Energetically, a new kind of empowerment begins when a client can stop coping with self-perpetuating, toxic energy flows.

Beyond that, consider the process involved in these 12 Steps. Clients are encouraged to take back their power at every opportunity.

Your perspective as a therapist will prepare you to notice how I sneak empowerment into other how-to portions of the book as well. Our little joke, right?

In preparation to go through the book when learning how to cut cords, I recommend that you first turn to the discussion of differences between psychological healing and Energy Spirituality in Step 10. I further invite you to preview Steps 9 – 12, seeking connections between your specialties with therapy and the skill set being offered here. Then, come back to this chapter's section on Technique Boxes (page 24), and read on from that point. You'll be psyched.

SUPPLEMENTING OTHER SERVICES

So many holistics are ready to become practice Energy Spirituality but don't yet know that the career path exists. Yes, there's a huge difference between doing energy work with a point of entry at the physical body, like advanced Reiki, versus developing expertise as a healer whose point of entry is the aura. Can you master both types of healing? Why not?

Likewise, psychic healers and medical intuitives stand to gain a lot from learning these 12 Steps to Cut Cords of Attachment. This completely different type of work will bring synergy to your existing skills. Check out the energy for you around making the choice to practice Energy Spirituality.

Whatever openings you have made as a holistic healer, techniques in this book are going to be a piece of cake. You may even be doing some work already, cutting cords, and you're reading just to pick up refinements from someone who has specialized in this field. I'm honored.

To deepen your perspective and become clear about the difference between my approach and what you're already doing, turn to some of the teaching stories in this book.

They're set off in boxes with italics.

Stories in the earlier chapters encourage new practitioners, so don't start there but instead begin at Step 6. These later stories will bring home the scope of these 12 Steps to Cut Cords of Attachment. After you have browsed to your heart's content, go to the part about Technique Boxes on the next page and read on from there.

BECOMING A SPIRITUAL HEALER FOR THE FIRST TIME

There's precedent for this, you know. Cutting cords of attachment was my introduction to Energy Spirituality.

And these 12 Steps are a great way to get started because of all the skills that this method will teach you, including:

- The empowerment of avoiding The Cosmic Excuse in Step 1.
- The protection of Get Big in Step 2.
- All you'll learn about working with clients in order to Assign Homework in Step 12.
- And, of course, this book can show you how to investigate the 50 vital databanks in chakras, as discussed in Step 3. Reading auras can bolster your intuitive sense about any religion or spiritual path that intrigues you.

Browse away in these chapters. I'd also recommend that you open this book at random for teaching stories. (They're set off in italics, with more of the juicy ones toward the last half of the book rather than the first half.)

Now you're ready to learn to cut cords, starting with a turn of the page, where I officially introduce you to the Technique Boxes.

TECHNIQUE BOXES

In this book, you'll find the main techniques in boxes. Just seeing those gray rectangles, you may start to salivate with delight. Well, that's optional, actually, but I do invite you to slow down and clear your throat or your mind or do whatever you typically do in advance of a thrilling new experience.

Technique Alert!

1. Read through the entire sequence of instructions, as you would before cooking a recipe.

2. Go back and follow the instructions, just as they are numbered in the box. Don't try for any particular experience. Innocence is the best way to learn.

3. After you go through each instruction, keep reading. Most boxed techniques are followed by information designed to *supplement your experience.* This will make better sense if you have first had an experience to supplement!

BUDDY SYSTEM

If possible, find a buddy to go through the 12 Steps along with you. Supporting each other, you'll learn faster. Besides, it's fun to have a friend for swapping ideas and insights. When ready, you can exchange your first practice sessions of cord cutting.

A buddy can also help by giving feedback when you receive insights. Reading auras is part of the skill set involved in cutting cords of attachment. Doing this, and reading the astral-level contents of cords of attachment, chances are that you're going to amaze yourself with how talented you are. Even if your goal is to cut cords only for yourself, working with a friend initially can help you to build confidence.

THE TEACHING STORIES

Yes, cutting cords of attachment is a real-life skill, helping real people, bringing real results. So I've included many teaching stories. Of course, to protect each client's confidentiality, I use fictitious names. Throughout this book, first names used on their own are always fictitious, and I have altered other details that might identify clients, honoring the confidentiality of their personal sessions. Stories are typeset in italics to help you find them... because some of us always want to read the stories first.

LET'S GET PRACTICAL

By now, I take it, you're committed. And I mean that in only the very nicest way. You definitely want to learn how to do the 12 Steps to Cut Cords of Attachment.

By now, you've also seen enough to tell that this is not your typical how-to book. American publishing today emphasizes books that are high concept. When publishers are primarily in the business of making money, they favor titles that are like iTunes—catchy, short, simple, designed for the widest possible audience.

I care more about fully delivering what I promise. In this book, you'll find the simplest possible how-to method to cut cords that does the full job, including that all-important quality control discussed in our first chapter.

Depending on your personal motivation, this chapter has given you suggestions about how to preview the book. Now that you are ready to learn, here's what I'd like you to do. Finish this chapter and then go through Steps 1 through 6, practicing as you go. *Read* at your own pace, with no limits about how far you read at a time.

Learn at your own pace, too, developing skills that will help you succeed right from the very first time that you physically cut a cord.

When will that happen? Step 7: In that chapter, you will actually cut your first cord of attachment, making this part of the book a major milestone. When you get there, I'm going to ask you to change your way of using the book. Here's a preview of what you will find.

Steps 7 through 12 need to be done in exact sequence, no detours along the way. At Step 7, you will find your first heading that says "LET'S GET PRACTICAL" and practical instructions will follow. Each subsequent Step will also give instructions with that heading, like this:

LET'S GET PRACTICAL

At this Step, you will be given special instructions for cutting cords.

1. Following these instructions, you'll start cutting cords in a quality way.

2. Depending on your present skill level, you will emphasize certain things, skim over others.

3. Your skill level will accelerate quickly as you proceed from Steps 7 to 12.

My goal is for you to cut your sixth cord by the time you complete Step 12. Proceeding in this way, you will really master the process by the time you have finished that chapter.

Admittedly, this is an unconventional way to structure a how-to book. Blame my 37 years of experience as a spiritual teacher, which has made my mind weirdly flexible. If you haven't ever encountered a book exactly like this one, don't feel intimidated. The "Let's get practical" stuff isn't complicated. You'll simply do one step at a time.

Altogether, let me reassure you that none of the techniques in this book is difficult. Learning to cut cords of attachment takes a little time, a little trust, that's all. Then you can lift negative patterns that have caused suffering for decades.

We're going to have fun together. And, to complete our view of possibilities, I'll end this chapter with an example of what it's like, cutting somebody's cord of attachment.

12 STEPS, AN OVERVIEW

In this book, you will be seeing the following diagram a lot. As I teach you step by step, I'll supply a pulldown menu for the particular step you are learning and show the key techniques involved. Here is a simple overview of all 12 Steps.

---

12 STEPS TO CUT CORDS OF ATTACHMENT

Step 1. Create a Sacred Space
Step 2. Make an Energy Sandwich
Step 3. Activate the Aura
Step 4. Choose Which Cord to Cut
Step 5. Locate the Cord
Step 6. Give Permission
Step 7. Remove the Cord
Step 8. Bandage to Rebalance
Step 9. Write the Dialogue Box
Step 10. Discuss the Relationship Pattern
Step 11. Impact Other Relationships
Step 12. Assign Homework

---

12 STEPS IN ACTION

Here is your sample of the 12 Steps in action. I'll summarize a session of Energy Spirituality that I did for a client, rather than one of many that I have done for myself. Helping someone else, the method is just the same but the dialogue definitely reads better.

Speaking of reading, I recommend that you breeze through this sample session. Watch it like a movie trailer, just without expecting special effects. Energy Spirituality isn't generally flashy.

Some technical terms are used. If you're not familiar with them, don't worry. Soon enough, you will own all these terms, all these Steps. My goal is to teach you very systematically. For now, any time you encounter something unfamiliar, relax and trust that you will soon master it as part of your becoming a really good cord-cutter.

Incidentally, this example will illustrate how my 12 Steps have way more substance than the "technique" of saying, "Archangel Michael, take away this nasty cord."

Step 1. Jessica's intention was to stop being emotionally dependent on Mel, her boyfriend.

We fine-tuned this intention. I asked, "Does that mean that your goal is emotional strength?"

"Yes," she agreed.

Sure enough, power turned out to be an important element in Jessica's session of Energy Spirituality.

Step 2. Jessica chose Buddha to be in charge of her session.

Step 3. Jessica's Before Picture showed a root chakra that was heavy and tense, a power chakra "like a hole." Emotionally, she felt confused.

I supplemented this Before Picture with a brief aura reading. Although she was coming to this session at a low point in her life, Jessica did have many life-long strengths encoded in her aura. Being reminded of them brought perspective for what was to follow. Besides, validating the truth about a client's aura starts to activate energy, and this will add oomph to your session.

Step 4. What would be involved in cutting Jessica's cord to Mel? I made sure that she understood clearly.

Step 5. Jessica's cord to Mel connected at her belly.

Step 6. Giving permission to cut this cord, Jessica teared up. When she was ready, we moved forward.

Step 7. This cord of attachment came out easily.

Step 8. For her bandage, Jessica chose to be rebalanced by a large blue sapphire with a "mountain crystal" on top.

Step 9. Energy patterns within a cord can be summarized as a Dialogue Box, with numbered cord items that come either from the client or the cordee. It took me about three minutes to diagram this cord.

1. *Jessica: Rejected and alone.*
2. *Mel: Give me energy, Jessica.*
3. *Mel: Keep trying to please me.*
4. *Mel: Jessica, I want you to look for every possible sign that I care about you.*
5. *Mel: You give so much in return for so little. I enjoy having this power over you.*
6. *Jessica: I feel left out of this relationship, socially excluded. (Major life theme.)*
7. *Jessica: Can't I have even one person loyal to me?*
8. *Jessica: Life is so unfair.*

Step 10. Discussing these cord items, Jessica could relate to everything except the last part of cord item #5.

She asked, "What did power have to do with this love relationship?"

My answer? "Everything!"

Like many clients, Jessica needed some coaching to understand that **power** is another word for a balanced give-and-take in relationships.

Step 11. We expanded our conversation to include having power versus being dependent. Didn't Jessica have a right to equal give-and-take?

She considered this. "Mel never brought me flowers. But once he did bring me a few pieces of fruit. I was really grateful. After I told my therapist, he teased me. He said that I was awfully easy to please."

Step 12. Jessica's homework was a quick ceremony to reprogram her subconscious mind about give-and-take in relationships.

- Her old programming went, "I give and give, getting back very little." Over!
- Jessica's new programming would be, "I give and receive in equal balance."

Jessica also received the standard follow-up instructions. To conclude her session, what remained was the After Picture. At the solar plexus, Jessica felt the stirrings of a more positive new energy. Emotionally, she felt more vibrant. But the real triumph showed at her root chakra, where tension had changed into feeling relaxed and "cushioned," protected. Jessica had begun to approach life with more emotional strength.

As you'll discover, removing a cord of attachment isn't just about taking something away. The goal is adding something positive: Personal growth, both immediate and long-term.

With Energy Spirituality, change starts in the energy field, then gradually works its way through the rest of a person's mind-body-spirit system.

What can you gain by cutting cords of attachment? More benefits than you can count, one cord at a time.

Step 1. Create a Sacred Space

Like following a recipe or solving a Sudoku, Energy Spirituality flows best when you patiently work it one step at a time. As we move into our first Step, let's start with some practical tips.

Throughout this book, I'll describe each Step as if you were working with a client. Of course, that "client" could be you. Whoever is being healed during your session, your success at cutting cords depends upon your desire to honor and empower your client.

- Explore what I have to teach you before you start tinkering with it. Otherwise, you're not really learning these 12 Steps, so you'll never find out what they can do.

- And speaking of common sense, no amount of metaphysical woo-woo will improve life unless you're also willing to cope with reality. Fortunately, we'll explore some techniques that can help to heal the healer. I've needed them, and they may help you, too.

- More common sense: It is your responsibility to seek out legal advice before doing sessions for anyone, even a friend. Every locality has legal requirements that healers must fulfill. Check with the government's requirements for healing in your locality. Will you need a minister's credentials? If so, one possible resource is a mail order degree from The Universal Life Church, www.ulc.org.

- When you have practiced enough to set fees for your work, you will need a business license and protection against liabilities. You might ask your attorney to help you to prepare a waiver that you give each new client without exception.

Even if you only cut cords for yourself, you're entering a new profession, Energy Spirituality. To me, this means teaming up with spiritual Source, or a Divine Being, to create permanent healing on the level of someone's energy field, or aura.

CREATE A SACRED SPACE

Physically and energetically, a spiritual healer must set the conditions for a session to take place. Energy Spirituality requires a sacred space.

SANCTIFY THE ROOM

1. Find an appropriate room.
2. Use words to create a sacred space.
3. Activate your Deeper Perception to appreciate what happens during the 12 Steps to Cut Cords of Attachment.

To do a session of Energy Spirituality, here's what you don't need:

- Designer furniture
- Museum-quality crystals
- Bells and smells
- Perfect silence
- Beautiful music

You do need:

- A room with a door you can close
- No animals present
- Comfortable chairs for yourself and your client
- A recording device, should you wish to make a CD or tape of the session
- Notepads for yourself and your client.

Of course you'll want to make your session room physically comfortable with little things like ventilation, adequate heating or cooling, and the absence of really weird smells.

Also, please move any pets into a different room. Although your pet's influence is probably magnificent, it can also be unpredictable. Who needs a wild card? Trust me. Things will become wild enough when you do the 12 Steps.

What if your environment isn't as perfect as you like? Either cry or go ahead and do the best session you can.

Howling Cats

In 1971, as a teacher of Transcendental Meditation. I was doing the most important teaching session of my career so far. In Miami, Florida, a colleague and I had interested public school officials in offering an accredited course based on TM. At this critical point in our negotiations, I had to personally initiate the Superintendent of Schools and High School Principal.

As a traveling teacher, I used to rely on volunteers to make their homes available for instruction. After arriving on this particular Saturday morning, I learned that my host had recently acquired two cats. There is no polite way to put this. The house simply stank. Moreover, the only room with a door was the bedroom where I would be teaching. (Oh, yes, it was the 70s.)

So I had to send the cats outside. Rain poured. The cats howled.

At such times, denial comes in handy. I stopped thinking about the high stakes for today's initiations. As for the lack of litter box hygiene, forget it. I focused on my sacred role, to teach each student. Both guys learned just fine, along with the rest of the class, and we did succeed in establishing that TM-based course at Miami-Dade High School. It became the first program of its kind in America, and in the long run that mattered far more than a little nasal distress.

How can words create a sacred space? If you were selling furniture, words alone couldn't create what you needed: "Ladies and gentlemen, here we have a gorgeous Lay-Z-Boy recliner that will cost you only $5,000." Abracadabra, and here comes your sale.

But vibrations of energy are free, and whatever you request spiritually will come into the room by decree. Here's a simple way to start off:

"Let's close our eyes. We fill this room with a sparkling new white light of healing. Let's add violet flames for transmuting stale or negative energy, placing one at the center of the room and others by each corner and window. Finally, let's seal the energy here with gold and silver light, like paint on the ceiling and walls; this will symbolize the presence of God as Father and Mother. Only energies of the highest vibration may enter this place."

Can you just think these words? Words in your head will create a fine energy space … in your head. But don't you want that energy right in the room, where it can help cut a cord of attachment?

Besides, if your client is so squeamish that words like these horrify him, better to have him flee now. Get it over with early, so you won't waste half an hour doing your session and then have him run out screaming. (Fortunately, I've never had a client end a session early … or screaming. Chances are you won't either.)

SET AN INTENTION

Cutting a cord is not an intention, it is a means to an end. An intention is a powerful statement of purpose, made aloud. When you set an intention, you gain Divine support. You also prepare your subconscious mind for changes. So don't be shy and don't ask small.

1. Say out loud one or more specific goals for this session.
2. Trust that this intention, once expressed, will manifest—either precisely what you've requested or something even better.

The rest of the techniques in Step 1 are useful for working with clients. Even if you're cutting cords of attachment for yourself alone, I encourage you to read them anyway. These techniques may help you to release limiting old patterns.

REQUEST A CLIENT'S INTENTION

Your client's intention matters enormously. She will decide on the goal, not you. Still, she may need prompting to make a clear statement of intention.

1. Ask your client, "How can I be of service to you in this session?"
2. Let your client speak for a while. (Most clients will want to talk a bit.)
3. Guide your client to set a specific intention, a purpose for the time you'll spend together.

Won't that intention usually be "to cut a cord of attachment"? That's like saying "I'd like to travel over a bridge." A bridge to where? With no specific destination in mind, how will you know when you get there? Unless she sets a clear intention, your client won't have a context for appreciating the results of a healing session.

TURN NEGATIVE COMPLAINTS INTO POSITIVE INTENTION

Some of the clients who come to you will be in enormous pain. Having suffered so much, they can't imagine a positive outcome. As you listen compassionately, the client's most hopeful intention may sound to you like wailing and gnashing of teeth.

Listening is one thing, aiming another. Take a leadership role and help your client to upgrade that intention. You're the healer, right?

REFINE INTENTION

1. Alternate listening to your client's ideas with your own questions.
2. For each request your client makes, guide him to find a positive element.
3. Keep refining until your client can choose at least one positive intention for this session.

What does your client want most? Surely, it can't just be to complain. For instance, perhaps a client tells you, "I'm unhappy in my marriage." After you listen to him, ask questions to find out what he wants, not just what he doesn't want.

Your client may not have thought much about this. Ironically, he's unlikely to overcome the unhappiness until he can choose a more positive goal. This could be:

- Feeling free to choose what to do about the marriage
- To summon the strength to get a divorce
- To stay married, but feel better

What if your client's version is still negative, like, "To stop feeling like I have no freedom" or "To find out why I lack strength" or "To learn why my life is fated to never improve"?

Well, you're halfway there. Help your client to rephrase that goal into something more positive, such as "So, could we say that your intention is to feel better?"

But which is it then, to feel better while staying married or feel better by not being married any more?

If you're confused, imagine how your client is feeling. Ask follow-up questions, like "To clarify your intention for now, do you aim for X or Y?"

What if the opposite happens and your client supplies an impossibly huge list of problems to solve?

Help your client to choose one or two for this particular session of Energy Spirituality. Admittedly, if a client is in crisis, it can seem as though there are a zillion problems, all of which must be solved right now:

- I hate my life.
- I'm bored.
- My boss is a monster.
- My boyfriend doesn't appreciate me enough.
- The upstairs neighbor makes too much noise.
- I'm too fat.
- My hair is too fat, etc.

Everyone has been in that crisis mentality. Sometimes the client needs to dump out that long list before she can hear a word you say. So just listen.

AVOID PROMISING

Listening doesn't mean that you promise to solve all your client's complaints. Deep down, both of you know that you are one human being, just one. And this is only one session. (Each of mine usually lasts 55 minutes.) Making a lifetime commitment to solve every smidge of difficulty isn't in your job description, is it?

Eventually, your client will reach the end of her list, however exhaustive. If that list is really, really long, I might say calmly, "That's all?"

A client must be pretty far gone not to laugh.

And, certainly, ask your client, "If you were going to choose, which would be the single most important area for us to focus on helping today?"

Sticker Shock

The first time I offered sessions in Japan, there was so much for me to get used to, like learning that houses on every street, if they were numbered at all, received numbers in the order they were built rather than a sequence like 1, 2, 3.

Strange and wonderful, that was every day for me in Japan. Out of all the weirdness, one thing stood out: The wish lists. Clients would bring the most extravagantly long lists of intentions. As my interpreter translated them one after another, I felt increasingly helpless. What was it with these Japanese clients? Did they think I was God?

On the final day of that trip, my interpreter couldn't resist asking me, "Rose, do you have any idea how much your clients pay for their sessions?"

I hadn't given this matter much thought. VOICE was the marvelous company that sponsored me, publicized the sessions, handled the payments, supplied the interpreter, etc. VOICE was paying me $80 per one-hour session. At home I charged $125, so I figured they were simply taking a chunk of money off the top and clients were paying about the same as at home.

"Tell me," I said.

"It's $450."

Eureka! Interpreters don't work for free, and neither does the staff at VOICE. From this simple mathematical reality check, I learned a valuable tip. If you want clients to bring a really long list of intentions, simply raise your fee!

While discussing intention with your client, make sure he understands that an intention is different from a promise. You cannot promise results, not ever. Watch your language throughout every session. Avoid claiming to bring particular results. If you need examples of carefully chosen language, let politicians inspire you! Watch their interviews on TV for role modeling.

As a spiritual healer you can have the purest intentions in the world, even more pristine than the intentions of those selfless, saintly people who run for public office. Still, promising is tricky. It's fine to say you will do a particular action, like cutting a cord of attachment to somebody's spouse. And it's better to agree on an intention like "To gain clarity about whether or not to stay in this marriage." But it's something else entirely to promise that, as a result of your session, your client will have the happiest marriage in all the world.

Unrealistic expectations aside, make sure your client knows from the outset that certain problems won't be solved simply by cutting a cord of attachment.

- If a medical problem is involved, recommend that your client see a doctor. Make it clear that this session is not meant as a substitute. Clinical depression, for instance, can require medical intervention. Alternative healing, such as cutting cords of attachment, is not an alternative to common sense.

- When someone asks for help with alcoholism, or has another complex emotional or physical problem, do not claim that one session will be an instant fix. Explain that you can, perhaps, remove a cord that contributes to the problem.

- For a client who is desperately seeking a husband, your session can help remove obstacles to being in a healthy love relationship. But she might still need to place that personal ad.

- What if your client already has a husband and he's the problem? He could be abusive or take drugs. Make it clear that no amount of cord cutting from you will change that. Cutting the cord between an abused wife and her husband can give her more freedom to decide what to do about the relationship. This could help her inwardly. Still, if she's in danger, recommend that she protect herself physically.

■ Finally, there's the ever-popular desire to lose weight. Alas, there is no cord of attachment to the extra 50 pounds. Regardless of your skill as a spiritual healer, there will be no cries of "I'm mellllllting" followed by a puddle of discarded grease on the floor. Sure, your session may help with weight issues, but these can involve complex problems and, frankly, other methods might prove more successful.

In short, clarify what you can and can't do toward fulfilling a client's intention. Give referrals, as appropriate. Then, ask your client the pertinent follow-up questions, like "If you did lose the weight, what would be different in your life?" Ta da! Your client just might find a deeper intention.

AVOID THE COSMIC EXCUSE

Wherever in the world I offer sessions of Energy Spirituality, clients bring intentions like this:

"What am I supposed to do? Tell me the purpose of my life."

Of course, it's natural to be curious. Which spiritual seeker wouldn't like all of life's mysteries to be solved right now? Then he could get on with the other pursuits that are so much more interesting, like ice-fishing.

Seriously, why do I consider it a problem when a client expects his session to deliver The Big Answer?

Personally, I have a red flag go up because I have never advertised myself as someone who supplies these answers. No matter who sponsors me, no matter how many interviews I give or which article appears on the Net, regardless of how often I blog during any particular month, never ever (anywhere) do I ever claim to find anyone's purpose in life.

So why would a client believe that such an answer is available from me? (Or from anyone, actually?)

Energy Spirituality does not mean doing a psychic reading or an astrology reading, both of which can be wonderful. But let's not confuse apples with oranges and pomegranates.

If life were more like a quiz show, One Big Answer would solve all your client's problems. You'd explain his cosmic purpose and perhaps he would never have to think again. However, as far as I can tell, spiritual evolution is more like a journey, accomplished through individually paced spurts of progress.

No matter how great your skill at cutting cords of attachment, you will never be able to cut a cord of attachment to The Cosmic Excuse. All you can do is initiate some common-sense conversation. Eventually, your client may appreciate that the moment of power in her life is the human here-and-now.

Requests to "Tell me what I'm supposed to do" are common when people are new to spiritual seeking. The question can return painfully while someone is in crisis, or has severe problems at work, if she is going through a divorce or suffers health problems, feels bored or overwhelmed.

You get the idea. There can be innumerable reasons why someone asks you a Cosmic Question. But I have only one favorite question to ask in response: "What is happening in your life right now that makes it feel so urgent for you to figure out this 'supposed-to' business?"

As a spiritual healer, you need never accept the role of all-wise guru, instructing your client in how to live. My preference is to hand the power right back.

New spiritual seekers act a lot like teenagers. They start expressing their "individuality" by dressing and talking just like everyone else in their group. Yet, with encouragement, these seekers can learn to trust their own hearts and minds, becoming empowered as adults.

When this happens, you'll watch them move from expressing clichés like "Tell me my purpose" to asking about more personal concerns.

Loving Mother Earth, learning from life, graceful surrender to cosmic forces—all of this can be beautiful, a sacred path. Each spiritual seeker has golden moments of knowing that all is right in the world. And if you were to read that seeker's aura right then, you would find something glorious. However, when a client starts talking "meant to be" and his aura shows blockage galore, that's your cue to gently poke beyond the Cosmic Excuse.

Really Valuable Guidance?

Gail told the most astonishing story about why she came to my workshop. She had searched online to learn about becoming skilled as an empath. This led her to my website and then my book, Empowered by Empathy.

Reading FAQs at my website, Gail found the information to be tremendously helpful. Yet she still didn't know if studying with me was "meant to be."

Beaming, Gail told me that days later she happened to browse in a bookstore that was sponsoring me to give a workshop in Massachusetts. Empowered by Empathy *was on display.*

"Because I saw your book right there, right where I could touch it, I knew that studying with you was meant to be," she said triumphantly. "That's why I signed up for your workshop."

Why did I find this story so astonishing? Let's play it back. Gail had found knowledge that spoke to her, knowledge that resonated deep within her soul. Common sense told her that this work could make her life better. But what really excited her was that my book was physically close enough to touch?

Of course, Divine guidance will adjust to support a prayer or requests. As long as Gail requires it, she can always wait to receive obvious outward signs and flashy synchronicities. And thus she will inch her way forward.

But when Gail feels ready to grow by leaps and bounds, she won't demand that her next teacher must travel hundreds of miles to her very doorstep. She won't need to follow whatever fad is currently popular and, therefore, readily available at her local bookstore.

Interacting with all that the world has to offer, while trusting your own heart, mind, and soul—isn't that a valid source of spiritual guidance?

In Step 2, you will connect with a kind of spiritual guidance that is indispensable for cutting cords of attachment. I love this method because it is effortless, simple, and foolproof. Use it as a supplement to your favorite method of connecting to Higher Intelligence. Or, if you don't already have a favorite method, you can start right here. Everyone can benefit from learning to make an Energy Sandwich.

LIFE FORCE ENERGY

You may prefer to call it life force energy, chi or prana, or one of its other innumerable names. For convenience, I refer to life force energy simply as "energy." Whatever the name, human life depends on it (as does all life). Technologies expressly designed to move energy may become one of the defining discoveries of the 21st century. Consider the array of energy healing methods available to us today.

Gary Craig and David Feinstein are pioneers of **Energy Psychology,** a holistic system of self-help that changes inner lives, healing psychological problems. Even though the full mind-body-spirit system becomes engaged, the *point of entry* is the desire for psychological health and wholeness.

Energy psychology produces results by changing energy patterns within an aura. Other energy techniques with a psychological point of entry include EMDR, Neuro-Linguistic Programming, Regression Therapy, Holographic Repatterning, and Transformational Breathwork.

Donna Eden's **Energy Medicine** is another system of self-help that changes a person's aura. Here the *point of entry* to the mind-body-spirit system is the physical body, with the main intention being to align physical health, correct imbalances, keep energy flowing.

Other energy techniques with a physical point of entry include Reiki, Healing Touch, Pranic Healing, Bio-Energetics, Qigong, Tai Chi, and Homeopathy.

Energy Spirituality uses the aura itself as a primary *point of entry* for healing the mind-body-spirit system. This matters because an aura can contain blockages to spiritual clarity that will be left untouched by mind-body-spirit approaches with a different point of entry.

Cords of attachment are the most common, and important, kind of blockage to remove. And the consequences of freeing up energy in this way can be enormous, as you'll soon see.

Whether about psychology, medicine, or spirituality, all energy healing methods are holistic. Whichever the point of entry, the full mind-body-spirit system will benefit.

Furthermore, these holistic technologies are accessible to anyone who wishes to learn them. Personally, I love that aspect. Most of us have neither the time nor the inclination to get extensive professional training simply to be able to work on ourselves. It's hardly a casual hobby to earn a Ph.D. in Clinical Psychology or become a physician. The 12 Steps to Cut Cords of Attachment take some time to properly absorb, but like any other quality technique for energy healing, the education is relatively brief and painless. It is also (usually) relatively inexpensive.

You learn at your own pace. You may choose to learn just enough to help yourself. Or you can move beyond self-care to helping others.

THAT TRICKY WORD "SPIRITUAL"

Now that you have a context for understanding Energy Spirituality, let's clarify just how "spiritual" you must be to engage in this form of self-help. For starters, do you have to be religious?

Religion requires structure. Worship, ritual, belief, and faith are other components. By contrast, spirituality aims for direct experience, connecting to something greater than oneself, however defined.

Spiritual seekers may, or may not, follow an organized religion. They may prefer to participate in what I call "disorganized religion" or none at all. However practiced, spirituality is more a path than a place. Someone travels or rests at will, choosing from all appealing beliefs, techniques, teachers, and more.

Therefore, Energy Spirituality doesn't demand religious affiliation but can deepen it. To my knowledge, all forms of energy healing work this way. I remember interviewing Janet Mentgen, the founder of Healing Touch, after observing one of her classes. The group represented a wide (and wild) variety of belief systems, evidenced by different types of religious jewelry, even a turban or two.

When talking privately with Janet, it became clear that, personally, she was an extremely devout Christian. I asked if fights ever broke out among her students, since clearly some of them were strongly committed to very different beliefs. Janet laughed.

"Never. They come here for only one reason, to learn to heal."

Well, it's just the same with Energy Spirituality. You don't need to graduate from any particular divinity school any more than you would need professional licensing to do Energy Psychology or Energy Medicine. Just bring to your healing journey all of the skills you have gained so far.

How do you access inner truth now? Do you request intuitive messages? Listen to your inner guidance or angels? Do you muscle test or use truth signals or contemplate? Excellent.

What if you haven't found your way in yet? It will be my delight to coach you. Should you feel trepidation, here's some perspective. The company I founded to teach my various techniques of Deeper Perception is called "Women's Intuition Worldwide." Well, I've stopped counting how many people who telephone me refer to this company as "Women's Institution."

Does it seem possible that you could open up intuitively without suffering mental derangement? Then I'm reasonably sure I can help you. Specifically, at our next Step, I will teach you the technique of Questioning, a super-easy way to obtain accurate information about spiritual energy.

Step 2.
Make an Energy Sandwich

12 STEPS TO CUT CORDS OF ATTACHMENT

Step 1. Create a Sacred Space
Step 2. Make an Energy Sandwich
  Get Yourself Big
  To help clients: Help Your Client Get Big
  Vibe-Raising Breaths
  Questioning
  Instant Emotional Insight
  Extra Cycles of Questioning
Step 3. Activate the Aura
Step 4. Choose Which Cord to Cut
Step 5. Locate the Cord
Step 6. Give Permission
Step 7. Remove the Cord
Step 8. Bandage to Rebalance
Step 9. Write the Dialogue Box
Step 10. Discuss the Pattern
Step 11. Impact Other Relationships
Step 12. Assign Homework

All metaphysical frequencies are not created equal. To cut a cord of attachment effectively, you must position your consciousness at the appropriate level.

It's common sense, really. Doing a routine load of laundry won't require the same attentiveness as dressing for your wedding day.

Usually we don't think about levels of vibration. Instead we take energy cues from the situation around us. If things we attempt on the surface don't go all the way through into subtle reality, so what? Most people focus on the surface level of life. They won't notice.

A surface approach works fine for practical life because energy patterns remain more or less constant. Even without probing the auras of people you talk to, you will usually find that the energy stays reasonably familiar. It's part of the setup at **Earth School,** a planet set up for super-intense spiritual evolution at a dense vibrational level.

To cut cords of attachment, however, you must use energy to *transform* the status quo. Energy Spirituality requires that you show leadership, initiative and presence of mind. Conscious leadership begins with two fascinating spiritual principles. The first is this: Here at Earth School, *physical action can change spiritual energy.*

For example, a typical bride might prepare for her wedding day by wearing special clothes, carrying a bouquet of flowers, prominently displaying a wedding cake. A Bridezilla might spend $10,000 or more on "her special day." However elaborate a bride's preparations, they can help her to bring higher spirits to the occasion.

Regarding the room where you do sessions of Energy Spirituality, you already know that no elaborate rituals are necessary. It is enough to close the door, bring in recording equipment, and state an intention to create healing. As you read in our last chapter, special trappings like bells and smells aren't required.

In general, the 12 Steps to Cut Cords of Attachment don't demand that you do a lot on the physical level. It's more efficient to supplement physical actions with high-vibrational energy, a level of consciousness higher than whatever is contained in a cord of attachment. How will you accomplish this if not by taking elaborate physical actions to change energy?

Energy and action have a reciprocal relationship, so you can work primarily at the level of subtle energy. Here comes our second principle: At Earth School, *energy can also be used as a cause, producing consequences for physical reality.*

If you experiment with using this second method, rather than the first, you'll find it works faster. Only people who are very earth-centered will have better results from working primarily from the slow, sweet level of physical reality.

Step 2 for Cutting Cords of Attachment will make it easy for you to use energy to change physical reality. For instance, I rely on the following technique whenever I cut cords of attachment.

Get Yourself Big

In less than one minute, you can raise your vibrations to the most effective level for cutting cords of attachment. Who knew it could be so easy?

1. Close your eyes and briefly notice how it feels to be you.
2. Think the name of a Divine Being. Once. In your head.
3. Take a deep breath.
4. Again, notice how it feels to be you.
5. Open your eyes.

Immediately you will be connected for the rest of your session. That Being will arrive instantly, with a body made of the highest-vibrational light and do all the heavy lifting for your session of Energy Spirituality.

It's the principle of making an Energy Sandwich, which I'll define after giving you context. First you need to be briefed on a very ancient understanding from India known as The Three Worlds, a concept as old as the Vedas, which may be the most ancient wisdom tradition on earth.

THE THREE WORLDS

World One, **human life,** is the most familiar to us. It had better be! To play the game of spiritual evolution here at Earth School, you require a physical body. To win the game, you must develop mastery at the level of earth life. Which kind of mastery will that be? You decide.

Yes, you are the one who defines the game here, one incarnation at a time. Will this lifetime teach you most about relationships or sex or money or power or social status or wisdom? Human life will support your chosen growth path.

World Two, **psychic planes,** contain angels, spirit guides, astral entities, ghosts, and so forth. (Another familiar term for this second world is the **astral** realm.) Astral beings can be higher or lower in consciousness but, in general, their frequencies are one realm higher than human life. This brings practical advantages like these:

- Angels can tune into practical information, like predicting the future, helping to find lost objects, assisting with physical healing. Serving as guides, angels will team up with anyone who is receptive to working with them.
- Mediums can heal aching hearts (or solve crimes) by making authentic contact with the deceased.
- Channelers bring wisdom by connecting with astral beings and sharing information from this higher plane.
- Shamanic practitioners and psychic healers bring results by working with astral-level guides and angels.

World Three, the **etheric** realm, is home to Divine Beings. When you make contact with any Ascended Master or Archangel, the vibration will be different from those of the other two worlds. Etheric contact brings spiritual experience. Love, light and power, creativity and inspiration—these emanate from Divine Beings as clearly as the unmistakable scent of a fragrant flower.

Any conscious connection at this vibration brings a super-concentrated experience of God.

But isn't God everywhere, at every level of creation? Certainly, and when you have the desire to experience God you can always find that presence. It is omnipresent, omniscient, all in all. But spiritual experience becomes super-clear when you consciously connect with a Divine Being, God in a personal form, at the etheric level.

Admittedly, this isn't fashionable. Angels are far more trendy. Yet there is much to be said for bringing awareness to the level of spirit. Consider the saying, "Know an action by its fruits." When you work with any help from the Other Side, the results will be clearly related to the World from which that help comes.

If, in the past, you have mainly depended on human or angelic support, I think you will be pleasantly surprised by the fruits of co-creating with Divine Beings. Certainly their help is invaluable for cutting cords of attachment. Divine Beings are, quite simply, the most appropriate helpers. And you'll avoid some of the problems we discussed earlier, such as: *"We have to keep re-cutting the cord of attachment to my mother."*

Understanding about The Three Worlds brings perspective to most of the problems of quality control we considered earlier. Think frequencies, just for a moment. Being a resident of Earth School, you bring *human frequencies* to cutting a cord of attachment, whether for yourself or for others. Cords of attachment exist at the astral level. If you team up with an *astral-level* guide to help you cut cords, she can have trouble moving things out at her own level, but *etheric* beings effortlessly move out energies at a lower frequency.

Hence, doing the 12 Steps to Cut Cords of Attachment you will make what I call an **Energy Sandwich.** Collaborate with a Divine Being when you do techniques of Energy Spirituality. For this kind of healing, both you and the Divine Being could be compared to one of the slices of bread in a sandwich. A cord of attachment serves as the filling.

What, you don't like the flavor in that old filling? Working as a spiritual healer, connected to both outer edges of the sandwich, you can scrape out what's in the middle, and replace it with a new, improved flavor. Because you work with both pieces of "bread," the grounded human slice plus the slice from an etheric vibration, your Energy Sandwich will hold together.

Stable and portable—that's why a sandwich is so convenient. A food item that actually makes its own plate, how great is that? And, in terms of this analogy, you can upgrade the flavor significantly. Your old sandwich could have tasted like moldy cheese with liverwurst and pickles. What an aftertaste to carry with you for the rest of your life! Bring on the peanut butter and jelly.

Admittedly, my approach to Energy Spirituality is controversial. Many people who have heard about cords of attachment make no distinction at all between World Two and World Three. They're satisfied by asking for help, any help, from The Other Side.

But I'm going to invite you to become more discerning in your request for assistance from **The Other Side,** life beyond earth. Start by paying careful attention to the names people use. Sometimes those names aren't accurate.

Spiritual healing is very different from psychic healing. Both types of healing depend upon collaboration with beings from The Other Side. But the similarity ends there.

You don't have to clairvoyantly see these beings to become a smart consumer of healing services. When having a session with a practitioner, just ask, "Who, exactly, is on your team?"

Listen carefully, mighty consumer. Then decide for yourself which type of healing is actually being done. For instance:

- "Psychic healers" from the Philippines co-create healing with Jesus, which makes them really *spiritual* healers.
- A so-called "spiritual healer" could be personally very devout, and she could excel at doing Shamanic work, angelic healing, guided readings, or Reiki. As a healer, however, she would be doing *psychic*-level work.

Why bother to make this distinction? My purpose is neither to criticize psychic activities nor to claim that spiritual activities are superior. Each has its place. Nevertheless, when cutting cords of attachment it is important that you know the difference... and that you position yourself energetically to do spiritual healing.

How can you change modes if your usual comfort zone is psychic healing?

Ask. That's all you need do.

What if you have never done either kind of healing before, nothing psychic and nothing spiritual? You don't have to work your way up the ladder, putting in several years with flower fairies, then being promoted to your first assignment with an angel and, eventually (perhaps rewarded for good behavior), being assigned to an excellent spirit guide before you, gulp, go big time. No, you can ask right now to connect with a Divine Being. It will happen instantly.

Just for This Sacred Work

Marilyn Cooley is one of my talented students who has turned pro. After studying with me three years ago, she developed a practice as an animal empath, animal communicator and healer. Now that she's had a lot of experience professionally, I asked her how she relates to Get Big. She said:

"The closer to Earth, the denser and lower the vibration. In terms of the inter-dimensional physics, Ascended Masters are at a higher vibration than those at an astral level. But, as a very Earth-based practitioner, and one who finds those denser vibrations the closest to God for me (for now, anyway), I do think that each Lightworker has her own best place.

> *"When I do any 'Rose work' such as cutting cords of attachment, I do so with the full knowledge that I am choosing a workspace that is beautiful and nurturing, although it is not my native and most comfortable land."*
>
> *And that's all I'm asking of you, Reader, when using the skills from this book. Come play at this level, with one or more Divine Beings. Just for now. Just for this.*
>
> *Please know how much I honor the sacred work that you do, whatever it is and however you do it. Never do I mean to suggest that working with Divine Beings is always the best way or the only way. While you are cutting cords of attachment, however, work with these Beings. They will help you to succeed at this particular form of sacred work.*

Which Divine Being is best to choose? I recommend calling on the highest vibrational kind of person with an individual form, either an Ascended Master or an Archangel. Always do this before you cut a cord of attachment.

If you're working with a client, before your client comes for the session, privately connect with your choice of Divine Being. After your client comes, you'll ask for your client's choice, and invite that, too, as we'll discuss later.

Who are **Divine Beings** anyway? Examples of **Ascended Masters** are Jesus, Mary, Buddha, Kwan Yin, Tara, Lakshmi, Krishna, Ganesh, Athena, Isis, St. Francis, Babaji. **Archangels** include Archangel Raphael, who brings healing; Archangel Gabriel, who facilitates communication; and Archangel Michael, who is great at removing things you no longer need or want. (For more details, and a technique to experience Divine Beings, see the Online Supplement.)

Why not simply call on Almighty God when cutting a cord of attachment? God is omnipresent, omniscient, unlimited creativity and love. Of course, it helps to call on That, whether you call it the Great Spirit, Source, Hashem, The Holy Spirit, the Universe, etc.

Terms like these bring forth a connection with the *impersonal* aspect of God.

For cutting cords, it's even better to work with *personal* expressions of God. Most clients (and healers) relate more easily to someone in a light body who does healing, rather than to visualize help emanating from the abstract, shimmering, un-localized Field of God.

Getting Big produces results instantly. True, many new students don't notice them. Over time, however, you'll grow used to staying awake inside while functioning at higher frequencies. Then your experiences will come clear. Meanwhile, every time you do the Get Big technique, you're investing how much time, a big three seconds?

What can you expect to notice, as an experienced healer? Will it be like having Superman arrive on the scene, only inside your head?

Unfortunately—or maybe fortunately—no. You will simply notice the distinctive presence of whichever Divine Being you have invoked. It's a gentle, natural merging with your own self, like the familiar sense of being with someone you love, hanging out with a favorite family member or friend. Unless you live in a comic-book world, your best friend doesn't seem like Superman, does he?

Help Your Client Get Big

Your personal source of inspiration is your business. Likewise, it's important to let the client make his own choice. Which Divine Being does he prefer?

1. Ask your client, "Which Divine Being would you like to have in charge of your session?"
2. Discuss the concept, if necessary. Some clients know all about this, others will understand it immediately, and a few will need a fair amount of conversation.
3. Once your client has made a choice, say it out loud, e.g., "I call on St. Germain."
4. Instantly That presence will arrive, a magnificent and distinctive expression of Divine love.

What if your client insists on Almighty God or nobody? You could do worse than enlisting Almighty God for your session of Energy Spirituality. Only one choice would really disallow your moving forward in session: if your client refuses to invite God in any form.

Atheism is a path I respect enormously. But how can someone who doesn't believe in God have confidence, deep down, in cutting cords of attachment? If a client doesn't have faith even as big as a mustard seed, you're not going to grow a whole lot of healing.

Cord cutting happens on a human scale, supplemented by spiritual help. The sacred place where you do your sessions is cooler than anywhere on earth, even the intersection of Hollywood and Vine. It's where human intention is supplemented by Divine intervention. The street sign doesn't only read "Energy" but "Energy Spirituality."

Sometimes it becomes clear that a client doesn't feel worthy of calling on a Divine Being. Then I'll ask the client to humor me and allow me to bring in a Being just for myself. A client doesn't need to believe in this part of a session any more than he must believe in a water faucet before taking a bath. Besides, it can be enormously empowering for a client to watch me calling forth a Divine Being. No lightning strikes me dead, after all.

In American pop culture today, Fundamentalists appear to own the conversation about God. But does it really have to be a choice between believing in televangelists or nothing? I delight in presenting an alternative. My message is "Connect to God any way you choose. You're just as entitled to do this as anyone else who has ever lived on earth."

From Aimless Pothead to Awesome Healer

When Susie first studied with me, her idea of a good time was to hang out with friends and smoke pot. Yet she became fascinated by the idea that she could call on Divine Beings whenever she liked, needing no special qualifications before she had permission.

Susie began to call on Archangel Michael whenever she felt down. It seemed to help more than smoking pot. Soon, she stopped puffing and started actively seeking. Shortly after that, she had sessions of Energy Spirituality with me that woke her up even more inside.

By now she has been trained to use the 12 Steps to Cut Cords of Attachment. One of her favorite things to do is to let clients know that they can call on their choice of Divine Being. She told me:

"They'll ask, 'Could I really be allowed to call on this saint?'

"I'm like, 'Go for it.'"

Many spiritual seekers assume that they don't have the right to call on a teacher like Jesus or Buddha unless they follow a religion named for Him. This is absolutely not true.

Even more ironic, some people devote their entire lives to a spiritual path without realizing that they have the right to Get Big with the founder. What a delightful surprise, discovering how That presence becomes available with one quick thought.

Thanks For Dropping By

David was a helper for one of my workshops. For years he'd been studying Yogananda's course in Kriya Yoga. Paramahansa Yogananda was the first enlightened yogi from India to teach large numbers of people in the West. (If you're curious about him, I'd recommend his Autobiography of a Yogi.)

Like every Ascended Master whose work I have studied, Yogananda never demanded that people worship him. He was just an enlightened teacher who taught practical techniques. David practiced these techniques daily. During the workshop, when I explained to everyone about Getting Big, David thought, "Hey, why not call on Yogananda?"

He did. Of course, this great Master arrived instantly in a body of light. As luck would have it, David hadn't come to my workshop because he was particularly interested in anything I had to teach. He just worked for the company that sponsored me. But, as he told me later, that one tiny piece of my workshop changed his life. Something big may happen to your client, too, simply because you explain the option to "Get Big."

BREATH CAN HELP YOU TO HEAL

Breath can become one of your greatest resources for cutting cords of attachment. Let's begin to explore this through my favorite breathing technique, which I call Vibe-Raising Breaths.

Vibe-Raising Breaths

1. Close your eyes.
2. Pay attention to how you feel inside. No supposed-to's or intense concentration, please, simply interest. How does it feel to be you right now?
3. Breathe in through your nose.
4. Breathe out through your mouth.
5. Repeat this breathing pattern for a minute or so.
6. Return to regular breathing. Again, notice how it feels to be you right now. Any contrast?
7. Open your eyes.

After you try this once, let's go into some refinements.

Big Crown: Breathe as deeply as is comfortable. That's somewhere between a shallow breath and giving yourself a hernia. Vibe-Raising Breaths will open up your crown chakra, letting through extra life-force energy. This will increase your effectiveness for doing any technique of Energy Spirituality (A **chakra** is an energy center within your aura. The **crown chakra** is located at the top of your head. You'll learn everything else you need to know about chakras for cutting cords in Step 3.)

Posture: For best results with this breathing technique, sit comfortably with your spine straight and head upright, unsupported.

Awareness: Closing your eyes, you start to direct awareness within. By gently paying attention, you activate **consciousness**, that part of you which witnesses all your activity, awake from inside.

In-Breath: By combining posture and awareness with a simple breath in through your nose, you cause extra life force energy to come into your aura. So each in-breath helps you to wake up more inside, like turning up the volume dial while you listen to music.

Out-Breath: Again, context counts. Your attention has been drawn inward because your eyes are closed. Plus, by gently paying attention, you have activated the huge power of your awareness. Without stimulation from the outer world, your body starts to relax. Therefore, each out-through-mouth breath will help you to release stuff like everyday worries, self-doubt, planning what you're going to eat for a snack later, etc.

Unfortunately, Vibe-Raising Breaths won't necessarily remove all the pain and suffering of your entire lifetime. It's a pretty good technique, but if it were that great, we'd have to charge an extra three cents for this book.

Although simple to do, Vibe-Raising Breaths have many uses. Any time you wish for more clarity (except, perhaps, when driving a car), Vibe-Raising Breaths will help. Personally, I use this breathing pattern during every one of the 12 Steps to Cut Cords of Attachment. It's particularly vital for our next technique, my favorite way to gather information from spiritual Source.

Questioning

Questioning is an enormously flexible technique for learning deep truths. Once you get into the flow of this technique, it couldn't be easier. Close your eyes and relax for a moment. Get Big. Then:

1. Think one question at a time.
2. Let go of the question
3. Accept what you get. Open your eyes and write it down.

Ever make lists for Santa Claus? Here's where all your years of practice can come in handy. You didn't just tell the jolly old elf, "Bring me whatever." Remember?

Similarly, you'll need to ask specific questions when you cut cords of attachment, like, "What are the dynamics of my client's cord of attachment to her mother?"

Thinking a question need not be a big deal. Just ask inside, using the same tone of voice you would use to think anything else, one sentence at a time.

Do you have to be extra precise? Or extra respectful?

No, your job is simply to think in the way that is natural for you. Let's use a book-style analogy. Ordinary thinking to yourself looks like this: "What are the dynamics of my cord of attachment to my mother?"

Thinking this question, you do not have to go through mental screaming, akin to:

Inner Experience Made Strange

The very idea of bringing awareness deeper can make people wildly self-conscious. Then they may doubt the most ordinary, effortless aspects of thinking.

For instance, I still remember a woman who came up to me after a talk I gave on meditation at the University of Miami in 1971.

"I don't think you can teach me to meditate," she said. "I'm not like other people. I have thoughts. They're inside my head. And nobody else knows what they are."

Please, take it easy with the Questioning technique. Trust that your ordinary way of thinking—those regular thoughts inside your head—will do just fine.

What about the "let go" part of the Questioning technique? This helps you to get an answer from yourself plus the Divine Being who is helping you. Otherwise, you would answer your initial question quite differently, searching through your regular set of thoughts about everyday life. This would not allow you to make that cosmic Energy Sandwich we've discussed before, which would diminish your healing power for cutting cords.

Questioning helps your consciousness to shift. When you think the original question, you think in your usual way. Releasing the question helps your awareness to open up. You remain yourself, with your normal inner tone of voice, only now you're thinking as a bigger, more expanded version of you.

Okay, by now you agree with me in theory. Letting go sounds great. But how, exactly, can you do it?

Real-life situations give us many opportunities to learn about letting go. Suppose you're taking care of Sonny, your two-year-old. He has grabbed your car keys and is holding onto them for dear life. Suppose that your goal is to get him to physically let go.

Struggling won't help. Tussle with a two-year-old over something that he considers "mine"? Forget it. A smart grownup takes a different tack: Offer the kid something else, like an exciting rock.

"Ooh," he'll say, grabbing it. Of course, in the process, he'll drop your keys.

Even if your social skills as a grownup have become more advanced than Sonny's, your mind works similarly. Give your mind something new to think about, rather than your original question, and automatically you will let go of your original thought, the question. For our technique of Questioning, "something different" can be that breathing pattern you've learned.

Vibe-Raising Breaths are easy. Plus they open up your crown chakra, remember? That makes them a great choice.

Hence the best way to let go of your question is simply for you to take 2-3 Vibe-Raising Breaths and then return to normal breathing.

Continue to sit quietly with your eyes closed. Because this technique works automatically, whatever you experience next will count as the answer to your question. Your job is simply to accept this. Here are some tips to help the process along.

Alternating: If you're going through this book with a buddy, you can sit in pairs and alternate doing Questioning for each other. Your partner poses a question she's curious about. You close your eyes, Get Big, set the intention to help your partner, ask that question inside, take the Vibe-Raising Breaths and tell your partner whatever you get. Then trade places.

Recording: If you're alone, keep pen and paper handy. Open your eyes long enough to jot down whatever you experience with Questioning. Or use a recording device, like a digital recorder. Open your eyes long enough to turn it on, close your eyes, then talk away.

The Best Part

One fearless student who has turned pro told me, "When Questioning with my client, I've learned to welcome the part that doesn't fit. Some little detail won't make a whole lot of sense to me, but it will to my client.

"Sometimes she won't get the connection until the next day. So I don't worry about complaints that "I can't relate to what you said.""

"I'll answer, 'Think about it when you get home. If you ever do make sense out of it, send me an e-mail, okay?'

"And that's why I get so many nice thank you e-mails. Often my client will write something like, "Once I realized what that detail meant, I realized it was the very best insight from our entire session.""

QUESTION ABOUT EMOTIONS

Here's a chance for you to do some Questioning. It's based on some facts about emotions that you may not know yet. True or false?

- Any moment while you are awake, you can have many emotions, not just one.
- However many emotions you have, there will always be one deep, underlying emotion.
- You can always (yes, always) identify this emotion.

Yes, all of this is true. And discovering this deep, underlying emotion isn't difficult at all, not now, when you know Questioning. So get your recording equipment ready and go through the cycle.

Instant Emotional Insight

Close your eyes. Give yourself a moment to relax. Get Big. Then:

1. Ask, "What deep, underlying emotion do I have right now?"
2. Take 2-3 Vibe-Raising Breaths.
3. Return to normal breathing. Sitting in the silence, soon as you have your first thought, immediately write it down.
4. Open your eyes and look at what you got. Interesting and insightful or what?

Ta da! You've done it. Here are some other productive questions to use when you practice the Questioning technique:

- What special gift do I bring to Energy Spirituality?
- What obstacle do I face in learning to do the 12 Steps to Cut Cords of Attachment?
- What will help me to overcome this obstacle?
- Which person from my past can inspire me now, as I learn to cut cords?
- What song that I know can become my theme song when I do Energy Spirituality?
- Why is that particular song meaningful to me right now?

RESULTS-ORIENTED QUESTIONING

Questioning always works, once you feel comfortable enough with the process to trust what you get. Still, sometimes the answer received from Questioning will puzzle you. Does this make your answer wrong? No, you simply need clarification.

Dictionaries work the same way, right? Say you begin with "What does umbrella mean?" and the dictionary defines it as "An appliance used to fend off unwelcome precipitation."

The word "appliance" you understand, and "fend off" isn't an entirely unknown concept, but say that you're stumped by that term "precipitation."

Well, go back to your dictionary and look it up. Your trusty dictionary might say, "Rain, sleet, or snow."

Now you can put all the meanings together.

Similarly, the Questioning technique sometimes supplies an answer that needs clarification through an additional cycle of Questioning. Simply frame your question and go. In the set of sample questions above, the last pair included a typical follow-up question:

- What song that I know can become my theme song when I do Energy Spirituality?
- Why is that song meaningful to me right now?

Besides helping with meaning, follow-up cycles of Questioning can clear up a context: "What does X have to do with Y?"

For instance, say that you ask, "Which person from my past can inspire me now, as I learn to cut cords?" Your answer is, "My mailman, Joe." And suppose that this answer mystifies you. Then your next question might be, "What does Joe have to do with inspiring me as I learn to cut cords?"

Perhaps you learn, "He is really, really persistent."

There you have it, one successful answer because you did an extra cycle of Questioning!

Finally, follow-up questions can help you translate from one sense modality to another. "What does that image of a waterfall have to do with my gifts as a healer?" Or "What does that sudden pain in my belly mean about my having an obstacle to overcome?"

Extra Cycles of Questioning

Ask follow-up questions whenever you like, just as if you were using a regular dictionary. If a first cycle of Questioning doesn't satisfy you:

1. Create a new question, based on the answer you just received.
2. Think the question mentally.
3. Let go by taking a couple of Vibe-Raising Breaths.
4. Accept what you get.

Questioning, plus the other Energy Sandwich techniques, will be essential for doing the 12 Steps to Cut Cords of Attachment. So our next page will give you the complete sequence, set off in a box for your easy reference.

Comprehensive Questioning

Here's the full method to use for Questioning when you do the 12 Steps to Cut Cords of Attachment. You will be making an Energy Sandwich, gaining wisdom with the help of a Divine Being.

1. Close your eyes.
2. Get Big.
3. Set an intention, like "I choose to gain wisdom."
4. Cycle through the three main parts of Questioning
• Think a question.
• Let go of it by taking a couple of Vibe-Raising Breaths. Then return to normal breathing.
• Accept what you get. Either write it down or speak it aloud.
5. If necessary, do extra cycles of Questioning, using refined versions of your question until you receive an answer that makes sense to you.
6. When finished with this period of Questioning, say thanks inside to the Divine Being who has been helping you. Stretch your body. Then open your eyes.

Because Questioning is so important, I'd like you to practice it a bit more before going forward. Here are some sample questions for you to use for practice. Remember, if any answer isn't quite clear, just create a follow-up question to ask next:

■ When I think about cutting cords of attachment, what deep, underlying emotion do I have?

■ Do I carry any subconscious fear related to Getting Big?

■ How I can I release that fear?

■ What will help me to use my full potential as a practitioner of Energy Spirituality?

Ruined for Love?

After her love affair with Jack, Dolores had zero libido. Although she felt intu-itively that she needed to cut her cord to him, Dolores had no idea why getting over Jack was so difficult. Did she ever find out! Using Questioning, here is the pattern of dialogue that I found when doing Step 9 to cut cords:

1. *Dolores:* Wow! When I'm with this man, I seem so forceful. Loads of my emotions come out.

2. *Jack:* She expresses for me. I'm not in touch with a lot of my emotions. (After Follow-Up Questioning: We have an energy hook-up through this cord where some of my more unpleasant, stuck emotions go directly into her. Then she acts really angry or jealous.)

3. *Dolores:* My super-expressiveness alternates with a complete turnoff to my feelings, especially if Jack has been badgering me.

4. *Jack:* Often I'm remote, inaccessible. (After Follow-Up Questioning: This is because I want women to indulge me, the way my mother did when I was growing up.)

5. *Dolores:* Being in love is so confusing. Sometimes Jack acts close. Other times he's distant. The randomness is driving me nuts.

6. *Dolores:* I wish I could be like him, so confident about relationships.

7. *Jack:* Gloating. I am quite the expert about psychology. All my therapy has made me psychologically super-healthy.

8. *Jack:* Poor Dolores. She knows nothing. She's lucky that I can show her how to be in touch with feelings.

9. *Dolores:* I'm not like him, so I must be defective.

After I read these cord items to Dolores, she laughed. Turned out that Jack had bragged a lot about his years of therapy. Then she turned serious. "Do you suppose that maybe I'm not defective, after all? And maybe Jack wasn't as per-fect as he thought?"

Consciously, Dolores had let Jack go. But subconsciously that cord of at-tachment kept his presence alive. Now she could put the relationship into per-spective. Dolores told me, "For the first time since breaking up with Jack, I feel that I might have something worthwhile to offer a man."

APPROPRIATE QUESTIONS

Be sure to ask appropriate questions when you do Questioning. Remember our discussion about how Divine Beings, at the etheric level, differ from astral beings such as spirit guides? The former specialize in life lessons, not psychic flash.

Here are three principles to help you select productive questions. I'll follow each principle with examples that I'd consider productive versus unproductive. Appropriate questions for cutting cords are:

Open-ended rather than yes-or-no
- Productive question: Which gifts of my soul will help me to cut cords of attachment?
- Unproductive question: Can I do this or not?

Wisdom-oriented rather than prediction-oriented
- Productive question: What will help me to be of greatest service to my clients when I cut cords of attachment?
- Unproductive question: What will be the name of my first client?

Predicated on free will rather than fatalism
- Productive question: How can I develop most quickly at doing this form of Energy Spirituality?
- Unproductive question: Is it my destiny to cut cords of attachment?

QUESTIONING TO BENEFIT A CLIENT

When Questioning, sometimes you'll receive unexpected images or information. For instance, while reading your client's heart chakra you might flash on an image of a miniature ballerina. What will you do with that?

If you were doing a *psychic reading,* you might ask your client, "What does a ballerina mean to you?"

If you were having an *ordinary conversation,* you and your client might share a lovely reminiscence about ballerinas you have known; then the two of you might conjecture how any of this might apply to cutting a cord of attachment.

But for a session of *Energy Spirituality,* continue to benefit from your connection to a Divine Being. Use Follow-Up Questioning until the information comes clear.

Questioning Cycles with a Client

Uh-oh, there you are with a client. You've already done Questioning once, but the answer doesn't make sense to you. For instance, you were exploring your client's heart chakra and got an image of a ballerina. Here's how to refine this experience to make it practical.

1. Do an additional cycle where you begin with a question that puts your perception in a context, like "What does a ballerina have to do with my client's heart chakra?"
2. Take the 2-3 Vibe-Raising Breaths.
3. Note your answer.
4. Only then tell your client what you have received from Questioning. In this example, you might hear this answer, "When young, she wanted to be a ballerina, but it didn't happen. This kind of longing dominates her emotions right now."

Information is what your client needs to hear, not your personal process of receiving it. She's the client, not you!

Do You Know a Tony, a Tom?

Most often, it's new mediums or psychics who go fishing for answers, but sometimes a beginner at cutting cords is tempted to do the same. Let's say that you are the client. The medium says, "I'm getting the name Tony. Does that mean anything to you?"

"No," you say. "I've never had an important person in my life named Tony. Sorry."

"Maybe not Tony, then," says the practitioner. "It could be Tom. Okay, how about this? Teddy."

"Gee, I wish I could say yes, but I can't."

"Hmm, not Teddy. Okay, no problem. Would you happen to know a Tim-Tim?"

Sometimes a medium might need to go on this kind of fishing expedition. His role is that of a reporter. He's connecting with an unknown entity who feeds him information.

Tim-Tim could be "physically" standing there, in his spirit body. What will motivate Tim-Tim to keep talking? He needs to be recognized. Otherwise, he might act like a fish that gets away. If, during a reading, a note of desperation creeps into a practitioner's voice, you can sympathize.

Fortunately, you're doing something entirely different by using the technique for Questioning. You are reading something right there that won't flit away any time soon. The information is located in your client's aura.

The same goes for any of the 12 Steps to Cut Cords of Attachment. Instead of fishing for something in the hereafter, you're reading something in the here-and-now.

So relax and do Questioning Round Two or Three or even Four until you find something that makes sense.

NO TORTURE ALLOWED

Have you been tempted to repeat Questioning simply to test yourself? I've had students ask themselves the same question repeatedly, just to make sure they would receive the same answer.

Hold on, you're not practicing scales. Also, spiritual inquiry isn't the scientific method. Your job is to make an Energy Sandwich, then open up trust. Whenever you test yourself or belittle something you have received, you're blocking yourself.

So ask today's questions only once. You'll receive as much as you can at this time. Give thanks for it. Gratitude will help you to do better next time. Trust and skill are cumulative.

A first grader doesn't criticize himself because he doesn't read like a college student. The only way that will happen is if he is willing to let reading skills develop, beginning with whatever degree of literacy he has right now.

Occasionally one of my students will act super self-critical. If you're inclined to torture yourself, you might ask a professional at Energy Spirituality to help you cut cords of attachment to any horrendous school teachers from back in the day.

But sometimes there is no deep reason for putting yourself through unnecessary testing. It can just be a bad habit. You might be able to bypass the problem simply by remembering the purpose of cutting cords of attachment. Do you want to help people or not?

And those people you are hoping to help—do you really want them to wait until you have satisfied yourself that you are absolutely, totally perfect?

With Step 2, all the "perfection" you need is to feel reasonably comfortable using the techniques offered here. Energy Spirituality is unfolding, bringing its own kind of grace. And you are learning to allow this.

If, inside, you are willing to say "Yes" to making an Energy Sandwich, you are prefectly ready to proceed to Step 3.

Step 3. Activate the Aura

12 STEPS TO CUT CORDS OF ATTACHMENT

Step 1. Create a Sacred Space
Step 2. Make an Energy Sandwich
Step 3. Activate the Aura
  Discover Your Gift Set
  Call It, Read It
  To help clients: Teach Call It, Read It
  Before Pictures
  See It, Read It
  Touch It, Read It
  To help clients: Insist on Reaching the Soul
Step 4. Choose Which Cord to Cut
Step 5. Locate the Cord
Step 6. Give Permission
Step 7. Remove the Cord
Step 8. Bandage to Rebalance
Step 9. Write the Dialogue Box
Step 10. Discuss the Pattern
Step 11. Impact Other Relationships
Step 12. Assign Homework

Cords of attachment fasten into auras and are made of a similar substance—psychic-level energy encoded with bits and bytes of data. So aura reading is indispensable for cutting cords intelligently. Not only will aura reading keep you from cutting blindly, but you will activate an aura by reading it, in preparation for healing.

Whenever you pay attention to someone, it subtly wakes up the aspect under scrutiny. For instance, when someone stares at you, don't you notice? The one who stares can avert her eyes, but you'll still notice. Why? You feel an energetic activation.

Activation happens whenever and wherever you pay close attention to someone. You will trigger greater self-consciousness. Why not do this to others? It has certainly been done to you.

For instance, when a woman stares at you as a sex object, don't you feel it? If you stare back, she might pretend to be fascinated by the nearest wall instead of your body. Yet subliminally (and maybe consciously, too) you will respond to the sexual charge, sensing an energetic activation.

What about someone who pays close attention to the status value of your clothing, checking for designer labels? Or how about being evaluated professionally, when the "stare" concerns whether you are incompetent at your work? Friendly or hostile, admiring or critical, however someone pays attention to you, you will feel it. The more awake you are inside, the more you will feel it.

So what happens when, as a healer, *you* pay attention to someone and your attention is aimed directly at that person's aura? You can activate a highly beneficial kind of self-awareness. Receiving attention can make a client self-conscious. But if the healer has a loving intent, that will be felt, too.

Activation can be either partial or holistic. Have you ever looked in the mirror and seen, mostly, a zit? As if one zit were all that mattered! That's an example of partial activation. In Step 3, you do the holistic version. Aiming deep, going all the way to a client's soul, you can activate the whole person, not just his problem.

Aware and Activating

Before turning pro as a practitioner of Energy Spirituality, my last full-time job was working as a secretary for AARP, the largest association in the United States. During the years I worked there, I had several bosses including Horace Deets. After I left AARP, he was promoted to Executive Director.

Although I liked Horace a lot, we never exchanged a word after I stopped working for him. I had, however, made friends with another AARP executive, Elliott Carlson. Years after I left AARP, he invited me over for lunch. To begin our visit, he gave me a tour of AARP's new national headquarters.

As we entered an extremely long hallway, I saw Horace Deets from the back. He, too, was walking, only near the opposite end of the hallway. Deets appeared to be deep in conversation with another AARP executive.

Recognizing him, I smiled affectionately. Of course, I wouldn't have dreamed of talking to him. The man was now one of the most influential CEOs in America, while I had merely been his lowly secretary, and for just a few months at that.

Abruptly Horace stood completely still. He turned around. Then he scanned the hall until he saw me and locked eyes for a second as if to say, "Oh, that presence belongs to you." Executive Director Deets didn't stop to wave or smile. We weren't officially friends, after all. Having satisfied his curiosity, he turned around and kept walking.

Haven't you had experiences like this, too? Here is how I explain it. When someone is very aware, he recognizes the energy presence of people he knows well. I believe that my brief but affectionate gaze at Horace Deets activated awareness within him.

My presence was familiar because we had worked together closely for months, although it had happened some five years before. Because Horace had a highly developed level of consciousness, he felt someone checking out his aura, recognized my presence and turned around just long enough to satisfy his curiosity.

What, precisely, is the effect of appreciatively reading a client's aura before cutting a cord? I leave that research project to the scientists involved in Energy Spirituality. What I can tell you is this. Clients feel deeply validated. They remember their strengths. Even skeptics begin to respect the healing potential of what lies ahead with the remaining Steps.

In Step 1, you harnessed the power of intention. In Step 2, you positioned your awareness to make an Energy Sandwich. With Step 3, you're ready to direct that appreciative, focused awareness toward the aura where a cord of attachment lies waiting.

What if you're not totally comfortable yet with the whole topic of reading auras? I'm going to help you change that right now. Your birthright is to become really comfortable at decoding the human energy field… also justifiably confident and effortlessly skillful.

Just as mathematics is the language of science, aura reading is the language you'll need for Energy Spirituality. If your experience has been limited until now, the problem could be as simple as how you define auras in the first place.

WHAT IS AN AURA?

Auras are three-dimensional bodies, made of electro-magnetic energy, layered all around your physical body.

Aren't they also colors? Isn't the whole point that auras are colors?

Definitely not! In today's metaphysical marketplace, most people would define auras as colors. OK, it's a start. But, with all due respect to those who haven't been taught anything more, equating auras with colors is a kindergarten understanding, like those color-by-number paintings back when you were a kid.

Equating auras with colors makes about this much sense: Imagine that The Mighty Aura Reading Authority enters the room where you are right now, glances at your skin, hair, and eyes, checks out your outfit, and then announces, "Okay, I've seen your colors. Now I know everything about you."

Seeing auras doesn't matter nearly as much as **reading** them. After you perceive something about an aura, what then? You can think of aura reading like an equation:

Perception + Interpretation = Aura Reading

Perception means receiving information. Seeing is just one way for senses to register a perception. However it comes will depend upon your personal gift set. But even the clearest perception has no value without **interpretation.** This turns a simple perception into something meaningful.

The human energy field is crammed with bits and bytes of information, and the senses through which you get that information don't matter nearly so much as making that knowledge your own. Think about helping your client. Is the goal having your client say, "Oh, my session was really valuable because the healer saw my colors"?

Or would you prefer something like this? "My session was really valuable because the healer accessed profound and accurate information about me, and that became a basis for improving my life."

Having helped thousands of students to have breakthrough experiences with aura reading, I can tell you another reason why reading matters far more than seeing:

You can definitely be good at reading auras.

Will you excel at seeing auras in color? That's more chancy. I don't, for instance.

God has given each person a distinctive built-in gift set for learning—and that applies to life, not just aura reading. However you are set up to process Deeper Perception, that's what I will help you to discover as part of Step 3.

Now, if you already read auras in depth and detail, you know that popular fantasies about aura reading don't do justice to its usefulness. And if you haven't had that treat yet, let the discoveries begin. Consider these counter-culture ideas:

- The most valuable information in auras is located in the concentrated sources of data called **chakras.** (You can pronounce this like CHA-kraz or SHAH-kraz. I prefer the former because it sounds more like "chocolate.") Right in front of your body, at different locations, you have a full collection of data at each chakra.

■ This data storehouse is organized into databanks. Yes, every chakra contains a number of **databanks.** We can make an analogy to savings accounts, where each chakra is like a savings bank. Your solar plexus chakra could be like Lloyds of London. You might have several accounts there: one for savings, one for checking, a Christmas Club to save money for holiday gifts. Databanks in a chakra are valuable, too. They contain information.

■ People who define auras as colors rather than information don't know **the best-kept secret in aura reading.** Here it is: Every chakra contains at least 50 different databanks of information. We'll be revisiting this concept later because it will help you to develop superb skills for cutting cords of attachment.

QUESTIONING CHANGES AURAS

In Step 2, you began using the Questioning technique. Now that we're bringing auras into the picture, let's deepen your understanding about how Questioning works.

Each chakra databank projects a certain distance from your physical body. Depending on how much you use that particular databank, more or less energy will project from that chakra. So the way you use your heart, mind, or spirit will affect the size of the corresponding parts of your aura.

Remember how Questioning has you consciously release a question in order to receive the best answer? An aura reader, observing you do the technique, could tell if you were cheating by not releasing that question. Your aura would shift, depending on whether you did regular thinking about the question, analyzing it, or truly letting go.

An example of **regular thinking** is asking a question inside like, "What are the dynamics of my client's cord of attachment to his mother?" You do this by using your everyday conscious mind.

Asking just one question with regular thinking won't affect your aura, but if you ask a whole series of questions (as kids do during that stage when they ask questions like crazy), aurically you will activate the related databank at your solar plexus chakra. It will pop right out, extra big.

By contrast, consider **analytical thinking,** the mental process used to solve puzzles. As an example, you might think, "What are the dynamics of my client's cord of attachment to his mother? Hmm, I already know he said that she was controlling. What else has my client said about her? And what are my client's weaknesses? How would her control irritate him?"

With several seconds or more of analytical thinking, you will expand the databank related to your intellect. This databank, like the one for the mind, is located at the solar plexus. Consequently, there will be a temporary expansion at this part of your aura.

But let's say that you ask that same question, only this time you really let go. Using the Questioning technique, you think, "What are the dynamics of my client's cord of attachment to his mother?" Then you follow up with Vibe-Raising Breaths which help you to release the question completely.

Which chakra databank expands now? It's the **spiritual wisdom** databank at your third eye chakra. What fun, doing Energy Spirituality with a great big forehead!

MYTH VERSUS GIFT SETS

Ready to learn the truth about your distinctive gift set for aura reading? Start by releasing **The Myth about Auras.**

Supposedly, talented healers see auras. One quick look instantly reveals everything important.

What a weird idea this is. Limiting! Confusing! Wrong!

In the light of common sense, the notion is even comical.

Auras aren't some TV show with the sound off. They're energy bodies around your physical body, encoded as abstract bits and bytes of information. Each human being has been given an instrument for decoding these bits and bytes, but here's the tricky part: Each person's instrument has a unique way of working.

If you're not fully using your instrument yet, I know I can help you. Having taught aura reading on three continents, I've helped many students who tried and failed with other methods. And I've also helped aura readers who had seen colors for ages but become stuck in their development. (Many aura readers with some clairvoyance ignore all their other gifts because, according to The Myth About Auras, only clairvoyance matters.)

Here is the single most important thing I've learned from teaching aura reading over the past 20 years: Everyone has been given a complete **gift set for Deeper Perception,** a collection of abilities and sensitivities which has been hard-wired into your mind-body-spirit system. Like your handedness or your sexual orientation, your gift set is no mere whim. It deserves respect as a sacred expression of who you are as a person.

You can trust that your set of gifts is perfect. It's related to your **spiritual mission,** ways that you have come to Earth to serve humanity.

What does it mean to respect your gift set? Be willing to accept these basic facts of life:

- Everyone was created *equal,* given a perfect and complete gift set.
- Yet everyone was not created *identical.*

This is where confusion sets in. We could diagram each person's gift set for reading auras within an equal-sized rectangle like this:

A TYPICAL GIFT SET

Major Gift #1	Major Gift #2	Major Gift #3	Major Gift #4	Other Gifts

Few people have a gift set that is mostly clairvoyance. Even fewer gift sets emphasize the specialized kind of clairvoyance about seeing colors. One such example is Doreen Virtue. From studying her work, I would diagram her gift set like this:

DOREEN'S GIFT SET

Clairvoyance	Other Gifts

Another famous aura reader is Sylvia Browne. Based on reading her books, I'd map her gift set like this:

SYLVIA'S GIFT SET

Clairvoyance	Clair-audience	Other Gifts

Both Sylvia and Doreen are psychics. Another American psychic, renowned for physical healing, is Barbara Brennan. Based on what I've read of her work, I would diagram her gift set as:

BARBARA'S GIFT SET

Clairvoyance	Analytical Awareness	Other Gifts

Yes, all three women are very talented. But why have they become so enormously influential? It doesn't hurt that every one of them happens to possess a gift set that matches The Myth About Auras.

Until people know better, they will assume that clairvoyance is the only valuable gift set for aura reading, which makes about as much sense as saying that a woman can't be beautiful unless she is tall, thin and busty, plus she happens to have straight blonde hair and big blue eyes.

What if your gift set doesn't fit the clichés? Don't sob yet. What you have is just as good. It fits with your spiritual mission, distinctive qualities of your soul, and exquisite ways that you can serve humanity.

Your gift set is expressed in how you live your life all the time, not just which gifts appear when you are learning how to cut cords of attachment or developing skill as an aura reader.

Enough suspense already! Let's explore what you have in your personal gift set.

Your Gift Set A QUIZ

Imagine yourself at a beautiful beach. It's a gorgeous day. You're visiting with a dear friend and having the most wonderful time. What makes the visit special for you? Circle each answer that applies. (Choose as many as you like.)

1. How it smells when you're near the water.
2. The sound of the waves.
3. Letting the water rock you, ride with you.
4. Noticing the progression of waves, plus how the tide moves in or out.
5. How you feel, emotionally, being here.
6. What sea air does for you physically.
7. Simply enjoying being a part of nature.
8. Noticing how the seagulls move as a group.
9. Observing how other people act at your part of the beach.
10. Feeling the contagious joy of babies at play.
11. Fascinated by the distinctive qualities of the beach. (Every beach has distinctive qualities not found elsewhere.)
12. Thrilled by how the beach looks. (Note: This question is trickier than it first seems. Does the sight of the beach interest you as an *association*, i.e., it triggers your interest in everything else? Or do you *minutely observe* the sand and the sea? Only the latter counts as being thrilled by how the beach looks.)

Turn the page for a brief description
of gifts for Deeper Perception
that correspond to these questions.

Your Gift Set ANSWERS

1. How it smells when you're near the water. **Gustatory Giftedness** means receiving deep knowledge through smell and taste.

2. The sound of the waves. **Clairaudience** means learning through listening.

3. Letting the water rock you, ride with you. **Clairsentience** brings insight through the sense of touch.

4. Noticing the progression of waves, plus how the tide moves in or out. **Analytical Awareness** means that you naturally combine Deeper Perception with curiosity.

5. How you feel, emotionally, being here. **Emotional Intuition** is one of many empathic gifts for Deeper Perception.

6. What sea air does for you physically. **Physical Intuition** is another empathic gift for Deeper Perception.

7. Simply enjoying being a part of nature. **Environmental Empathy** is—you guessed it—one more empathic gift related to Deeper Perception.

8. Noticing how the seagulls move as a group. **Animal Empathy** is yet another form of empathy that can be hard-wired into a person's aura and soul.

9. Observing how other people act at your part of the beach. **Truth Knowledge** is a no-frills form of Deeper Perception where you get straight to the point.

10. Feeling the contagious joy of babies at play. **Holistic Knowing** is a gift for effortlessly reading many auras at once.

11. Delighting in the distinctive qualities of the beach. **Spiritual Oneness** brings celestial knowledge, an empathic gift that could be the sweetest kind of Deeper Perception.

12. Thrilled by how the beach looks. **Clairvoyance** is the

technical name. Clairvoyant forms of Deeper Perception include seeing patterns of light, geometric shapes, seeing colors, or any other way that you find more refined truth visually.

Thus, seeing colors is one specialized type of clairvoyance. And no type of clairvoyance matters more than any other gift for Deeper Perception... not unless you believe in The Myth About Auras.

Do you get the picture/hear what I'm saying/have a sense of what this gift set business is all about?

Unless all that thrills you about a beach is seeing the colors, your gift set has more to it than most people expect.

Consider this an understatement, actually. Based on my experience with students, I have found that most human beings aren't set up as mostly clairvoyant.

This is not because they lack talent but because most people don't fit into a limiting stereotype.

Given what you know now, let's revisit:

A TYPICAL GIFT SET

A wide variety of gifts including the one universal gift for Deeper Perception (Something new, something wonderful, something that I will describe soon.)	Clair- voy- ance

CELEBRATE YOUR GIFT SET

Now that you understand how gift sets work, you can appreciate why The Myth About Auras is so limiting. However your perception works, this is a most intimate part of you. Your personal gift set explains a lot about how you learn, which types of vacation would be fun for you, what turns you on sexually, and more.

Have an extra day to spare? You could spend it by looking back over your life story now that you understand more about your personal gift set. It has been in place from Day One. Family members, teachers and others may have expected you to be different, perceiving more in their way, causing pain that you can now re-evaluate. (Also make note of these people for when you choose cords to cut.)

In the present you can quickly diagram your gift set. Mine goes like this:

ROSE'S GIFT SET

Clair-audience	Clair-sentience	Various forms of empathy	Other gifts

Now it's your turn. Fill in your own diagram about your gift set.

MY PERSONAL GIFT SET

Reality Check

Aura reading is not the only area in life where a person can be limited by myths. In 1988, I went back to Illinois on vacation—Illinois, where I'd first lived with and, later, divorced, my second husband, David. Now I was visiting my dear friend Hilma Hawkins, an enormously perceptive woman who earned her living as a social worker.

For the past five years, I'd lived in Washington D.C., and much of that time I had been in a relationship with a nice kid named Mitch. We had a great relationship, except that we broke up and got back together frequently. Right now, we were on the outs. As I bemoaned my pathetic love life, Hilma listened sympathetically.

Finally she asked, "What do you think it means to love someone, anyway?"

Whatever I'd experienced with my friend Mitch, that didn't seem to qualify as love. By contrast, with each of my two ex-husbands, I had definitely been in love.

I explained to Hilma how, with Mitch, all we had was best-friend intimacy, shared interests, tender sex, not taking our relationship too seriously. This scarcely added up to my definition of "love."

"How come?" Hilma asked.

Hey! Maybe my definition of "love" was the problem.

I apologized to Mitch. We got married. Since 1990, we have had a real-life happily-ever-after.

Gift sets are hardwired into your soul, not likely to change. So you may as well accept yours, rather than worrying about whether you were born with the sensory equivalent of blonde hair and blue eyes.

Self-acceptance won't only save you confusion and anguish. Self-acceptance is wise. Only your gift set can lead you to the fullest personal experience of life. And, of course, using your personal gift set is the only way that you can develop superb skill at cutting cords of attachment.

What if your dream has always been to see auras in full color? Then, with all respect, it's time to get yourself a new dream.

Some salespeople make money by supplying whatever a person requests, even an unrealistic dream that can never fully be realized. If you're unwilling to put aside the dream of "Clairvoyance or nothing," you can find people who will take your money. Instead, I invite you to put aside dreams about having a different person's gift set. Give my techniques—and your own gift set— a chance. You can grow faster that way, and gain meaningful results.

Recognizing distinctive gift sets has been an important feature of my work right from when I developed the method of Aura Reading Through All Your Senses.® You can be sure that I designed the 12 Steps to Cut Cords of Attachment to work for you no matter what your gift set might be.

From Step 3 onward, I will honor your distinctive gift set by giving you a variety of techniques to choose from so that you can find what suits you best.

Here's one last reason to celebrate your gift set: **Synesthesia**. At the level of auras, all gifts become fully activated. When you bring your awareness to the level of auras (whatever technique you may use), you will activate your full gift set.

So you might explore a technique where you first use clairsentience, clairvoyance, clairaudience or another sense. Once you are using that technique, you could have experiences of emotional intuition, gustatory giftedness or any of your other gifts.

This will happen automatically... provided you're not trying to be a particular kind of clairvoyant.

Despite all you have read about gift sets, some readers still may be skeptical. You may have been strongly programmed to believe in The Myth About Auras. Well, dare to be counter-culture. Dare to question what you've been told. Or, at least, dare to experiment at least as long as you're reading the rest of this book. If you do, what will you gain?

Accepting your gift set will help you to fulfill your *deepest* desires to serve humanity as an aura reader.

START READING AURAS

Now you are ready to read the aura of the person whose cord of attachment is going to be cut. If you have a technique that you already love, use that. Your experience may be enriched by new appreciation of your full gift set.

Otherwise, here is an outrageously simple (but effective) way to read auras, "Call It, Read It." You can start by practicing on yourself or else experiment with a buddy. Later, if you work professionally with clients, you may find yourself using this super-easy technique in just about every session.

My inspiration to develop this technique was Tarot readings. Have you ever had one? The reader starts with three things: A deck of cards, a client to read for, and a **spread.**

This last part means a specialized form of intention, a chosen meaning that each card will have for the particular Tarot reading.

A spread is chosen before any card is drawn. For instance, the reader may call a spread this way:

- The first card will summarize your present situation.
- The second card will reveal a hidden conflict.
- The third card will provide insight into your hopes and fears about this situation.
- The fourth card will predict what happens over the next six months.

Lo and behold, the cards will reveal precisely that information.

Once the Tarot reader calls a spread, whether she chooses the cards or the client does, the cards will show up perfectly to support that chosen sequence.

This kind of meaningful coincidence has a name, thanks to Carl Jung. He coined the term **synchronicity.**

Because of synchronicity, Tarot readers can choose any spread they like. It will work.

I asked Robert Place, author of *The Tarot: History, Symbolism, and Divination,* about the importance of choosing a spread. He told me:

> A spread creates meaning before you put a single card down. You're creating a context for the cards so they will talk about the specific subject that you need to know about. Then you can read the story.

With Call It, Read It, any databank in someone's aura will reveal its story.

Call It, Read It

1. Close your eyes. Get Big.
2. Set the intention to learn about your aura.
3. Name a chakra databank (e.g., "How I communicate") followed by the databank location (e.g., "My throat").
4. Close your eyes and pay attention to that body part.
5. Notice how that body part feels to you physically. Is it heavy or light, tight or loose, large or small, comfortable or uncomfortable? Do you notice emotions or colors or words as part of the experience?
6. Say aloud whatever you get. This will be information about the chakra databank you have called out.

You can easily adapt this technique to call and read different databanks. Just name any databank that interests you.

For best results, speak your choice aloud or write it down. Do the same with the information you receive.

When receiving information through your body, stay in flow. Feel the sensation. Put it into words. Please note: This is different from straining to figure out what the sensation means at the same time as you're experiencing it. Just blurt those words out!

Call It, Read It works because of synchronicity. Because you have set up a spread, your Higher Self projects information about your aura right onto your body. The "screen" for this movie is located at the body part you have named.

Receiving this information could be compared to watching a movie, except that you're engaging your complete gift set. And synesthesia will be triggered automatically.

Therefore, physical sensations might just serve as a springboard for your other gifts. You might mostly smell the data or notice emotions. And, unlike a real-life movie, you may not see a thing. However, The Myth About Auras no longer limits you, right? You understand. All that matters is that you receive information.

If you are willing to "watch" with all your senses, the movie of your aura will be projected onto body parts like your throat, your heart or even your butt. Who knew that your butt could become so deeply informative?

LOADS OF INFORMATION

Just how much data can you read from an aura? Using your full gift set, you can easily read 50 databanks per chakra (except, perhaps, for the crown chakra, which isn't quite so packed with personal data).

My set of 50 will be different from yours because each of us specializes—in aura reading, in life. An athlete, for instance, can read nuances about a person's coordination, movement, steadiness. When that athlete becomes an aura reader, he will give brilliant interpretations of these databanks and more.

If you're not that athlete, don't be jealous. You have your own specialties, too, no doubt about it... except, perhaps, for doubts in your own mind when you start out. Aura reading can bring up loads of doubts. (Doubt those doubts.)

See the following chart for examples of databanks, chakra locations and corresponding body parts.

Chakra Databanks to Explore

For any question you might have, there is a databank with an answer! To read it, think of the chakra that would correspond to the data you seek. Create a name for the databank. Then use Call It, Read It to get the information. Here are some sample databanks to get you started.

1. Root Chakra
Chakra Location: Tip of tailbone
Body Part: The butt (Or to put it more politely to your client, "Notice how it feels right where you are sitting on that chair.")
Sample Databanks:
His world (What is his relationship to physical reality?)
Sensuousness (How does he relate to his physical body?)
Prosperity vibe (How likely is he to attract money?)
Trust (Under what conditions does he trust strangers?)
Groundedness (To what degree does he allow himself to feel physically present?)

2. Belly Chakra
Chakra Location: Two inches below the navel
Body Part: The lower belly
Sample Databanks:
Creativity in life (What is a gift of her soul for creativity?)
Frustrations (What blocks her creativity right now?)
Wholeness (How comfortable does she feel expressing her inner child?)
Sexiness (What is she like as a lover?)
Belief (How much confidence does she have about attracting love?)

3. Solar Plexus Chakra

Chakra Location: Between navel and breastbone
Body Part: The rib cage, at the front of the body
Sample Databanks:
Public power (What power style does he show at work?)
Power when it counts (How does he deal with conflict in a relationship where he has invested a lot?)
Mind (Under what situations is he willing to use simple mindfulness?)
Intellectual creativity (What are his creative strengths?)
Vulnerability (What discourages him intellectually?)

4. Heart Chakra

Chakra Location: Center of the body, at the breastbone
Body Part: Around the area of the heart. Note: Initially, clients may think this means the upper chest. It's not. By contrast, the last chakra on our list is at the upper chest. Explain the difference, if necessary.
Sample Databanks:
Giving (What are her patterns with giving love?)
Taking (What are her patterns with receiving love?)
Specialties (Which types of information is she especially good at receiving emotionally?)
Walls (Which kinds of blockage are stuck at this chakra?)
Empathic abilities (Does she have any empathic gifts that involve emotions?)

5. Throat Chakra

Chakra Location: The throat
Body Part: The throat!
Sample Databanks:
Public truthfulness (What happens with verbal truthfulness when he is at work?)

Truthfulness in personal relationships (How about his verbal truthfulness with people he knows well?)

Intimacy style (Does your client feel comfortable sharing information that might make him seem vulnerable?)

Facades in public (What size and kind of facade does he use to impress strangers?)

Assertiveness (Which communication patterns come up when he faces conflict?)

6. Third Eye Chakra

Chakra Location: Between and above the eyebrows
Body Part: The forehead
Sample Databanks:

Evolution (What helps her along her spiritual path?)

Reality check (How willing is she to take responsibility for her human life on earth?)

Timing (What is her preferred speed for evolving right now?)

Limitations (Does she carry fears related to religion?)

Insights (Which conflicts does your client have about co-creating with a Higher Power?)

7. Soul Expression Chakra

Chakra Location: Halfway between the throat and heart
Body Part: The upper chest
Sample Databanks:

Specialties (What are his soul-level gifts for enjoying life as a human being?)

Sub-Programs (Are circuits in place that re-route seeking his own happiness to... helping others instead?)

Self-Awareness (Does he pursue what thrills his soul?)

Obstructions (What blocks his experience of joy?)

Allowing (What will it take for him to choose happiness?)

You get the idea. Once you choose a particular chakra location, inquire about any databank that you believe might be related. Not only are you accessing information that can prove very important for cutting a cord of attachment. You also awaken a person's aura, and prepare it to change, just by the act of reading it.

ACTIVATE YOUR CLIENT'S AURA

Once you have become familiar with Call It, Read It, go ahead. Teach it to your client. You can put her in touch with underlying experiences.

Besides, the very process of paying attention at the level of her own aura will activate it, preparation for the major aura surgery to come.

Especially if a client usually spends a lot of time in her head, worrying or analyzing, this technique can bring a reality check.

Teach Your Client Call It, Read It

Here is a way to teach your client how to do this technique:

1. Call It, Read It is a way to explore what goes on within you. I'm going to name one databank at a time. Then I'll pair one aspect of life with that part of your body. After I call it out, you tell me what you notice there. We'll talk more later. For now, let's just go step by step.
2. The first databank to explore is called "How I communicate."
3. Now close your eyes and pay attention to your throat. Notice how that body part feels to you. Is it heavy or light, tight or loose, large or small, comfortable or uncomfortable? Do you notice emotions or colors or words?

4. Now, I'm going to ask you to pay attention to your butt. How does your body feel, right where you're connecting to that chair? Whatever sensations you feel will give us information about your prosperity vibe right now, your deep-down willingness to attract money.

5. Remember, physical sensations have meaning for the technique we're using. Whatever you physically feel there, right in your butt, will count as information. You don't have to think about the topic, because my mentioning it was enough to direct your inner consciousness. Just close your eyes, pay attention to the sensations in your body, and tell me what you get.

6. Finally, pay attention to your chest. This will supply information about how it feels to be you right now, the emotional experience. Because we're using the Call It, Read It technique, whatever you feel in your body will automatically be about your emotions. Close your eyes. How does it feel in that part of your body? Tell me.

To summarize, the basic instruction for reading any databank is:

"You'll pay attention to X part of your body. It will give information about the Y databank in your aura. Whatever you feel there will be about what I've said. You don't have to think about the topic, once I have said it. Just pay attention to your body. Tell me what you get."

I invite you to play client with yourself, right now. Do a big set of Before Pictures. Choose at least one databank per chakra and record what you get for each item. Save the record you make.

Starting with Step 7, you will be cutting your own cords of attachment. So long as you are doing the practice sessions recommended for this book, do a new After Picture for each of the databanks you have chosen. That's a new After Picture for every time you cut a cord. You may be amazed at the difference.

An important principle of healing is that you will only be able to go as deeply into a client's experiences as you are willing to go into your own. This holds true for physical, psychological and spiritual types of healing.

Using Call It, Read It, you can deepen your own self-awareness. If you should go on to teach the technique to clients, your ability to understand any client's experiences will be enhanced by your own process of self-discovery.

Taking out Garbage

A quick scan of Jeff's aura revealed problems with his solar plexus. So, at the start of his session, I had him research two different databanks there.

Using the Call It, Read It technique, I asked him to put attention at the front of his ribcage to check out personal power during a conflict with someone he cared about. I told him, "Whatever you feel there will describe the databank I've named. You don't have to think about the topic, once I call it out. Just pay attention to your body and tell me what you get."

"Something is stuck," Jeff said.

Then I asked him to feel the front of his ribcage again, only this time the databank would be about how he expressed himself when angry.

"Tension," he noted.

Jeff's intention for this session was simple: To release anger. Which cord did he think was related? The one to his mother.

We cut it. In Step 10, I described the following dynamics. Jeff laughed a lot... apparently out of pure relief to have these familiar feelings depart.

1. *Mother: Constantly yapping and fussing, like an overexcited small dog.*
2. *Jeff: Feeling a similar discomfort himself.*
3. *Jeff: I must avoid these excessive emotions.*
4. *Mother: You don't care enough. You're so insensitive.*
5. *Jeff: Instinctively knowing that he is very sensitive, Jeff reacts with rage: "How dare you? Nobody will make me feel guilty again. In fact, the more someone demands things of me, the less I will give. Ever."*
6. *Jeff: Circuits were installed for passive-aggressive behavior, e.g., If mother asked him to take out the garbage, and he felt angry, he*

wouldn't confront her directly with "No way! I refuse to take out your garbage." Instead, he would say, "Sure, in a moment" and let that "moment" last forever. If she repeated her demand, he would repeat the polite stalling tactic. Passive-aggressive behavior may not be informative for the person being punished but it sure can feel effective as vengeance.

7. Jeff: Feeling guilty: I shouldn't get so angry at her—or enjoy my revenge so much.

When we discussed the consequences of cutting the cord, Jeff felt hopeful. His old behavior pattern didn't really work well for him. Previously, he'd recognized the problem but hadn't been able to stop. With the cord gone, that could finally change.

To give Jeff closure, at the end of his session, we used Call It, Read It again at the two solar plexus databanks. Nothing was stuck there any more, and his chronic tension had gone.

QUALITY CONTROL

How can you evaluate the benefits of cutting a cord of attachment? Only half the results (or less) will consist of new ideas. We're all used to valuing these ideas, and they have great significance for psychological healing. But in the words of Bill Bauman, my greatest inspiration in developing the field of Energy Spirituality, "New ideas are good for about two hours."

To change someone's life, don't just change his mind for two hours. Change his aura.

You are doing that when you use all 12 Steps to Cut Cords of Attachment. Still, who among us is going to automatically recognize the full extent of what has changed aurically? Not most of us, not without a little coaching. Therefore, I encourage you to include Before-and-After Pictures, even when you are your own client. It's a 21st century procedure for quality control.

Before Pictures

Ideally, Step 3 of Cutting Cords of Attachment includes doing a Before Picture. This activates the aura, as well as providing quality control for your session.

1. Introduce the idea of Before-and-After Pictures.
2. Teach the Call It, Read It technique.
3. To help you gauge the success of your session, make a simple chart to record your client's responses. (See the next page for examples.)
4. Ask for a total of three readings, ending with one about how the client feels emotionally.
5. Congratulate the client.
6. At the end of your session, do an After Picture.

To keep track of Before-and-After pictures, I like to make a simple chart. Since you don't show this to your client, it doesn't have to be beautiful. Just jot down the information as best you can so that you can compare before and after.

You will need a couple of columns, one for Before and one for After.

Then make a few rows, labeling both the chakra and the databank in question.

Can you ever choose three different databanks at the same chakra? I've done that sometimes.

One thing I do almost always is to end with the heart chakra databank called "How do I feel, emotionally, right now?"

Let the client explore this one for herself, whether by using Call It, Read It, or simply by moving into present emotions in her own favorite way. Cutting a cord can bring your client significant emotional improvement, for the After Picture and well beyond it.

Chakra Databank	Before Picture	After Picture
High Heart: Expressing Your Soul in Everyday Life		
SolarPlexus: Connection to Personal Power in EverydayLife		
Heart: How It Feels to Be YOU Right Now		

Scary In-Laws

Gary's in-laws were giving him grief. His intention for the session was get along with them better. Mission was accomplished—or at least off to a good start. Subsequent sessions could help even more. But here is what he reported after only one session.

Chakra Databank	Before Picture	After Picture
Root: Your Confidence in Front of Family	Not too much.	More is there. And I feel calm.
Solar Plexus: Having Power with Your Wife's Family	A burning sensation.	Much better.
Heart: How It Feels to Be YOU Right Now	Tense. The energy feels compressed.	Relief. It really feels different for me, emotionally.

READ THE AURA OUT LOUD

To locate a cord of attachment, yes, you'll need aura reading. To diagram it after cutting, you'll also have to read auras. Besides that, aura reading will help you to activate a client's aura. Paying attention starts this happening. By speaking out loud about a client's aura, you activate it still more.

Altogether, the more comfortable you can become with reading auras, the greater your effectiveness at helping yourself and others with Energy Spirituality. Okay, you're willing. How do you go about doing something more elegant than Call It, Read It?

I'm going to share two more aura reading techniques out of the many I have developed to make Deeper Perception easy, natural and practical. These two techniques are based on something we've considered before, your personal gift set. Whichever technique you prefer, once you successfully connect to an aura through any one sense, because of synesthesia all of your gifts will become activated.

Both of the following techniques are equally powerful. I've put "See It, Read It" first because that's the order most readers expect but, personally, I strongly prefer "Touch It, Read It." If, like me, you are more touch-sensitive or sound-oriented than visual, skip ahead to that technique first. Probably you will enjoy it more, too.

Remember, you only need one of the following techniques to do hugely powerful sessions for clients. And, of course, if you already enjoy using some different method for reading auras in depth, use that instead.

See It, Read It

The following technique will appeal to you if visual abilities are a big part of your gift set.

1. Close your eyes. Get Big.

2. Set an intention, like "I choose to gain more wisdom about myself." or "I wish to be of service to my client."

3. Choose one databank to research. Here, I'll give the example of "Communication with intimacy" at the throat chakra.

4. Open your eyes and aim them (i.e., stare) at the part of your client's body corresponding to your chosen databank.

5. Begin the Questioning technique while you look. Ask inside, "What is going on with..." In this example, I ask,

> "What is going on with his ability to communicate with intimacy?"
>
> 6. As a novice, you would do well to close your eyes at this point. With more experience, you can keep your eyes open. Release the question with two vibe-raising breaths. Then return to normal breathing.
>
> 7. Accept what you get. That's valid information about your client's aura. Say it out loud.

Some visually-oriented people find this technique ridiculously easy, but others run into a few temporary difficulties. Does that include you? Let's do some problem solving.

All I got was an image, an apple with a slight dent near the top. Should I tell my client what I'm getting and ask what that means to him?

Definitely not. Your inner self communicates to you through a unique alphabet. The precise combination of letters is nobody else's business. As discussed earlier, never tell your client the equivalent of "I'm getting Tim-Tim."

But what if I don't know what an image means? Shouldn't I ask someone else to interpret for me?

No. Cycle through another round of Questioning. This time your question will be, "What does that apple mean about my client's communication?"

Uh-oh, I just got another image. This time, it was a whole orchard. I saw one apple tree up close. One of the branches on the right was slightly broken, twisting off to the side. Why would I get multiple images?

It won't happen for long, not when your conscious and subconscious minds become clear on one very important point:

You have a goal here.

Energy Spirituality is not some quaint hobby, where you can summon infinite patience while meandering through the ethers. You are reading auras to get results, correct?

Some of the sweetest spiritual seekers in the world get lost in imagery. Some analyze dreams; others train as psychics. Whatever the discipline, they can spend hours on pretty pictures, never bringing forth anything so practical as a single concrete result. That's a hobby, like having a lovely time hanging out in the Olde Curiosity Shoppe.

The human mind will accommodate any kind of hobby. But if you're very clear that you aim to get results, your full mind will support that, too—your conscious mind, subconscious mind, and Higher Self.

What if I'm scared to interpret my image, and that's why I keep getting new ones? Could this be a way to put off being put to the test?

Very perceptive. But remember, your client isn't some harsh schoolmaster about to grade you. This is a person who has come to you for help. When your work is accurate, your client will be helped to the max. Should your work be less than accurate, your client is perfectly capable of sloughing it off.

That would be a relief, but can I really trust a client to compensate for my inadequacies? What if he's instinct impaired?

Come on! You think your client can't handle TV commercials, Internet spam, newspaper ads?

What, he never has to walk through a crowd of strangers or drive on a road full of cars?

To function in the post-modern age, each of us has learned a great deal about how to select and how to toss.

After a couple of cycles of Questioning, use your common sense to interpret. Go back to that first image: Context is communication about intimacy. Questioning gives you "an apple with a slight dent near the top." Get a grip. Put it together.

Remember, once you set the intention to serve your client, everything that happens will be for good. And the more you move into a state of flow, the better you'll do.

The Big Question

Once a TV reporter interviewed me for a couple of hours. She'd driven down from Baltimore with a camera guy. Ultimately, only six minutes from our interview would be used on the air. I knew that. When she finished, I knew which part of our interview would definitely make the cut. Sure enough it later appeared on Sweeps Week.

How could I tell which particular question was so very important? The reporter asked it three times. First time, she had the cameraman film a close-up of her asking. Second time, he took a close-up of me. Third came a long shot to establish that we were talking together about this urgent matter.

Three times, then, the pretty young reporter leaned towards me confidingly and said, with thinly veiled condescension:

"Rose, we know you think you read auras. You say that you get information and it helps people. You seem satisfied with what you do. But tell me, don't people sometimes ask you, 'ARE YOU CRAZY?'"

Lucky me, I got to answer this very shrewd question three times in a row. I told her, "That very fear of being crazy is what keeps so many people from reading auras in the first place."

Consider yourself warned. Do you have fears about your sanity or doubt your spiritual worthiness? All kinds of nasty stuff deep within may come up when you start reading auras. What's the fastest way to heal it? Simple. Ignore fears and doubts. Keep on reading auras.

When that blockage is gone, it will go for good. What a blessing to have those fears finally disintegrate! Even for the sake of the rest of your life, you'd want to read auras.

CONNECT THROUGH TOUCH

Now let's shift to our second aura reading technique. You'll be connecting to an aura through clairsentience, rather than the clairvoyance of the See It, Read It technique. Instead of both eyes, you'll use one hand. Which one? I call that your **Hand of Preference.** Here's how to find it:

Hand of Preference

Sometimes you will read auras by using one hand as a tool. I recommend that you use your Hand of Preference.

To find out which one this is, imagine yourself being reunited with your true love after a long absence. If you were reaching out with one hand to touch his or her face, which hand would you use? The hand better suited to tender touch is your Hand of Preference.

Don't automatically assume this is your right hand (if you're right handed) or left (if you're left handed). Take a moment to fantasize touching your love with each hand. The inner experience is quite different.

Which hand would enable you to receive more information, going all the way to the depths of your love's soul?

Whenever you are going to use one hand to do an aura reading, use that Hand of Preference. The information will be clearer than if you were to use the other hand.

What if you still aren't sure which is your Hand of Preference? Experiment by using different hands, reading different databanks. Which hand brings quicker, clearer results?

Just don't ever test yourself by doing the same technique twice on the same databank, comparing the information you get with each hand. Testing is a way to block your development, remember?

Alternating different investigations with different hands is fine until you decide on one Hand of Preference. Most of my students find that one hand is definitely better than the other for taking in data from auras. If you don't strongly prefer one hand after the first few experiments, arbitrarily pick one and stick with that choice.

Having established your Hand of Preference, you are ready to move into the technique for aura reading that I, personally, use most often.

Touch It, Read It

1. Close your eyes. Get Big.

2. Set an intention, like "I choose to gain more wisdom about myself" or "I wish to be of service to my client."

3. Choose one databank to research. (Here, I'll give the example of "Communication with intimacy" at the heart chakra.)

4. Move your Hand of Preference, palm toward your client, a few inches in front of her body, at the place corresponding to your chosen databank. Leave your hand there and know that you won't need to *feel* anything in your hand in order for you to get information. The palm of your hand is simply a conduit. Information will flow *through* your hand.

5. Begin the Questioning technique while your hand is placed within your client's aura. Ask inside, "What is going on with…" (In this example, I ask, "What is going on with her ability to communicate with intimacy.")

6. As a novice, you would do well to close your eyes after you ask the question. (With more experience, you can keep your eyes open.) Release the question with two vibe-raising breaths. Then return to normal breathing.

7. Accept whatever you get. Write it down and count the information as valid.

Remember, you are the world's expert at interpreting what you find in auras. Trust your wisdom and it will grow. Allowing yourself to read auras daily will accelerate full ownership of your gift set. You'll advance most rapidly as a practitioner of Energy Spirituality.

Yes, I know that some famous teachers train their students to be just like them. Supposedly, the more precisely students can duplicate their teacher, the better they are doing. This makes about as much sense as thinking that true beauty for a woman requires that she squeeze herself into a corset or, these days, get cosmetic surgery until she superficially resembles her favorite star.

I have enormous respect for Donna Eden, a medical intuitive and healer who has been described as having a one-in-a-million talent. She has trained thousands of students without ever demanding that they imitate her. Here's what she said when I asked her whether it would be desirable for every aura reader to receive identical information:

> While it might be desirable for everyone to be consistent, and it would certainly make it easier to get this work recognized as having a scientific basis, it is not possible. We all have our own special way of taking in information and we see through our own aura with its unique intensity and personal color scheme—which, of course, causes us to perceive colors differently from one another.
>
> In the synesthesia of energy perception, some see energy as colors, some see geometrical shapes, some see a glow or variations in brightness, while others hear it, taste it, or smell it. Many feel it. We each have our own filters, which makes it all very interesting, plus it requires us each to be our own authority."

AIM FOR GIFTS

Admittedly, when you read a client's aura, inspiration may not always be your first reaction. When doing Touch It, Read It or See It,

Read It, you may feel overwhelmed by fear, pain, sorrow or other negative qualities.

But healing involves making choices, and nowhere is this more evident than with Energy Spirituality. Remember, hundreds of databanks live within your client, available for you to call and read. Insist on finding gifts of your client's soul.

The following technique can help you. The context is our discussion in Step 2 about making an Energy Sandwich. Mostly, auras are astral. But they contain some etheric-level information as well.

In other words, auras mostly inform you about a person's experience in everyday life, with past influences and problems showing up prominently. That's the psychic-level portion.

However, auras also reveal gifts of the soul. Well, you have the membership card to enter here, at the etheric level, when researching an aura. Why? You Got Big, which connected your consciousness to a being who lives at the etheric level. So all you need do now is use the following technique.

Insist on Reaching the Soul

Right at the moment when you realize that you haven't found anything positive in a client's aura, stop and do this technique.

1. Close your eyes. Get Big. And set an intention, like "I choose to find a gift of my client's soul."
2. Go back to the databank you were researching. Here, I'll give the example of "Communication with intimacy" at the heart chakra.
3. Connect by touch or vision (whichever is your favorite). Begin the Questioning technique by asking inside, "What is a gift of his or her soul with..." (In this example, I'd ask, "What is a gift of her soul for communication with intimacy?")

---

4. Release the question by taking two Vibe-Raising Breaths. Then return to normal breathing.

5. Accept what you get. Count it as valid information about your client's aura.

6. Choose this information to tell your client *first*.

Never let something negative be the first thing you tell your client about her aura. Ultimately, your client's aura is about magnificence, not problems. Long after the problems are healed, that magnificence will remain.

Will I Ever Be Able to Express Myself?

Bruce blamed his "bad" throat chakra for how awful he felt. He was wrong. One clue came from his own Before Picture:

*Throat databank: **Speaking up for himself at work.***

"I don't feel much."

*Throat databank: **Speaking up during conflict** with people important to him.*

"I don't feel much."

*Emotions: **How does it feel to be you?***

"I feel nothing at all."

Here were the cord dynamics between Bruce and his mother:

1. *Mom: Crabby*
2. *Bruce: Headache from being bullied.*
3. *Mom: You are bad, bad, bad.*
4. *Bruce: I feel criticized.*
5. *Mom: Delight in son's pain.*
6. *Bruce: "Nothing I do changes things. The only way to feel better is to close myself off from how I feel." (Like an ostrich with its head in the sand, Bruce would wait out the situation.)*
7. *Bruce: Trying very hard not to hate Mom.*

When we discussed the cord items, Bruce had a big aha! Both hatred and de-nial of hatred were locked into that cord of attachment, repeating 24/7. These negative feelings had Bruce energetically tied up in knots, blocking his heart chakra even more than his throat.

By the After Picture, Bruce began to feel his emotions again. All his prob-lems weren't solved yet, not by a long shot, but he had become someone who could speak up for himself. More growth would follow.

Don't let aura reading intimidate either your client or you.

- Problems at the level of auras can cause difficulties with emotions, communication, health, you name it.
- Improvement at the level of auras will give your client a better life.

Soon, you will be doing surgery to bring forth that soul beauty. On to Step 4!

Step 4. Choose Which Cord to Cut

12 STEPS TO CUT CORDS OF ATTACHMENT

Step 1. Create a Sacred Space
Step 2. Make an Energy Sandwich
Step 3. Activate the Aura
Step 4. Choose Which Cord to Cut
  Distinguish Minor vs. Major Cords of Attachment
  Avoid Ego Hooks
  To help clients: Assess Stability
  To help clients: Screen out Drama
  To help clients: Preview the Process
  Identify Which Cord to Cut
  Inner Permission
  To help clients: Preview the Next Steps
Step 5. Locate the Cord
Step 6. Give Permission
Step 7. Remove the Cord
Step 8. Bandage to Rebalance
Step 9. Write the Dialogue Box
Step 10. Discuss the Pattern
Step 11. Impact Other Relationships
Step 12. Assign Homework

Steps 1-3 have prepared you to use Energy Spirituality to trans-form an aura. Now you need to choose wisely which cord to cut at this particular time. Whether you're working on yourself or help-ing someone else, you'll find Step 4 indispensable for facilitating the psychic-level surgery of cutting cords of attachment.

But isn't it obvious which cord to cut first? Don't you want to go straight to the most horrendous, nastiest relationship of all?

Slow down, mighty healer! As someone developing this power-ful skill set, it's extremely important to begin with minor cords. Find examples on the following list. Undoubtedly, you will think of oth-ers, too.

I strongly recommend that you do at least 10 sessions on what I call Minor Cords before you attempt to remove a Major Cord.

Minor Cords of Attachment

Practice by cutting **minor cords,** not major ones. These re-lationships are no big deal but not pleasant, either. Your set of minor cords could include:

1. Annoying politicians or celebrities
2. Irritating co-workers, bosses or customers
3. Minor friendships from your adult life that ended badly (even if they were otherwise good relationships)
4. Neighbors or acquaintances, from your adult life, who got under your skin
5. People who have wasted your time or money, or betrayed your trust in minor ways

---

As you learn this new skill set, let your timing be slow. Whether you are doing sessions for yourself or exchanging with a friend, never begin by cutting major cords of attachment. Begin with the minor ones *especially* when your long-term goal is to cut major cords.

Remember, cutting a cord by the method you're learning is permanent, a one-time opportunity. If you were practicing for your first piano recital, would you choose to perform Rachmaninoff's Piano Concerto No 3 in D minor? Any complicated set of chords/cords is best left until later, when you've had more experience.

The Top 15 Cords

The following list will give you examples of **major cords of attachment,** very important to (eventually) cut.

1. Anyone who has hurt you through violence or abuse
2. Any major accident or trauma. (You bet there can be a cord to an event. If a particular person was involved, there will be a cord to that person. The name isn't necessary, not if it isn't known. It's enough to say something like, "The hit-and-run driver from the accident when I was nine.")
3. Mother
4. Father
5. If you were adopted, both biological parents
6. Every sister, brother, half-sister or brother, step-sister or brother
7. Any children, including any who died or were given away for adoption
8. Any developing babies who didn't make it to term—miscarriages, abortions
9. Any sexual partner involved in conceiving a child
10. Every ex-spouse or former live-in lover, including the person with whom virginity was lost
11. Any cult leader or other person with undue influence over your life
12. Childhood friends, especially anyone involved with first

drugs, first cigarettes, first experiments with hard liquor
13. Any spiritual teacher, therapist, or healer who put ego hooks into you
14. Outstandingly difficult relationships from work, like horrible employers or employees, plus any co-workers or clients who betrayed you
15. All bullies from childhood, including any harsh teachers or others involved in hurtful relationships

EGO HOOKS

In the list of The Top 15 Cords, you may have noticed my reference to **ego hooks.** These are energy-draining structures within cords of attachment. The person who hooks will fasten energetically onto people, setting up cords of attachment in relationships that otherwise would be so minor that no cord would be present.

Hooks can also cause a routine cord of attachment to become extra draining, even debilitating. Typically, ego hooks drain a client's power, sexual energy, or emotional vitality.

During Step 7, hooks will automatically be pulled out and destroyed along with the rest of the cord of attachment. Definitely a relief!

Are ego hooks created on purpose? Not always. For example, say that you have been working with a well intended teacher, healer, psychic, therapist, etc. This practitioner has subconscious emotional or sexual needs that create a hook. Or perhaps the two of you have unfinished business from a past life. Whatever has caused you both to be connected now, ego hooks can drain your energy significantly. Consider yourself warned:

- Even if no harm is meant, ego hooks can hurt you.
- Even if you and the cordee are equally unaware of your energetic connection, that doesn't keep you from being drained.

What if you are tremendously fond of the cordee, ego hooks or not? The fondness forms a spiritual tie, remember? So fear not. Spiritual ties will remain long after you have removed a cord of attachment, ego hooks and all.

Worried about reprisals or harm that could come from removing ego hooks? Cutting a cord of attachment, using the 12-Step method, will free you permanently. And the cordee will not be harmed in any way.

Not all ego hooks are innocent, of course. Many charismatic people hook others on purpose. This is especially common with:

- Cult leaders
- Greedy or highly ambitious business people
- Performers and politicians (terms that you can define as broadly as you wish)
- Sociopaths
- Anyone with oversized sex appeal
- Alas, charming people of any kind may attach ego hooks, but they have such winning ways it's hard to spot.

In addition, so-called "toxic people" also attach ego hooks, whether consciously or not. Surely you've encountered at least one super-draining teacher from school, a relative who cheerfully clobbers you energetically each time you meet, or some power-hungry boss at work.

Anyone's ego hooks can cause a major cord of attachment to form. And if you have been hooked by a manipulative relationship, however temporarily, you can be sure that a cord still connects you.

To remove these gotcha-appliances, will you have to become a hook specialist like some kind of fly fisherman of the soul? No, ego hook removal is easy. Hooks automatically come out with the rest of a cord of attachment.

But learning about ego hooks in the context of cords explains a lot, doesn't it? How often have you told yourself something like this?

"Avoid Mr. X. He's toxic."

Yet you simply couldn't stay away. Maybe you blamed yourself, called yourself "weak."

Why blame the victim? Cords of attachment really do pull and tug. Ego hooks, especially, can land you like a trout. Energy Spirituality to the rescue!

PROTECTION

When cutting cords of attachment for clients, might *you* inadvertently put in a hook of your own?

The 12 Steps to Cut Cords of Attachment include safeguards against this, including "Get Big" and "Set an Intention." Beyond that, you bear sole responsibility for your personal integrity. Avoid ulterior motives in dealing with clients. Choices accumulate into a reputation, so make yours the best it can be.

Psychic Healing with Hooks

Roger had done many sessions with me over the years. Psychologically he was in great shape, and it was always a treat to spiff up his already magnificent aura. This time, however, Roger looked worried in a way that I'd never seen before. His story:

"I just came back from a two-week seminar with a famous psychic healer, Zachary. During the seminar I felt great, but since coming home I've had the sense that something was wrong. Could you see if I have a cord of attachment to him?"

The answer was a resounding "Yes." Here's what I found, after re moving the cord at Roger's belly chakra:

1. The Healer: You must keep learning more from me.
2. Roger: Yes, I must keep learning more from you.
3. The Healer: To do my healing, I work with a group of astral-level beings, the Committee. Once I initiate you, I form an energetic linkage between you and the Committee. They feed off your aura for the rest

> *of your life. In return for receiving energy from my students and patients, the Committee does healings for me.*

Scary, I know. Many forms of healing come with strings attached. It isn't just psychic healers, either. Good old M.D.'s can throw out ego hooks, too.

Choosing any healer, always ask your gut "Where she is coming from?"

Sometimes you will feel the need to inwardly ask some follow-up questions.

- Is the healing done selflessly or as an extension of the healer's ego?
- Does the healer give out her own energy? Does she seem tired or drained at the end of your session?
- If she teams up with help, where does that help come from?

In Step 2, you learned how to make an Energy Sandwich by teaming up with Divine Beings. Not everyone has the training (or inclination), to work this way. Some of the scariest auras I've met belong to preachers or healers who team up with low-level astral beings.

Studying with his renowned teacher, Roger never considered the possibility that astral strings would be attached. During Step 10 of our session, Roger told me that, as soon as he returned home from studying with Zachary, he decided to end the relationship. But that hadn't felt sufficient. With the cord gone, Roger finally felt clear of Zachary's influence.

AND MORE PROTECTION

Before you discuss cutting a particular cord of attachment with a client, be sure to assess her first. Is she emotionally and physically stable enough for this type of work? If not, problems could develop later. Do the smart thing and check.

Read Your Client for Stability

Sometimes a client isn't ready for you to cut *any* cord of attachment. During Step 3, you've read your client's aura. That should have told you a lot about her stability. But if you didn't focus on her stability before, use the following technique now, at Step 4. This assessment can be kept private. Satisfy yourself that this client is stable enough for you to do surgery on her aura.

1. Get Big.
2. Set the intention to tell if your client is stable enough for cutting a cord of attachment.
3. Choose your favorite aura reading technique, like Touch It, Read It or See It, Read It. Check out these three databanks:
• Root chakra: Connection to Reality databank
• Throat chakra: Truthfulness databank
• Third eye: Spiritual Connection databank
4. Supplement whatever you find here with all you have learned so far from your client's behavior and body language. Does your client seem weepy, prone to rage or extremely fearful?
5. If anything seems like a cause for concern, *do not* attempt to cut any cords of attachment. Use other techniques from your personal skill set or simply end the session.

Don't expect warning bells to clang loudly in your session room, like a fire alarm. You'll hear warnings only if you pay attention.

Hyper-vigilance isn't needed, for a client's aura can be loaded with turmoil yet stable enough for cord removal. I can assure you, back when Joanna Lester cut all those cords of attachment for me, I was no model of fortitude. Basically, consider yourself warned if:

- At the root chakra, your client doesn't connect much to reality, or if any databank at the root chakra shows big cracks (representing major unhealed traumas).
- At the throat, if your client seems extremely untruthful, slimy, etc. Although stable, he may so hard to satisfy that you're better off not working with him.
- The spiritual connection databank can also show deep psychological problems, with major cracks, leaks or tears at any layer of your client's aura.
- If your client is drunk or high on non-prescription drugs, don't cut any cords of attachment at all and ask that, next time, he comes with his regular "naked" aura.
- If your client expresses wildly unrealistic expectations of what the session will do, don't cut any cords of attachment.
- Finally, don't cut any cords of attachment for a client who has major trouble dealing with reality, e.g., She turns the process of making an appointment into a complicated mess. She arrives late after much turmoil. She can't manage to sit on the chair in your office without falling off. Hmm, is this beginning to sound like a real-life client? Yep. Luckily, my session room has a soft carpet.

Basically, any time a client gives you a bad feeling inside, pay attention. Your intuition is speaking. Sometimes intuition may prompt you to avoid scheduling a session in the first place. No fancy explanation is needed. Just say, "I don't feel I can help you at this time."

A client could be very miserable but still remain a perfectly fine candidate for a session. What matters is that, in his own way, he is stable.

Yes, it is a huge responsibility to use Energy Spirituality to transform an aura. Don't let anyone pressure you into cutting a cord of attachment unless you personally feel comfortable doing so.

SCREEN OUT DRAMA

If a client calls to schedule a session because he's in crisis, think twice before pulling out your calendar. My policy is to refuse to take on any new client while he or she is going through drama.

Why? Think about typical life situations where someone might be in crisis:

- A wife has just asked for a divorce
- A child has run away from home
- A husband has started beating his wife
- An alcoholic spouse hit bottom
- Bankruptcy proceedings have just begun

For problems like these, immediate solutions come from taking action in the outer world. No amount of cord-cutting will bring back a wayward spouse. Sometimes your would-be client really needs psychological counseling, debt counseling, or the police.

Once you feel satisfied that cutting a cord for a client *will* be appropriate, make sure that her expectations are appropriate as well.

REFINE EXPECTATIONS

Energy Spirituality isn't physical. It is also relatively new to most clients, so they can have some wild ideas about what to expect. Clients can bring expectations that would be more suitable for a visit to Disney World.

Even the most realistic clients may not be clear about the difference between how a psychic would approach cords of attachment in contrast to a practitioner of Energy Spirituality. Well, here goes my standard explanation:

"In just one session, a psychic could *describe* many cords of attachment in minute detail. This could be really meaningful. And learning about a whole lot of cords at once sounds like a great deal. Still, describing without healing may not be such a great value. At best, this knowledge will contribute to psychological healing, rather than spiritual healing." (Read more about psychological versus spiritual healing in Step 10.)

Whatever your client's expectations, it's your job to find out what they are or, at least, clarify what you can do. Complicating this need is the possibility that your client may be in a big rush, demanding that you do something dramatic and do it fast.

You're in charge, however. So take the time needed to prepare your client properly. If you're being pressured to rush through Step 4, it might be better to stop the session right there.

Preview the Process

Even if a client has had previous experience with cutting cords of attachment, he may not be familiar with *your* way of doing it. Begin by explaining what cord cutting will and won't do. Here are the most important points to make:

1. When you have an important relationship, the Cosmic Phone Company comes in to install a cable, or cord, between yourself and the other person. This cord attaches to your aura.

2. Energy flows back and forth through this cord. This is not unconditional love but the toxic part of a relationship. For instance, a cord could be sending *you* the equivalent of a ton of anger. As if this weren't bad enough, the energy pattern in a cord will usually repeat 24/7 until the last day of your life.

3. But here we're using the technology of Energy Spirituality to remove a cord of attachment permanently. This will free you from the energy imbalance that has affected you subconsciously, through your aura.

4. Cutting a cord of attachment brings freedom. How you use that new freedom will be up to you.

WHICH CORD TO CUT

By Step 4 in your session, the choice of which cord to cut may be obvious—or not.

If your client is concerned about a particular relationship, choosing a name is easy. Confirm the choice with your client: "You've talked about your mother. Are you interested in cutting a cord of attachment to her?"

What if the choice for this session isn't obvious?

Ask your client: "Given your intention for this session, who comes to mind as a candidate for cord cutting?"

Often, you'll need to fine-tune this question, for example:

- "Since your intention is to reclaim your power, who comes to mind as a candidate for cord cutting?"
- "You've mentioned that releasing anger is important to you. Which person's name comes up for you when you think about anger?"
- "Greater intimacy is your goal for this session, as you said before. Let's consider cutting your cord of attachment to the person who has made intimacy most difficult. Who would that be?"

Usually a client will include a bit of information to clarify the person's role in his life. If not, ask. "And the type of relationship here is son, father, what?" You wouldn't interpret a cord to a son the same way as a cord to a father.

Also ask, "Is this person still living?" This just helps you correctly refer to the cordee in the present or past tense. Technically, there is no significant difference between how you cut a cord to someone who is deceased, alive, closely related or estranged.

Use the following quiz to supplement your preview. You may be surprised at the answers supplied by a hopeful client.

What Will Cord Cutting Do? A QUIZ

Here's a quiz you can give your client to clarify further what is reasonable to expect. Answer TRUE or FALSE.

Will cutting a cord of attachment:

1. Remove unconditional love, the spiritual learning, between you and the other person?

2. Hurt the other person?

3. Change the other person, turning him into somebody who is really nice to you?

4. Make you instantly closer to the other person? Or break off your relationship?

5. Cause suffering? Is there a spiritual price to pay?

Turn the page for answers.

What Will Cord Cutting Do? ANSWERS

1. Will cutting a cord of attachment remove **unconditional love,** the spiritual learning, between you and the other person?
NO. Spiritual ties are sacred, as much a part of you as your very soul. Nothing can remove spiritual ties, but cords of attachment are different.

2. Will cutting a cord of attachment **hurt** the other person?
NO. It won't affect the cordee in any way. (If your client worries about this, explain Divine Homeostasis, discussed in Step 6.)

3. Will cutting a cord of attachment **change** the other person, turning him into somebody who is really nice to you?
NO. For that, we'd have to charge an extra nickel.

Actually, no amount of money could force a spiritual healer to change anyone without consent. You know who must make the decision in order for a person to change, don't you? (Coach your client, if necessary, that each person is responsible for her own life. Some clients need to hear this again and again. With each cord cut, they will hear it better.)

4. Will cutting a cord of attachment make you instantly **closer** to the other person? Or will it break off your relationship?
NO and NO. You'll simply have more choices about how close you wish to be.

5. Will cutting a cord of attachment cause suffering? Is there a spiritual **price** to pay for moving out a cord of attachment?
NO and NO. Cutting cords of attachment is a sacred form of surgery, done with Divine blessing. This is Energy Spirituality, after all. If you're seeking enlightenment in your spiritual life, you can appreciate how important it would be to gain freedom from energies that distort your aura.

INNER PERMISSION

Think of it like a vote: A candidate for cord cutting has been named. But will that candidate win the election? Remember, you co-create healing sessions with a Divine Being. Consult that wisdom before agreeing to cut any cord of attachment.

Question Twice, Cut Once

Tailors and carpenters are advised to measure twice, cut once. When I suggest that you question twice, I don't mean that you should test yourself unnecessarily by asking the same question twice.

Horrors! Never! But two vital questions must be answered before you agree to cut a cord of attachment.

1. Get Big
2. Set an intention to learn the truth.
3. Ask *"Is there a cord of attachment significant enough to be worth cutting* between my client and this person?"
4. Take 2 vibe-raising breaths.
5. Accept what you get. Inside, your answer could show up as physical sensation, words, colors, etc. Know that you can receive information about degree of intensity, not simply a yes-or-no reaction. No energy at all means that the answer is "No." There can be many degrees of yes, as you will discover through experience with cutting cords.
6. Ask, *"Do I have Divine permission to facilitate cutting this cord of attachment?"*
7. Take 2 vibe-raising breaths.
8. Accept whatever you get. Here, you'll only need a simple yes or no. Nearly always, the answer is "Yes." Still, check just to make sure.

Questioning in this way can help you decide which cord of several is the one to cut. You know that energy flows back and forth in any cord of attachment. However, you'll find that all cords aren't equally intense. The one you research could send your client just a little whimper of jealousy from the cordee. Alternatively, that cord could be dumping major emotional sewage, the equivalent of five tons daily.

If one proposed cord isn't a big deal, choose another.

What is the biggest number of cords I have ever cut in one session, for myself or anyone else? Three. Never cut more than three cords of attachment in one day, and leave at least three days before you facilitate cutting another. Cutting even one cord of attachment counts as major surgery for an aura; your client's whole mind-body-spirit system must recuperate afterwards.

Wouldn't cutting three cords give your client the most value for a session? Actually, cutting just one cord properly will help your client more than racing to cut two or three. Focus on doing a really good job, giving quality feedback. Never skimp on going through all the 12 Steps in this book.

Remember, this aura-level technology is enormously powerful. One cord cutting could give your client the same benefit as a year of psychotherapy.

COMMON QUESTIONS

Here are answers to questions, or worries, that you may have:

Can't a client ask about a cord that was already cut by somebody else?
This happens fairly often. Remember, different practitioners use different techniques, and many well-intended healers repeatedly cut cords of attachment only to have them return. By questioning, you'll discover whether or not a particular cord of attachment is there now. If so, you have the training to cut that cord in a way that will be permanent.

Is Divine permission ever NOT given?

Occasionally this does happen. One of my clients, a psychothera-pist, was feeling an uncomfortable degree of transference with a par-ticular client. The cord definitely existed. It was mildly nasty. But permission to cut that cord wasn't forthcoming for nearly a year. My client returned twice more. Every time he asked if we could cut that cord. By the third time, we finally had clearance.

Mysteries are involved in life's energy exchanges. You don't have to understand them all to be an effective practitioner of Energy Spiri-tuality. Asking permission at Step 4 helps to compensate for not being omniscient. Should you feel doubts about cutting a cord of attachment, to quote Nancy Reagan, "Just say 'No.'"

What if you receive permission but still feel iffy about cutting a particular cord?

Especially when new to this work, you may not feel secure enough yet to deal with a difficult client or cord. Let a sequence of successes bring you confidence. If you feel any strong doubt about cutting a cord of attachment, don't do it.

The Cord My Student Wouldn't Cut

Of course, Holly didn't start by telling me that one of my students had declined to cut a particular cord. Instead, this new client told me her goal. She wanted to cut the cord of attachment to her boyfriend Terrence. After I finished Step 4 and was ready to move forward, Holly blurted out, "I'm so glad you're willing to do this for me. Last week, I had an appointment with one of your students, Claudia. She told me that she didn't have permission to cut it."

Uh-oh.

Years of experience or not, I squirmed inwardly for a moment, doubting myself. How stable had Holly's aura been? Borderline. Yet I had definitely re-ceived a "Yes" to go forward and cut that cord. Still, what if Claudia had been right and I was wrong?

Hey, what was happening to my spiritual self-authority? "Yes," when it comes from inside, means yes! So I went ahead and cut the cord.

Terrence's pattern with Holly involved emotional abuse, plus a complicated array of push-pull power dynamics. When discussing cord dialogue with Holly in Step 10, she had trouble understanding a word I said. Evidently, she only wanted to hear something like "You can blame that monster Terrance for everything wrong with your life."

It took every bit of clarity I had gained in 20 years of practice to work with Holly. Quietly but persistently, I clarified which relationship changes were reasonable to expect and which were not. Assigning homework at Step 12 was a struggle, and equally touchy was finding an effective way to explain to Holly why I strongly recommended psychological counseling.

Bless her heart, this client fought me every step of the way but succeeded in reaching a terrific outcome by the end of our session. Even though she needed an exceptional amount of encouragement, here's what mattered: Holly found new strength to take responsibility for her life.

In retrospect, Claudia, my new graduate, had been right not to attempt to cut Holly's cord. As a more experienced healer, I had been ready. Inner guidance for both of us had been correct.

GIVE AN OVERVIEW

Now you and the client are ready to cut a particular cord of attachment. It's the perfect time to preview what will happen next. You'll demystify the process and help your client to become comfortable with an unfamiliar procedure.

For the following example, I'll use Hercules for the name of the Divine Being in charge of the session. You would, of course, substitute your client's choice.

Note: To break up the long description, I like to include my "big joke." If it makes you laugh, this can become one of your big jokes also.

To make sure you can even *recognize* what is supposed to be my big joke, I will italicize it. In Japan, this joke goes over really, really well. Really! If you come up with good jokes to use in other parts of the world, please let me know. The 12 Steps to Cut Cords of Attachment work universally. If my jokes were as successful, guess I'd be in a different line of work.

Preview the Next Steps

1. First, I'll locate where the cord of attachment connects into your body.

2. Then I'll ask you to speak out a Permission Statement, to satisfy spiritual law.

3. Next, Hercules will help me to cut the cord of attachment.

4. After cutting the cord, I'll reach in and remove any bits of that cord still attached to your aura. You can watch me fling this stuff into the nearest violet flame.

5. Following this comes the creative part, and you'll be the one to do it. I'll ask you to name any gemstones you like, such as diamonds, rubies, emeralds, amethysts. Then Hercules and I will bring this into your aura for a bandage.

There's good news and bad news about this bandage.

Good news is that you can ask for whatever you like. It could be the biggest diamond you've ever seen, yet it won't cost you a cent because the complete price is included in the fee for your session.

The bad news is that you can't go to a store tomorrow and sell it all, like second-hand jewelry, because this bandage will only exist at the level of your aura.

6. Validation is the next step. I'll go into your aura to record the destructive energy pattern that was stuck in this cord of attachment. This isn't everything about the other person or you or the relationship, only the ways in which you have been stuck repeating a toxic pattern. We'll discuss this pattern, plus the implications for having your life improve as a result of the session.

7. Finally, I'll give you some very simple homework, plus going-home instructions. Do you have any questions?

ENJOY THE SHOW

When giving clients a preview of what I'm about to do, I usually add these pointers.

- You may or may not see the Divine Being standing next to me now, and sending special energy into my crown chakra to help me cut this cord of attachment.

- You may or may not see the other energy that flows into my crown chakra to help me do this session.

- You may or may not see the laser light that pops out from my fingers (or laser wand) when I cut this cord of attachment.

- But here's what you will definitely see, provided that you open your eyes and look. I'll circle my crystal around the outside of the cord three times to cut it open. So if you look, you can see where the cord is and how big it is.

- Remember, this cord of attachment is being cut permanently. I recommend that you watch because this particular form of entertainment can never be repeated.

Congratulations. You've conscientiously prepared yourself to cut cords up through Step 4. Now the rest of the 12 Steps can proceed smoothly.

If you are like me, you'll find that healing with Energy Spirituality is one of the greatest delights in life.

Step 5. Locate the Cord

12 STEPS TO CUT CORDS OF ATTACHMENT

Step 1. Create a Sacred Space
Step 2. Make an Energy Sandwich
Step 3. Activate the Aura
Step 4. Choose Which Cord to Cut
Step 5. Locate the Cord
 Locate a Cord by Questioning
 One Simple Choice
 See the Cord of Attachment
 Feel the Cord of Attachment
 Locate the Cord by Feeling It Inside Yourself
Step 6. Give Permission
Step 7. Remove the Cord
Step 8. Bandage to Rebalance
Step 9. Write the Dialog Box
Step 10. Discuss the Pattern
Step 11. Impact Other Relationships
Step 12. Assign Homework

Before you can *cut* that cord of attachment, you had better *find* it. That's not as hard as you might think. Step 5 presents you with four different techniques to choose from, so that you can experiment and, eventually, choose your favorite. Along the way, I'll intersperse some practical ideas about the nature of Deeper Perception.

Besides finding your best way to locate a cord, Step 5 will help you to make one vital choice. Simple though it is, this choice affects whether you will do a mediocre job at cutting cords of attachment versus developing truly professional skills.

Don't just read through the techniques in this chapter. Try each one. Try it once, at least. Techniques could be compared to clothing displayed at a store. On the page, a technique may not seem like much. But when you try it on, wow! That's IT.

Locate a Cord by Questioning

You're already familiar with Questioning. Well, that same process can help you to locate a cord of attachment.

1. Close your eyes.
2. Get Big.
3. Set the intention to be of service to your client.
4. Ask a specific question inside, e.g., "Where is Romeo's cord of attachment to his favorite hair stylist, Bob?"
5. Take 2-3 Vibe-Raising Breaths.
6. Accept whatever you experience next as your answer.

Yes, Questioning is the simplest of our four methods for locating a cord. But what if you're not confident about what you find? Simply go forward. It's like riding a bicycle. Keep pedaling. Through movement, balance comes.

What if you tried to perfect your balance *before* you let yourself ride? Would you ever manage to ride at all? Balance is a process, not an object that can be acquired once and for all.

Remember, too, how you are taking your first rides with Energy Spirituality. You have been advised to start by cutting cords that are relatively minor. Also, doing these first 10 practice sessions, you're either doing a trade with a buddy or working on yourself. This will be no high-pressure concert at Madison Square Garden. So relax, trust, and have some fun experimenting.

Perfect Locations

Lyle's cord of attachment to his drug-taking son was at the third eye. That's where drugs especially mess up a person's aura. So, in retrospect, that location isn't surprising, is it?

A second cord of attachment connected Lyle to his bullying father. This was stuck at Lyle's solar plexus, on the left side of his body. Power center and personal life—in hindsight, that connection seems reasonable, too.

Often, you will find a connection between a chakra databank and the location of a cord.

Would it, therefore, be smart to figure out where a cord should logically be? Should you work backwards from there in order to choose a location? Never. Until you have cut a cord of attachment and read the dynamics within it, you won't know for sure what that cord does energetically. Your clever and logical choice could be dead wrong.

Granted, a cord's location will always make sense by the time you have finished Step 12. At Step 5 you won't know most of the story yet. Nor will you necessarily understand how a particular cord relates to your client's intention.

So keep things simple. Put the horse in front of the cart. Find a location at Step 5. Read that cord at Step 9. Probably you won't fully appreciate the cord location until Step 12.

Whether you find the location through Questioning or one of the other techniques that follows, certain fears are common for beginners. Let's do some problem-solving about questions that might be bothering you right now.

Shouldn't I just ask the client where the cord is?

Quality control—that's why. If asked, most clients would guess at a cord location and (to put it bluntly) guess wrong. Do you want to base your professional services on information that may be inaccurate? Seek to empower your client in ways that cannot detract from quality control. Our 12 Steps are loaded with ways to do this.

What if you are the one who is wrong about the location of a cord? If you're off by an inch or two, could that ruin everything?

Remember who is teaming up here. You are cutting this cord along with a Divine Being who will compensate for any slight mistakes or inaccuracies. Just make a good faith effort as you co-create the healing.

I still don't get why you can't figure out the cord location logically. Like wouldn't a cord to your mother usually be at your navel? Wouldn't a lover usually attach at your sexual organs? Why should I use techniques to locate cords of attachment when you could have just given me a simple chart?

Here's a deeper explanation about why we locate a cord through experiential techniques rather than referring to some chart. It's time to consider **states of consciousness**, the overall way that your mind-body-spirit functions.

Common examples of states of consciousness are when you are awake versus sleeping or dreaming. Beyond these three, some additional states of consciousness are available as well.

Knowledge is different in different states of consciousness. Say that you're talking about spaghetti. Admit it. Even half asleep, you could come up with an intelligent sentence about pasta. But contemplating that same bowl of spaghetti when wide awake and inspired, your words will become far more interesting.

This example shows the *potential* for higher states of consciousness. Content of conversation matters but so does consciousness. Very awake, you'll be wiser than semi-awake, but you will still be functioning from the waking state of consciousness.

Whether you're groggy from a hangover or juiced up on a huge latte from Starbucks, in this example about Spaghetti Speak you are using variations on the waking state. This means your nervous system functions in a particular way.

The **waking state of consciousness** is an everyday, common-sense way of being in the world. Coming so naturally, this state of consciousness is usually taken for granted. Physiologically, lab tests show there are certain brain wave functions, breathing patterns, etc. corresponding to the waking state of consciousness.

ONE SIMPLE CHOICE

To be effective when you do a session of Energy Spirituality, your success depends upon being able to move into a higher state of consciousness.

That isn't because your client can necessarily tell the difference. On the basis of words alone, a state of consciousness doesn't show. Whether you talk about a cord of attachment or a strand of spaghetti, you might be half asleep.

Frankly, unless your eyes physically close, most people won't notice if you are in a fuzzy version of the waking state of consciousness. It takes an aura reader, or someone with years of experience at doing spiritual practice, to discern a person's level of consciousness.

But if you are dull inwardly, *you* will know. And you are responsible for your state of consciousness, especially when doing surgery on somebody's aura.

Realize that you are fully capable of working from higher consciousness rather than the ordinary waking state. Mostly it comes down to a simple choice. Are you willing to stretch yourself a bit?

This book is my way to team up with you, but I can't pop off the pages to tell if you're going to slow down, stretch yourself, and test all the techniques offered here. Some readers, I know, would prefer a Cord Cutting for Dummies approach. To them, nothing matters more than a quick 'n' easy way to be able to say, "Sure, I can cut cords." Readers like this may wonder, "Why doesn't Rose get to the cutting part, already?"

Here's why. It takes time and intention to move into the state of consciousness for doing quality work. Some people buy designer clothes that cost thousands of dollars; others shop at Wal-Mart. Economically, such choices are necessary. Spiritually, however, there is no reason to settle for anything but the best.

Energy Spirituality requires that *concepts* about spirituality must be supplemented by *energy*. And where does that energy come from? The practitioner functions from a higher state of consciousness than the everyday waking state.

The 12 Steps to Cut Cords of Attachment are sequenced in a way that automatically moves you into a higher state. Right from the time you began to create a sacred space, you have been lifting your vibrations. All the way through Step 12, you will move into the highest state of consciousness of which you are capable at your present stage of spiritual development. (And, if you're working with a client, she will do the same. It's a kind of contact high.)

As long as you read and try each of the techniques, rather than speed-reading through them, you will develop professional-level skill outwardly and inwardly. I hope you will give it your best and truest shot!

Now that you appreciate the importance of states of consciousness for cutting cords, you can understand why Step 5 has you use Questioning or other techniques to locate a cord. Not only is it desirable to have high-quality information—the side effect is that using any of these techniques will help to move you into a higher state of consciousness.

By using expanded awareness to locate a cord of attachment, instead of figuring things out from the waking state, you will do your best work. That includes clarity at finding cord items, insight when viewing the logical consequences of cutting a cord, even affecting the quality of homework you give at Step 12.

Still not clear about what it means to work from a higher state of consciousness? As variations on the regular waking states of consciousness, two altered states are readily available:

- Your **subconscious** mind collects all of the experiences of a lifetime, like making an inner video of all that happens to you. This vast amount of information lurks just beneath the surface of conscious awareness. It corresponds to experiencing at the astral, or psychic, level. (Remember our discussion back in Step 2 about The Three Worlds? Any astral type of experience means that awareness has shifted to some portion of The Second World.)

- Your **Higher Self** is a more expanded version of your personal mind. This is where you co-create with a Divine Being. When you Get Big, set an intention, and then use a technique to wake up more inside, you access the etheric, or spiritual, level. (The corresponding state of consciousness positions you at the highest of the Three Worlds.)

As soon as you start Questioning, for instance, your neuro-physiological functioning begins to change. Automatically, you move into a state of consciousness in which you can make the clearest possible contact with your Higher Self. When you take Vibe-Raising Breaths, awareness will go even deeper.

- As an advanced spiritual practitioner, you will need only a couple of breaths to recognize that familiar experience of being awake inside and as deep as you can be.

- And if you're not such an advanced practitioner, at least you'll go *deeper* inside.

Either way, the goal is for your answers to come from a relatively expanded state of consciousness. Just how far within will you go?

Here's where we come to the tricky part. Remember, your subconscious mind is inner, too, not only your Higher Self. What will happen if you choose not to bother with the steps of Questioning and, instead, ask a question based on your regular, eyes-open, every-day state of consciousness? Probably you'll go within only slightly.

Consequently, the answer you receive will come from your sub-conscious mind, just beneath the surface.

Such an answer could be triggered from past experiences, like memories, hopes and fears from your own personal storehouse of impressions. Sure, it's a slightly higher state of consciousness than the waking state, but you can do better.

With Energy Spirituality, it's important to connect with your Higher Self. That way, you'll receive the highest wisdom possible about your client, rather than half-hidden leftovers from your own past.

Trying to guess which ideas come from where could be crazy-making; don't even go there. Instead, simply do all the steps of the Questioning technique.

- Close your eyes.
- Relax.
- Ignore any quick answer that comes before you take your Vibe-Raising Breaths.
- If an answer really does come from your Higher Self, it will return after you take those breaths.

What counts is your very first experience *after* you take those Vibe-Raising Breaths.

CLAIRVOYANT LOCATION

Questioning gives you a cord location purely as information. But sometimes a spiritual healer prefers a more sensuous approach, us-ing sight or touch.

Keep in mind that your senses will be observing something subtle in either case.

Only in Fantasyland

Over the past 37 years, I have taught students in a great variety of settings, from juvenile offenders at a halfway house to the privileged, pampered guests at one of America's premier resorts, Canyon Ranch. Often I have taught adult education classes in public schools.

My most shocking experience yet occurred in a Virginia schoolroom in 2006 when I taught aura reading. The students didn't seem to be listening to a word I said. As a joke, I asked them:

"When you came here today, did any of you expect that I would just switch on auras for you? Did you think our class would be like watching TV, where you would sit back after I switched everything on for you and then you could just sit back and watch the pretty colors?"

Hands went up. I stifled a scream.

At least I knew what the problem was, so I could help my students adjust expectations. (After this, they managed to learn just fine.)

TV and movies are great, but all their special effects have given some people the nuttiest expectations. Nobody else can switch on a higher state of consciousness for you. Likewise, whether you see auras or feel them, hear them or smell them, don't expect it to be like a TV show.

You're at Earth School, not Fantasyland. So choose reality rather than fantasy. That's where the real miracles happen.

Myth notwithstanding, many people do have clairvoyant perception, in their own way, as part of their authentic gift set. When you use the following technique, your spontaneous experience may bring a quick inner image. Or, perhaps, a perception will linger. Certainly, because of synesthesia, other inner experiences will be activated. Remember to count this information, too.

I have heard some students refer to my techniques as "aura sensing." This shows they are not yet ready to fully relinquish The Myth About Auras. To them, clairvoyant techniques like the following one, represent "real aura reading" while other methods are how an untalented non-clairvoyant can cope.

Ridiculous! You can easily prove to yourself how false this is. Use all four of the techniques in this chapter to bring results.

And, no matter which technique you prefer, remember that any aura reading worth the name equals *perception plus interpretation*. Use a technique for perceiving a cord and, if necessary, supplement what you receive. Do some Questioning.

See the Cord of Attachment

When you prefer to locate a cord by *seeing* it with Deeper Perception, use this technique.

1. Close your eyes.
2. Take (what else?) a Vibe-Raising Breath.
3. Get Big.
4. Set the intention to be of service to your client and find the particular cord of attachment you name, e.g., "Juliet's cord to her nurse."
5. Open your eyes and look at your client's body. Accept what you see, a cord location.

Now let's consider some common questions about seeing cords of attachment.

How will that cord look to me?

Like any other experience with auras, the way you perceive a cord of attachment depends on your personal gift set.

Deeper Perception is also subtle, so please don't expect an illustration straight out of *Gray's Anatomy*. Any of the following examples would count as valid. Here are examples of how you might receive information about the position for a cord:

- One body part can light up, inwardly. Compared to the rest of what you are seeing on the client, you will find that one particular place is highlighted. Count this as your cord location.

- You could have an experience of magnetic intensity. As you scan your client's body, attention could be drawn to one particular area. Auras are made of electro-magnetic energy, after all. Having a place seem sticky or magnetic to your sight—yes, that counts.
- Or you may actually see a cord-shaped object that attaches into a part of your client's body.

Spiritual sight is not physical sight. Using human senses, like vision, we process auric information differently from how we experience•life physically. The customary channels are used, but with higher consciousness. That's why my method of teaching Deeper Perception is called Aura Reading *Through* All Your Senses®, not Aura Reading *With* All Your Senses.

Why didn't the cord look the way I expected it to?

For accuracy at cord cutting, release expectations. If you've been taught to see particular colors in certain places, forget it. Otherwise, auras will show up for you according to somebody else's rules. Although anyone can succeed at this if he works hard enough, here's the problem. Should you try to read auras as though you were someone else, your gift set will go into arrested development.

By analogy, you have a unique personality that expresses your soul. For a while you could choose to imitate somebody else you admire. You could dress like your hero, wear your hair the same way, copy that person's mannerisms, even get look-alike plastic surgery. Consciousness flows with intention, so you need not be a professional mime to do an extremely good imitation of your idol's personality.

Sadly, this would bring only a limited kind of success. You would give the desired impression yet be socially stuck for as long as you kept trying. Imitating your hero, how could you attract the people who would be interested in *you*? Until you revert to being yourself, you won't evolve past the thin slice of life that you're copying.

If you do actually see a cord, must it appear in full color?

Fantasy strikes again! Here are some of the many ways you might see a cord, using your personal gift set:

- Light shoots out of a particular place.
- There's an outline, like a grayed-out window on a computer screen.
- A cord can appear as a ghosted area, something you see inwardly, not quite physically.
- A symbol appears to you intuitively, like an arrow or an X to mark the spot.
- A blob of color shows up where you didn't see it before, and it's a contrast to other colors you're seeing in that part of the person's aura.
- You *feel* like you're seeing.
- You find yourself making up a story that you see something. For some reason, you choose a particular location. (Well, trust it. In this context, you're not making it up.)
- The language most commonly used is, "Somehow I see, yet I don't see."

Since cords of attachment are real, why don't they look the same to everyone?

No matter how many times I repeat it, most people need to hear this idea many times before it really sinks in, so here goes:

Deeper Perception is subtle. It is not like having somebody toss a football, where spectators all see the same thing. You can think of Deeper Perception as an intimately personal way that your Higher Power talks to you. That sacred language is nobody else's business. All that matters is that you are willing to get the message.

So Suave

I love the woman who taught me Healing Touch, Level One. For this funny story, I'll refer to her as Maggie. The Healing Touch Program® is a magnifi-

cent set of techniques for Energy Medicine, pioneered by the late Janet Mentgen, a brilliant healer and system builder.

During chit-chat at the start of the class, I mentioned that, although I never had studied Healing Touch before, I did have experience with reading auras.

Soon Maggie explained to our class how she wanted us to introduce ourselves. Everyone was supposed to answer a short set of questions.

When I began to take my turn, I could see Maggie pull a book close to her side. As I kept talking, she excitedly flipped through the pages, all the while pretending not to be looking at anything but me.

After I got to the end of my intro, Maggie thrust the book at me until it nearly poked me in the nose. Pages were open to a color illustration. Maggie asked, "Do you see... this?"

The book was Hands of Light by the renowned healer, Barbara Brennan. This had been a rather suave move on Maggie's part. Everyone in the class became excited. Would I pass the test? Could I perhaps be a genius like Barbara?

"Of course not," I said. "Why would I see things her way?"

Whoosh, there went our drama, deflating like a balloon that hadn't been knotted up properly. Collectively, the class sighed in disappointment.

Yes, even a sophisticated teacher like Maggie can believe in The Myth about Auras. Supposedly, every aura reader sees things in color, always the same colors, uniform for everyone. What nonsense!

If anyone asks you, don't be ashamed to tell the truth. As a spiritual healer, your job is to bring results. Never are you obligated to live up to another person's myth. And the test of your worth as a healer isn't "Can you duplicate another person's color illustration?" It is "Do you have the courage to use the gifts that God gave you?"

CLAIRSENTIENT WISDOM

Clairsentience means "Truth touch." Many people have a gift set which includes a great deal of talent for reading auras by means of touch. If you are strongly clairsentient, the two remaining techniques in this chapter will be easy for you.

Feel the Cord of Attachment

Any form of holistic healing is excellent preparation for identifying a cord of attachment by touch. You could be a chiropractor or massage therapist, study Energy Medicine with Donna Eden, do Reiki, Tai Chi, Qigong, etc.

Should you be familiar with reading auras by touch, you'll find it extra easy to be confident while you do this technique. Whether or not you're new to this, follow this sequence for best results:

1. Remember which is your Hand of Preference (as discussed in Step 3). Close your eyes.
2. Take a Vibe-Raising Breath.
3. Get Big.
4. Set the intention to be of service to your client.
5. Rub both hands together until you build up some heat. Open your eyes. Raise your Hand of Preference and position it a few inches in front of your client's body. (And, of course, this "client" could be you!)
6. Move that Hand around to explore the field around your client's torso, arms, wherever you feel guided. You'll start picking up lots of information, whether confidently or tentatively, e.g., textures, flows of energy, patterns of information. You understand by now, don't you? How you receive information is nobody's business but yours.
7. Once you have done your initial exploration, close your eyes again.
8. Set the intention to find a particular cord of attachment, e.g., "Romeo's cord to his fiancée."
9. Open your eyes and feel around again. The first *different* item you notice, that's it!

And here comes our last technique for finding a cord of attachment.

Locate the Cord by Feeling It Inside Yourself

Since you've mastered the Call It, Read It Technique, you know that information about auras can display according to the spread that you choose. Well, you can request that the location for a particular cord of attachment be experienced through sensations in your own body:

1. Close your eyes. Notice how it feels right now, in your physical body.

2. Get Big.

3. Set the intention to be of service to your client.

4. Ask for the location of the particular cord of attachment you're seeking, e.g., "William Shakespeare's cord to his fan club president." Request that information display quickly and comfortably in your own body.

5. Take 2-3 Vibe-Raising Breaths.

6. Notice any unusual sensation, image of your body, etc. It counts.

7. Ask the Divine Being you're working with to remove that experience completely, so you won't risk taking on your client's problems on any level. (Or, if you're working on yourself, so that you won't stay attached to energetic traces of the cord after the healing is done.)

Can you trust this kind of knowing?

Of course! You have set an intention to find information. You have given yourself a valid context. So trust it. You can also trust the Divine Being who is helping you. Another option which never hurts is to trust yourself.

Energy Spirituality flows most powerfully when you dare to trust.

Exactly Where It Should Have Been

Marian had traveled for hours to attend our session. She burst into the room and blurted out her intention. "I want to express myself better when I'm with people."

Where did I locate the cord of attachment? If you were to guess at this point in my story, you might think, "Self-expression is at the throat chakra. So that's where Rose is going to find a big, fat cord of attachment."

Nope! Doing the Before Picture, I asked Marian to describe how she felt emotionally. She said, "Dark and cold, like an empty hole in there. I've had that my whole life."

We wound up cutting the cord of attachment to Marian's mother at the heart chakra.

This released a hideous pattern, a recurring nightmare that had been stuck in Marian's aura since childhood: No hugs, no love, not even being allowed to cry.

In Step 10, I asked Marian for her reaction to what I described about the cord. Sorrowfully, she confirmed the unusual harshness of her upbringing. If caught crying, she was punished. Bad enough that she often cried herself to sleep, Marian also had to hide the tears.

More data from the cord revealed that Marian's mother successfully kept her cruelty secret. So nobody intervened to stop the abuse. As children will, Marian blamed herself, feeling that she deserved no better.

There is always a difference between stand-alone psychological insight and the conversations you'll have during Steps 10-12, after a cord has been removed. At her After Picture, Marian was asked to move back into her heart space and describe what she felt. "What about that hole in your heart?" I asked gently.

"Gone," she said, clearly amazed.

Now that the speaker was more whole, she would be able to speak as never before.

For Step 5, I have given you many techniques. But, remember, you only need one. After you have grown comfortable with that technique, Step 5 will become one of the quickest parts of the cord-cutting procedure. Step 6 goes fast, too, but don't skip it. To find out why, keep reading.

Step 6. Give Permission

12 STEPS TO CUT CORDS OF ATTACHMENT

Step 1. Create a Sacred Space
Step 2. Make an Energy Sandwich
Step 3. Activate the Aura
Step 4. Choose Which Cord to Cut
Step 5. Locate the Cord
Step 6. Give Permission
  Provide drama through a sacred ceremony
  Make a Spiritual Contract
  Activate Divine Homeostasis
  To help clients: Provide Guidance on Request
Step 7. Remove the Cord
Step 8. Bandage to Rebalance
Step 9. Write the Dialogue Box
Step 10. Discuss the Pattern
Step 11. Impact Other Relationships
Step 12. Assign Homework

Ceremonies make an impression. No matter how worldly-wise we may be, or how skeptical, everyone's conscious mind responds to drama. Even the most jaded theater critic becomes more alert when the curtain goes up.

Subconsciously we love drama even more. This simple fact can help you as a healer. Choose when to create a bit of therapeutic drama. Only take care to do it appropriately. You want to introduce just enough drama, neither too little nor too much.

In 20 years, I've never caused a client to run from the room, screaming, sobbing or firing gunshots into the air. Ultimately, a wise client values results more than flash. Nonetheless, a judicious amount of drama can improve results.

Ceremonies provide a solution. I'm not alone in discovering this. For instance, religions have long recognized the human need for drama. Otherwise they never would have created ceremonies like baptisms, weddings and funerals. Many spiritual teachers offer formal initiations.

Well, here's my equivalent, Step 6 to cut cords of attachment. Use a formal Permission Statement to make this act of Energy Spirituality into a unique and lasting ceremony.

Make a Spiritual Contract

Lawyers need not be present for this type of contract. Nor will you need any special license to officiate. Create any Spiritual Contract you like. Just be careful what you ask for.

1. Ask your client to repeat the following words, phrase by phrase. Fill in the blanks, as appropriate. For this example, I'll fill in the first blank with the name of Archangel Michael, but substitute your client's choice of Divine Being. The healer's name goes in the second blank. For the third, feel free to change the name I have supplied. All cordees probably won't be named "John Doe."

> 2. I now give permission
> 3. to <u>Archangel Michael</u> and to <u>your name, Healer</u>
> 4. to cut the cord of attachment between myself and <u>John Doe</u>
> 5. so there will be no more pulling and tugging of emotion between us
> 6. but only unconditional love.

Energy follows intention. You and your client have now officially set an intention for Energy Spirituality. This will cause spiritual help to flow in a way that permanently cuts, then heals, this particular cord of attachment.

Filling in the blank, is it enough to say the person's relationship to the client, like "my sweetheart"? How about substituting a romantic phrase, like "The only man I have ever loved"?

Sorry, but ceremonies work best with some degree of formality. Even a bride who holds her wedding in a park, wears blue jeans and no makeup, is unlikely to be so informal that her vow states, "I agree to marry, um, like, this guy. I guess."

Therefore, even if your client is an unrepentant first-namer, encourage her to state the full name of the cordee.

Of course, people involved in some of the grimmest cords will not have a name, as in the case of a hit-and-run car accident. But for cords like this, your client's memory has encoded an identity loud and clear. In such a case it will be enough to say something like, "The driver in that hit-and-run accident."

Do clients like saying a Permission Statement?

For some, it's no biggie—quick and routine. But other clients clearly need the chance. Subconsciously, or even consciously, some clients don't fully appreciate what's happening until they speak the official words of a Permission Statement.

Such a client may cry or come up with new questions. Good! You definitely want this to happen before moving on to Step 7.

When Samantha Knew

Samantha wasn't the most introspective person I have ever met. Objective reality is her thing, not inner nuances. I had known this about Samantha for some time. Still, I was a bit startled to hear her describe giving birth to her daughter:

"I knew I was pregnant. I mean, I could see that belly grow. Still it wasn't real to me that I was going to have a child. I just couldn't believe it.

"Fast forward to me in labor. It got to the point when I had to push. I gave a big push and my daughter's head came out. When I looked down and saw that head, finally I realized that it was true.

"I felt so surprised. I kept saying to myself, over and over: 'I'm having a child. I'm having a child.'"

Likewise, saying the Permission Statement out loud reminds a client that a big and permanent ceremony of liberation is about to happen.

No More Hiding

Juan was one of the most self-aware clients I've ever had. Yet he suffered from an acute lack of confidence, especially when dealing with women. The cord of attachment to an abusive mother attached at his throat.

Giving permission to cut that cord, Juan started to cry, then held the tears back. He could scarcely get the words out. I let him take his time. Healing was in progress. Why rush?

Did it make sense that this particular client would choke up? In Step 9, I learned that the worst part of his cord of attachment went, "If I put my soul in hiding, maybe I won't be attacked so much. Being myself is what seems to set her off."

Another pattern, replaying in Juan's cord 24/7, went, "Women will always like me better if I give them only a vague picture of who I am. I should say as little as possible, seem tough, avoid answering questions. Then we can pretend that I am whatever the woman wants. Not showing up as myself feels so much safer than exposing my real opinions and feelings."

In retrospect, it made perfect sense that Juan struggled to speak up and give his Permission Statement. Doing this helped set his healing in motion. As a result of our session, Juan found new confidence to speak up in front of women... anywhere, any time, any woman.

DIVINE HOMEOSTASIS

It takes two to tango, but stopping the dance requires just one person. Removing a cord of attachment between dancers is just a bit more complicated. The job will require additional personnel. You could be involved, as the healer. A Divine Being is also needed, and that is who will arrange for Divine Homeostasis.

Here at Earth School, energy is neither created nor destroyed. So what happens to the energy flow within a cord of attachment? Where does it go, once a cord has been cut?

Your client's share will be dispersed. That is an important part of the 12 Steps to Cut Cords of Attachment. You can help your client to recognize and regroup because the toxic energy is definitely gone for good. Farther into the future, this reorganization will protect your client against taking on a similar energy.

But how about the cordee? He has energy patterns, too, in that cord. That's where **Divine Homeostasis** comes in. This keeps a cordee's energy in the same balance as it was while there was a cord of attachment. Here are some examples to help you consider cord patterns from the cordee's point of view:

- Josie is married to an angry man who has been sending her the equivalent of a ton of rage daily. Where will he put that rage once the cord is cut?
- Ethan's son has been pulling on Dad's emotions for years. It has been a daily "Gimme, gimme," draining a swimming pool's worth of emotional energy. Now that the pool has a big "Keep out" sign, what will happen to the son?

■ Audrey's boss at work changes his attitude at random. Sometimes he sends her normal boss-like vibes, sometimes lust, sometimes hate. Maybe you would consider his behavior a form of sexual harassment. Certainly, Audrey has the right to free herself, but as a healer you don't have the right to change her boss, even if you could.

When Audrey, Ethan and Josie cut their cords of attachment, they will be freed from certain energy patterns. *They* are your clients, not the cordees.

Now, if those cordees come to you for help, you might help cut *their* cords to Audrey, Ethan or Josie. But no such request has been made.

Meanwhile your role as a healer, first and always, is to do no harm. That includes not confusing someone who happens to be on the other side of a cord of attachment. Divine Homeostasis takes care of this.

THEY DON'T ASK? DON'T YOU TELL

Only explain about Divine Homeostasis when a client asks. Most won't. They'll be more satisfied with a session if they can fill it with conversation about "Me-me-me." As the healer, however, you deserve to know, exactly, how Divine Homeostasis works.

It's a matter of rebalancing energy for the cordee. Soon as your client makes the official Permission Statement, the Divine Being who has been invited to cut the cord gets busy. He or She begins to reconfigure the energy flow.

That cordee, what does he need to receive? What must be discharged?

Agreements will be negotiated with people on-planet and off, until the precise energy configuration is created. Each participant agrees, on a spiritual level.

Yet one more reason to be grateful to be working with Divine Beings! Even if you could figure out whom to ask, and then locate each person's spirit to set up a quick conference; even if you had great skills for negotiation, so that a "No" would never faze you and you'd persist until receiving every requisite "Yes"; even if you had the math skills to tote up every ounce of give-and-take and therefore knew exactly when to stop making any more deals, don't you think that all this might take you longer than 10 seconds?

It's Okay, Mom

Tyler's mother had mood swings like crazy. This was driving him crazy.

Tyler was nearly 40, but still unmarried. Although he had managed to leave home, Mom still called him daily, treating him like a baby. Tyler wanted to get a life—his own life, as a grown-up.

After we cut the cord, Tyler wasn't surprised to learn that his mother had been dumping a lot of energy into him: Huge quantities of anxiety, depression and anger. Without all these feelings intruding at random intervals, maybe Tyler would finally stop feeling emotionally overwhelmed.

Having more energy might be a welcome change, too.

During Step 10, I pointed out these likely consequences of having his cord cut to Mommy. Tyler felt hopeful. Yet he was still a good son, concerned about selfishly hurting his mother.

As soon as I explained Divine Homeostasis, Tyler began to brighten up. But he wasn't satisfied quite yet. "How many other people does it take to handle all I used to receive from my mother?"

Using the Questioning technique, I got the scoop straight from Archangel Michael. "Nine people," He said, "Three on-planet and six off-planet."

I told Tyler. He was impressed. "I'm that powerful? Wow!"

> ## Activate Divine Homeostasis
>
> Divine Homeostasis may be my favorite technique of all, because you as the healer need do nothing extra to make it happen. Actually, you've *already* done it by:
>
> 1. Bringing in a Divine Being at Step 2.
> 2. Checking with Him or Her in Step 4 that cutting this particular cord is appropriate.
> 3. Receiving the client's official Permission Statement in Step 6.

Not only does this do-nothing technique work automatically, it protects you, the healer, from having emotions from a freshly cut cord be deposited into *you*.

Would it be healthy for you to receive all the energy and karma released when a cord of attachment is cut? Are you obligated to allow your client's problems to be deposited into your aura?

No, but without skill, this could happen. Three cheers for skill, maybe 12 cheers!

One way you'll know that you are staying clear is when, after a session of Energy Spirituality, you don't remember details about a client's cord of attachment. (If you think those details may come in handy for future reference, make a few notes right after your session.)

GUIDANCE ABOUT LIFE CHOICES

Right around Step 6, some clients discover doubts. It's important to deal with them.

In my experience, the most common doubt involves what, during Step 1, I called the Cosmic Excuse. Some clients start worrying, "Sure, I have this cord. But do I dare remove it? Since I have it, maybe it is meant to be. Where is my great big sign that I have permission to cut this cord?"

Well, it wasn't terribly long ago, historically speaking, that bathing was considered dangerous. Didn't all that grime serve some purpose? When someone expresses last-minute qualms about cutting a cord of attachment, maybe it's time to talk baths.

Or you might choose to give a wavering client the benefit of our next technique.

Call It, Read It, Compare It

Why expect God to supply dramatic signs about whether a choice is "meant to be"? Common sense is one of the ways that God remains anonymous. Still, you can supplement this when requested. Help your client by supplying clear, detailed guidance about any life choice, feedback that comes directly from your client's own aura.

1. Go back to your client's Before Picture. Note which databanks your client has already explored. Explain that you are going to research the impact of some life choices on her aura. Then you will proceed to research the impact of cutting, versus not cutting, that particular cord of attachment.
2. Ask your client to talk for 60 seconds about any choice that she is considering, other than cutting that cord, e.g., trying a particular career, reading a particular book, taking a particular workshop. The words don't matter. Instead, the very process of talking will morph her aura into the configuration created by that very choice being researched.
3. Coach your client to do Call It, Read it on the same databanks that were explored previously, back in the Before Picture.
4. Now have your client talk for 60 seconds about cutting that particular cord of attachment, e.g., Why does she want

to cut it? How long has she has known the cordee? Again, the words don't matter. Talking will simply intensify the vibrations related to that choice.

5. Have your client do Call It, Read it again on the very same databanks explored previously.

6. Ask your client to talk one more minute about *not* cutting that cord. Once again, your client's aura will morph to show the impact of that decision.

7. Coach your client to do Call It, Read it one more time, exploring the same set of databanks, as usual.

8. An improvement to your client's aura related to cutting that cord can count as "a sign." In general, a good choice makes a person's aura livelier and more balanced. A less desirable choice does the opposite.

Why do some clients look so hard for what is "meant to be"? Perhaps, onsciously or not, they divide life into "spiritual time," like meditation and prayer, versus "regular human life," with its unpredictable ups and downs.

Then a client assumes that ideally he will live only in spiritual time, as if this could lift him bodily off the planet into some happier realm. For decades, I had that goal. Once I let it go, my human life improved enormously.

Whatever your client's goals, Deeper Perception can bring clearer perspective about human life. It's empowering to find how easily your aura gives feedback on the consequences of any choice.

Deeper Perception may, therefore, be a client's best antidote to fatalism. By using Call It, Read It, Compare It to help your client, you may also motivate him to become an expert aura reader.

Meanwhile, when your client has completed his Permission Statement, he is fully ready for the only part of this procedure that he knew would happen for sure , when you facilitate physically cutting the cord, our Step 7.

Step 7. Remove the Cord

12 STEPS TO CUT CORDS OF ATTACHMENT

Step 1. Create a Sacred Space
Step 2. Make an Energy Sandwich
Step 3. Activate the Aura
Step 4. Choose Which Cord to Cut
Step 5. Locate the Cord
Step 6. Give Permission
Step 7. Remove the Cord
  Create a Laser with Your Fingers
  Cut the Cord of Attachment
  Meet the top 12 Spiritual Surgeons
  Choosing and Using Tools to Cut Cords
Step 8. Bandage to Rebalance
Step 9. Write the Dialogue Box
Step 10. Discuss the Pattern
Step 11. Impact Other Relationships
Step 12. Assign Homework

LET'S GET PRACTICAL

At Step 7, you will cut your first cord of attachment. Here is what I recommend:

1. Read quickly through Steps 7-12 without doing any techniques at all. You will be previewing, not yet practicing. Emphasize the technique boxes as you skim through the chapters. Add Post-Its or paper clips, any method you choose to highlight what you will do. (Soon the first page of a Step, with its list of subsections, will be enough to jog your memory.)

2. Take out your list of minor cords to cut for yourself or a friend. (Or make that list now, if you haven't already done so.) Select one very, very minor cord to remove.

3. Practice ideally begins with this Step. You will be doing an "Official Reading" of each *new* chapter, but skimming additional chapters before and after, just to get your bearings as you practice cutting cords.

4. Quickly do Steps 1-6, focused on the minor cord you have chosen. Then go ahead and *slowly* move through Step 7 for your "Official Reading." Follow up with quick read-and-do for the remaining chapters through Step 12.

Congratulations on cutting your very first cord using the 12 Steps to Cut Cords of Attachment!

Because you have prepared so thoroughly, you'll find it easy to remove cords of attachment. All you have done leading up to Step 7 helps to make you effective at doing aura-level surgery.

When doing Step 7 you can use either your fingers in "Laser Position" or else a dedicated crystal like a "Laser Wand." Even if you plan to use a crystal, it's good to start cutting cords by using your hand.

On the cover of this book, you can find a photograph where I am holding a Laser Wand. For a preview of Laser Position, note the position of my hand in the photo. How would the fingers look without that big crystal in the middle? Imagine the fingers moved closer together until they are touching. That's all you need do to move into Laser Postion. At the Online Supplement to this book (See www.cutcordsofattachment .com.) you will also find photos. Or look down at your own hand, your own personal visual, after trying out the technique below.

Create a Laser from Your Fingers

Laser Position turns an ordinary hand into a surgical tool. This technique is adapted from the form of Energy Medicine developed by Janet Mentgen, Healing Touch.

1. Choose your left or right hand, whichever will be more comfortable for you to use as a Power Hand for *healing* auras. (Probably this will be the opposite of your Hand of Preference for *reading* auras.)

2. Lightly touch together all your fingertips and the tip of your thumb, bunching them up together.

3. To check that you have the position correctly, turn your hand around, fingertips facing you. See how it looks at the business end. Do you see a tiny circle where all five fingers meet? That's what I call **Laser Position.**

> 3. When you're cutting a cord of attachment, a laser-like beam of etheric energy will shoot through your hand, perfect for doing psychic-level surgery.

How can your hand send out a laser beam strong enough to cut a cord?

Soon as your client gives the Permission Statement in Step 6, energy becomes available for cutting a cord of attachment.

This is comparable to the letdown reflex for mothers who nurse their babies; milk just flows toward the child. Similarly, when you have positioned yourself to do Energy Spirituality, you will feed *healing* to your client's aura.

While you were doing Steps 1-6, healing light began to enter your aura through the top of your head. By now it has moved through your entire body. This concentrated beam of healing energy has been gaining momentum. Here at Step 7, this energy will steadily move through your hand for as long as you hold it in the special **mudra**, or sacred symbolic posture, of Laser Position.

What form does this laser light take, when shooting out through your hand? The circle of fingertips held in Laser Position will direct a perfectly focused beam.

(If, later, you decide to hold a crystal in your hand instead of using Laser Position, healing energy will pass through this tool in a similar manner.)

Therefore, you are now prepared to bring through laser light. Steps 1-6 have prepared you and the client. At Step 7, etheric light, entering through your crown chakra, will blend with your human vibrations to create a high-level frequency that can remove anything at the astral level.

That includes any mere cord of attachment, however ugly.

Cut the Cord of Attachment

How will you switch on healing energy for cutting cords? You've already done it: Create a Sacred Space, Make an Energy Sandwich, Activate the Aura, Choose Which Cord to Cut, Locate It, Receive Permission to Proceed, and Locate the Cord. Yes, you are now in The Zone for Energy Spirituality, so cut that cord with confidence.

1. Move your hand into Laser Position or hold a Laser Wand crystal in your hand. Either way, you have a perfect tool for cutting a cord of attachment.

2. Place your tool a few inches away from your client's body, where the cord attaches. Circle around the cord of attachment three times. Activated laser light will slice through the cord, cutting it open. Put down the tool. (Either place your crystal onto a table or relax your hand out of Laser Position.)

3. Visualizing the shape you have cut—or seeing it, if that comes easier—clap your hands repeatedly to break the cord apart. Go from top to bottom.

4. The cord is now cut into two pieces. Divine Homeostasis takes care of the part attached to the cordee. Your responsibility lies with the piece still within your client's aura, so reach inside using both hands. Set the intention to pull out all bits of cord stuck in your client. Also ask inwardly to remove any related matter that has been deposited in your client's aura, like the ego hooks we discussed earlier.

5. Every bit of cord that you grab, immediately fling into the nearest violet flame. Throw it like a ball. (Remember that violet flame? You installed it back when doing Step 1.)

6. When done, thank the Divine Being who has helped you.

7. Immediately do Step 8 to Cut Cords of Attachment.

THE TOP 12 SPIRITUAL SURGEONS

By now, I hope you have practiced Getting Big with help from a variety of Ascended Masters and Archangels. It's like going to an amazing ice cream store with a great array of different flavors, all of them available to you for free. Each Divine Being has a story and, more important, an individual flavor of vibration.

Some Divine Beings are particularly superb at cutting cords of attachment. I've gone into detail about these Top 12 Spiritual Surgeons in the Online Supplement to this book, at www.cutcords ofattachment.com. There, you'll also find my favorite technique for connecting to the Divine Being of your choice. Why not get to know them all?

You could call on one per day, like eating huge ice cream dessert every day without gaining an ounce, amazing or what? Your gift set for Deeper Perception can help you to receive any Divine Being's distinctive blessings.

What if your client has chosen someone *not* on the following list for her session? Right before cutting the cord (or during Step 4, when you preview what will happen in the following Steps) explain that it would be wise to bring in an extra Divine Being just to do the cutting.

Invite your client to choose one of the 12 Top Spiritual Surgeons. The Divine Being already present can be assigned to do the bandage. Then start naming the list of surgeons, one at a time, until your client makes a choice. All the following Divine Beings do a magnificent job at cutting cords.

Top 12 Spiritual Surgeons

1. Archangel Michael
2. Ascended Master Jesus
3. Ascended Master Merlin
4. Ascended Master St. Germain

5. Ascended Master Buddha
6. Ascended Master Sananda
7. Ascended Master Socrates
8. Ascended Master Athena
9. Ascended Master Hercules
10. Ascended Master Ganesh
11. Ascended Master Krishna
12. Ascended Master Shiva

Trouble, Right on the Bedroom Wall

Ashley and Jacob had been having marital problems. Each approached me separately, requesting a session. I was delighted to help.

Her cord to him featured destructive tendencies in which her husband would mock things she did and sabotage plans that she made.

His cord to her emphasized impatience, in which his wife was constantly forcing him to go faster than his comfortable timing. Ashley didn't seem to care if his needs were met, so long as she got what she wanted.

All in a day's work for this spiritual healer, except for the little matter of their household decor...

Since I was on a book tour, my sessions for Ashley and Jacob were being done as a house call. I had needed to set up a makeshift sanctuary for Energy Spirituality, choosing their condo's biggest room with a door, the bedroom.

During both sessions, my back was to the main wall. So it wasn't until I turned to leave that I saw Him. Shiva was pictured on an immense art print, beautifully framed. Black, brown and red flames curled out from his image, stylized flames ready to lick you just for taking an impertinent look.

Even if the style of this picture hadn't emphasized His destructive power, Shiva is hardly the coziest of Hindu gods. I always treat him with extra deference. After all, he specialty is destruction.

"Ouch!" I said to Jacob and Ashley. "How could you keep that terrifying picture of Shiva in your bedroom? By comparison, a dragon would seem tame."

Jacob explained, "We met each other while studying in an ashram, so you could say that Lord Shiva brought us together."

> *"Great," I said. "And tell me, were you by any chance living as celibates while you studied at that ashram?"*
>
> *Understanding dawned on their faces, and I had a hunch that this particular item of home decor might be moved rather soon.*
>
> *True, Shiva is sometimes pictured with his consort Kali but it's hardly the kind of pairing you would find on a Hallmark card. They're the ultimate power couple. Don't expect them to model the marital tenderness that most humans require.*
>
> *Cord-cutting won't remove the energy frequencies of your home furnishings, so think twice before you decorate your boudoir with the personification of relentless purification.*

CHOOSING AND USING TOOLS

Only you can decide if you prefer to enhance your cord-cutting by using special stones as tools.

Usually I don't. I'm a hands-on kind of gal. My favorite advice from any cookbook comes from the great James Beard, who advocated tossing salads by using your hands. My dear, now departed, hairstylist Dale Hamel, used to run his fingers through my hair, crooning "Hands are the best tool God ever made." So you can guess whether I prefer cutting cords with a special crystal or using my perfectly portable gadget, hand in Laser Position.

Yet when I was new to Energy Spirituality, I was desperate for anything that would make me feel more confident as a healer. Soon as my teacher, Johanna Lester, said that I was qualified to cut cords of attachment, I raced out to buy a Laser Wand like the one she used. Money was no object. Luckily for me then—and maybe for you now—a good laser-shaped crystal costs far less than a grand piano.

If you wish to use a crystal to help you cut cords, you could actually program any quartz crystal to do the job. For best results, however, choose a long, clear crystal that comes to a well-defined point. For the very best results, purchase a Laser Wand, like the one I hold on the cover of this book. Use your cord-cutting tool exclusively for this kind of work.

What, exactly, is a **Laser Wand?** It is a long, tapering crystal which naturally comes to a point. Often the sides have curved or jagged edges, as well as a strong termination. These crystals might remind you of a craggy mountain peak, only this kind of mountain would be exceptionally tall, also skinny, plus small enough to hold in your hand.

As with all crystals, a Laser Wand's physical structure previews what it can do to move energy. Craggy edges gather momentum, like waves breaking onto a beach. When directed by your consciousness, this dynamic flow of energy will shoot out through the tip of the Wand, taking form as a laser-fine beam of light.

Cord Cutter's Shopping List

Using crystals is optional. Still, you may wish to use physical tools to supplement your work as a spiritual healer. If so, your complete shopping list looks like this:

1. One Laser Wand
2. Three agate slices
3. A purple plate or crystal cluster

Agate slices are colorful, thin cross-sections of a mineral that helps to rebalance the nervous system. You can use these slices for bandages. Agate is inexpensive. If you prefer something even cheaper, you could find some flat pebbles whose quality is pleasing to you.

Of course, you will need to wash and program any stone to make it suitable for psychic-level surgery, and instructions for doing this follow.

Purple plates are my favorite appliances for cleaning professional tools like Laser Wands, agate slices, any other crystals, plus all my personal gemstone jewelry.

An alternative is **crystal clusters.** These natural formations have many crystal terminations joined at the base, forming one piece. Again, instructions for cleaning *any* type of crystal will follow.

But first, let's discuss basic consumer smarts in a rock shop. If you're a born **crystal empath,** as soon as you pick up a stone it will take you on a journey in consciousness. (How can you know if you are a crystal empath? Go to a rock shop. Pick up one crystal at a time. Close your eyes. If adventures in consciousness begin spontaneously, know that you are this type of empath.)

Whether or not you are an empath of any kind, you can benefit from crystals. Moreover, you need not study them for years to gain enough knowledge to use a crystal to help you cut cords of attachment. (Of course, if you do like working with crystals, eventually you may wish to study with an expert. Brilliant teachers are available to help you develop a powerful skill set as a crystal healer.)

What do you need to know for now about using a Laser Wand? Crystals change auras. Selecting a Laser Wand is different from buying mere jewelry. Here, the emphasis will not be on the looks of your purchase. What matters is what a particular crystal does for you energetically.

Therefore, a savvy consumer will audition one stone at a time. Is there a special consumer technique to bring best results? You bet.

Audition a Crystal to Cut Cords

Aura reading to the rescue! Let your own energy field inform you as a consumer.

1. Start by doing a Before Picture on yourself. Be sure to read these databanks:

> • At the third eye: Spiritual connection to the Divine Being of your choice.
> • At the solar plexus: Personal power when cutting cords of attachment.
> • At the root chakra: Ability to stay grounded while cutting cords of attachment.
> 2. Hold one Laser Wand or crystal at a time. Place it in the hand you'll be using to cut cords of attachment.
> 3. Do After Pictures with the same databanks. A crystal worth your money does something positive to your aura.

Will the right Laser Wand make you more powerful, cutting cords of attachment? It might. Once you feel established in your spiritual connection, the extra amount of oomph is negligible. Still, most *clients* will feel that something special happens when you use a beautiful Laser Wand.

Showmanship for Healers

Packaging does impress people. I remember doing consumer research when publishing my first book, a cookbook. To test my dessert recipes, I used to fill up my car with home-baked goodies once a week and hold a bake sale at the Springfield, Illinois YWCA. When I asked my customers for feedback, the most popular suggestion by far was "More plastic wrap."

Yes, apparently each slice of cake would taste far better if, instead of being cut and served personally for each customer, the dessert could be pre-cut and wrapped, looking more like something you would buy in a store.

I took this as a lesson about showmanship. And it applies to healers as well as to cooks. Some clients will be impressed by the sheen of a Laser Wand. At least, using a special crystal is easier than covering yourself in Saran Wrap.

HYGIENE WITH CRYSTALS

If you're going to use a special crystal to cut cords of attachment, keep it clean. Otherwise you're definitely better off using only your hands.

Pain, fear, any of the qualities in the cord that you cut can temporarily penetrate a Laser Wand. It's the auric equivalent of a scalpel being plunged into some bleeding organ. Just because you don't see the grime with your naked eyes, could it still be there?

Hard As Which Diamond?

It would have given me a clue, if only I had been paying attention. My crush, David Ramsay, was a good man but not someone who would bring me happiness as a husband. The first present he gave me was a lovely necklace with a crystal heart. Within 24 hours, it smashed.

Oops, I married him anyway. For our engagement ring, he bought me a lovely aquamarine ring, set with two diamonds.

Fast forward to the divorce, some four years later. I was left with a pretty ring that I no longer wished to wear. When I took it to a second-hand shop, the jeweler studied the ring through his special magnifying glass and said, "Lady, I can't buy this."

"Why not?" I asked.

"Both the diamonds have cracked."

Yes, diamonds do have a reputation for being hard. But, like any precious or semi-precious gems, diamonds will store the wearer's vibrations. During my marriage to David, I didn't know this. Never, once, did I clean my ring energetically. Enough pain accumulated to crack both diamonds. Surely that lesson about cleansing crystals was worth the price of a ring.

For Crystal Cleaning Devices, here are three good choices:

A **purple plate** is a thin piece of specially treated, magenta-colored metal. These plates are said to emit positive energy that vibrationally affects any objects placed upon them. Purple plates range in size from rectangles the size of a file card to 12-inch squares.

Developed from the work of Nikola Tesla by the late Ralph Bergstresser, these plates are wonderfully portable. If your local rock shop doesn't carry them, you can find them online by searching for "purple plate."

A **crystal cluster** is a natural quartz crystal that contains several different points joined at one base. These are natural washing machines for smaller crystals, and will be completely self-cleaning. Once you program your crystal cluster, it will cleanse anything that you place upon it. (An amethyst cluster will do this in purple-tuity.)

Or you can give your stones a **salt bath.** Dedicate a non-reactive container to this use, e.g., a ceramic, glass or plastic bowl. The container should have a wide opening at the top. Fill your container with dry sea salt or kosher salt, either of which can be reused indefinitely. Gently bury your crystals and precious stones in the salt, with the most fragile parts uppermost.

Cleanse Your Tools To Cut Cords

1. Treat your tools for cutting cords of attachment as the special instruments they are. Keep them out of reach, so nobody can casually touch them.
2. Buy or make a Crystal Cleaning Device: a purple plate, crystal cluster or salt bath. Keep it available in a convenient location.
3. After each use of a crystal tool, place it onto or into your choice of Crystal Cleaning Device.
4. Allow 15 minutes for the cleaning to be complete. But don't worry about going over the time. You can leave your tools indefinitely without causing any problems.

Dress clean, too, when you cut cords of attachment. You can use your Crystal Cleaning Device for any precious or semi-precious stone that you might wear while doing sessions (or at any other time).

Cleaning your jewelry once a day isn't excessive. Remember, the cleaner your accoutrements, the clearer your aura, just what works best for Energy Spirituality.

If you happen to be a crystal empath, it will be especially important for you to dress clean. You were born with a gift for sensitivity to the energy flow in crystals and precious gems. Subconsciously (and maybe consciously, too) you can feel when stones are junked up with negative vibrations.

While you're doing sessions for clients, you might wish to educate them about cleaning gemstones and crystals. Tactfully, you might ask something like, "I'm finding your ring a bit distracting. It's lovely, but tell me, when was the last time you cleaned it?"

Probably you have placed your Crystal Cleaning Device in the room anyway, so it's simple to ask a client to place jewelry upon it. By the end of your session, that jewelry will be ready to wear, energetically fresh.

CRYSTAL POWER

To buy a crystal without programming it afterwards is like moving a grand piano into your living room without ever playing a scale. Such a waste, especially when programming a crystal is so simple!

You will definitely want to program your Laser Wand, plus any Wands or agate slices dedicated to cutting cords of attachment. If you wear jewelry with precious or semi-precious stones, why not program them as well? Both precious and semi-precious stones can be programmed. They'll become even more precious.

To Program Any Crystal

1. To prepare for your programming ceremony, collect all the crystals and jewelry you wish to program, the more the merrier. Use a purple plate, crystal cluster or salt bath to clean them up.

2. Find a room with a door to serve as your sacred chamber for this ceremony. No pets are allowed within, not even your favorite gerbil. Do whatever you feel is needed to create a sacred space, whether burning a candle or incense or simply saying out loud, "Be here actively, Spiritual Source, to witness this ceremony."

3. Choose the program for each item.

4. Get Big. Also, if other facets of your work involve collaborating with guides or angels, invite them to participate also.

5. Set the intention "To program these stones."

6. Hold in your hand one object at a time, be it a crystal, a piece of jewelry, or a decorative stone. Announce the program aloud. Allow a moment for it to stabilize within the object you're holding. Done! (Repeat this sequence until you have programmed the whole batch.)

7. Thank God and all the Divine and celestial beings who have helped you. Each program installed will replay permanently, unless and until you do another ceremony to reprogram.

What constitutes suitable programming for a crystal? Choose how you would like it to subtly alter your vibrations. Your program could be a wish, an affirmation or a specialty. For instance:

- A Laser Wand's program could be the wish, "to bring the highest caliber of healing possible, whenever and wherever I use it."
- A rose quartz necklace might be programmed with the affirmation, "I like myself."
- The double-pointed Herkimer diamond that you keep in your pocket might turn into a healing factory, thanks to a program like "To attract high-frequency healing vibrations that are compatible with my aura."

Whether you use a tool for your aura-level healing or you prefer using your naked hands, don't stop with the cutting. Your most fascinating Steps lie ahead. And the next one, Step 8, will be especially enjoyable as an act of creativity for yourself or your client.

Step 8. Bandage to Rebalance

LET'S GET PRACTICAL

At Step 8, you will cut your second cord of attachment.

1. Choose another minor cord to cut.

2. Quickly do Steps 1-7, then go ahead and slowly move through Step 8, doing your first "Official Reading" of the chapter.

3. Then pick up your pace for the remaining chapters through Step 12.

Notice how naturally you keep gaining more skill? This kind of learning is cumulative.

Does the sight of blood make you faint? Not to worry, you can still remain upright while doing the kind of bandaging in Step 8. There's no blood, no horror, and probably not much active work for you to do at all.

That's because you can ask your client to do the main work instead. This will bring him extra benefits, as detailed in this chapter. I'll start by mentioning my favorite benefit: Fun.

Aside from its serious therapeutic value, Step 8 can be the most playful part of the 12 Steps to Cut Cords of Attachment. Laughter, creativity, artistry and fun—qualities like these add juice to Energy Spirituality.

Apply an Energy Bandage

With your knowledge about cords of attachment, maybe you have started to think that human life has a lot in common with the book title, *Of Human Bondage*. Well, here's your chance to learn Of Human *Bandage*.

1. First, perform the spiritual healer's equivalent of washing your hands: Get Big, thinking the name of the Divine Being who will be applying this bandage. (Here I'll use the example of Archangel Raphael.)

2. Set up the **bandage-base,** establishing the physical site of the bandage. Move one of your client's hands, palm down, onto the part of his body where the cord was just cut. (Or, if you're using an agate slice as a tool, place it where the cord was cut and then guide your client's hand to hold the agate in place.)

3. Form a temporary **bandage lid:** With your hands facing away from you, move them together, thumb touching thumb, palms facing your client. Stand in front of him, positioning your hands just a few inches in front of the bandage-base.

4. Tell your client, "Choose whatever stones you like for your bandage, like diamonds, rubies, emeralds, amethysts. Archangel Raphael and I will put it on as you speak."

5. Each time your client names a gemstone, move the bandage lid away from his body. You're allowing space for the bandage to grow beneath your hands. The first stone named will be closest to your client, followed by the second, and so forth, with the final choice of stone the farthest away. For each new stone he names, take a step backward. Make each step as large as seems right to you. Stop when the last gemstone is named. You need not see or feel the bandage growing beneath your hands. Trust that it has happened.

6. End with a white stone. If your client hasn't mentioned one, give a prompt. "It's customary to top off a bandage like this with a white stone, like a diamond, pearl, moonstone or clear quartz crystal. This will let in all the frequencies of light."

7. After your client names the last stone, take one last step backwards. Archangel Raphael will finish constructing the energy bandage. All you need do is keep your bandage lid in position.

8. Announce a time frame for the bandage, "three days or better". The complete request would go like this: "Archangel Raphael, have this bandage be with Pat for three days or better, until this healing is complete. Thank you."

9. Remove the agate stone, if used. If a hand was used, tell your client that he may return to any comfortable position desired.

10. Sit where you were before Step 8, and proceed immediately to Step 9.

Quickly and effortlessly, you have brought closure to the physical cutting of the cord. This bandage will serve a real purpose, sending frequencies of light to balance your client's aura.

These energy bandages are as important as physical bandages would be for surgery in a hospital, so don't skimp on them, not even when you are your own client.

An extra benefit is the empowerment factor. Choosing the stones for a bandage is an opportunity for a client to ask himself questions like these:

- What do I want?
- What do I need?
- If I could have anything I wanted, what would I really prefer?
- Instead of thinking about the cordee, what do I desire for *myself*?

For some clients, this empowerment notion will seem like a stretch. Asking him to name gemstones that he cannot physically see, this is supposed to be empowering?

Actually, it is. I have noticed often that this playful act of creativity can be a big first step for some clients.

Remember, *you* are not the typical client wishing to be freed from a cord of attachment. You have already demonstrated exceptional courage by your willingness to learn how to use Energy Spirituality. Give yourself credit for your leadership. It may seem like no big deal, but it is.

You may be in much better shape than you think. Your client may be, too. I have had many clients like the one in the following story.

Patience With That Bandage

Madison was, frankly, a whiner. Yet I knew that she deserved healing as much as any of my easier clients. When we got to the bandage part of her session, it felt like pulling teeth. At least I was glad not to be her dentist; pulling real teeth would undoubtedly be worse.

"What would you like on your bandage?"

"I don't know. You choose."

"You can do this part, Madison. You know best what you need."

"No, I don't."

"Just pick something, whatever appeals to you."

"I don't know the names of any stones."

Although I seriously doubted this, I played along. "Really? Could it be a diamond?"

"I suppose, if you say so."

On went her diamond. "Mother Mary, please have this be with Madison for a period of three days or better, until this healing is complete."

When we got to the cord dynamics in Step 10, I described how Madison had a pattern with the cordee, her big sister, where supposedly nothing that Madison did was ever good enough.

My client was so grateful for the validation that she cried. And I felt my heart open up.

Guess what? The people who most try your patience can also be the ones you help most. If we had not been able to make a change to the energy flows in her aura, Madison could have kept whining for years. But cutting this cord of attachment enabled her to stop whining and reclaim her power.

If a client isn't particularly advanced, why would you want him to choose the bandage? You, The Modest Reader, may have spent years doing therapy or metaphysics or both. Wouldn't you choose better?

Whenever someone co-creates with a Divine Being, help is supplied instantly. True, spiritual help won't be enough to compensate for a complete lack of skill. But here your client is part of an Energy Sandwich, guided by a skilled practitioner (you), and the task is simply stringing together some beautiful astral-level gemstones.

No client, no matter how clueless, can mess this up.

This fact makes Step 8 a great chance to give your client an active role. It's empowering for your client to actively participate. But what if your client pulls a Madison and claims that she doesn't know the names of any gemstones?

Saying "a red stone" will work. Divine Beings work telepathically, and they're quite familiar with gemstones.

Never miss a low-risk opportunity to empower the person you're helping.

By contrast, your client could be wildly creative. What if she wants to add accoutrements like the vibes from her favorite camping trip or a Mozart sonata?

A Divine Being can manage that, too.

Bird, Beach and Bouquet

Marvin had a poetic streak. Whenever we had a session, I would look forward to his bandage creation. This one was typical:

• Daisies
• A really beautiful sunset at the beach.
• The call of a songbird.

Here, he paused. "I don't know names of songbirds. Is that okay?"

"Sure," I answered. "Archangel Raphael knows plenty of them. He'll find the right one for you."

To finish the job: "Archangel Raphael, have this bandage be with Marvin for three days or better, until this healing is complete."

Sometimes a client thinks for an awfully long time before naming any gemstones. You may suspect that she is trying to psych out what would help the cordee.

Don't interrogate her to find out. Simply say, "Remember, this bandage is just for you. The other person is already taken care of, as we discussed before."

Yes, despite all your previous conversation, some clients still feel guilty about cutting a cord. Or there can be very established patterns about always putting other people first. By asking your client to choose her own bandage, you subtly begin to retrain her. She can learn to put herself first.

Grunter Turned Bandage Designer

When Don cut the cord to his ex-wife, he wasn't in a great mood. The man didn't smile once until we got to Step 10, when I validated his side of the story in this painful marriage.

Meanwhile, at Step 8, Don looked and felt grim. He even sounded grim, answering most of my questions with a scowl and a grunt.

So did Don leap at the chance to name gemstones during Step 8? Hardly. But I wasn't going to let him grunt his way through. I coaxed him. Outright frolicking wasn't demanded, but at least the guy could name a gemstone or two.

Humoring me, Don chose a ruby, then a diamond.

I avoided saying, "That wasn't so horrible, was it?" Instead, I stayed with the program:

"Archangel Gabriel, have this be with Don for three days or better, until the healing is complete."

From that moment, precisely, joy began to enter Don's aura.

A BANDAGE OF YOUR OWN

The only tricky part of bandaging yourself is that you may be tempted to rush.

A client might need five minutes to select the crystal covering that is simply perfect for rebalancing. You, however, might say the fastest thing that comes to mind, just to save time.

Well, don't be a cheapskate. Do Step 8 with as much TLC as you would give a paying client. Apart from allowing enough time, here is what you need to know to bandage yourself properly:

Self-Bandaging

1. Get Big, thinking the name of the Divine Being who will be applying this bandage. (Here, I'll use the example of Archangel Raphael.)

2. To set up the physical basis for your bandage, the **bandage-base,** place one of your hands, palm down, on the part of your body where the cord was cut. Or, if you're using an agate slice as a tool, put that in position and hold it down with your hand.

3. Form a temporary **bandage lid:** Place your free hand, palm facing your body, close to the bandage-base.

4. Say aloud the sequence of stones that you choose for your energy bandage.

5. With each stone, move your hand a bit further away from your body. This allows space for the bandage to grow beneath your bandage lid.

6. End with a white stone to let in all the frequencies of light.

7. Adjust the size of the bandage. Your hand can only move so far away from your body but don't worry because you have simply set the initial proportions. To increase the size of the bandage overall, just ask. For example, "Archangel Raphael, please make this bandage five times as big as it is right now. Keep the proportions that we have used so far."

8. Announce a time frame of three days for the bandage, including the term "or better," e.g., "Archangel Raphael, have this bandage be with me for three days or better, until this healing is complete. Thank you."

9. Remove the agate stone, if used. If a hand was used, let it return to any comfortable position desired. Proceed immediately to Step 9.

EXTRA HELP FOR BANDAGING

To enhance Step 8, become a connoisseur of bandage-makers. Introduce yourself to them whenever you like, using the experiential technique in the Online Supplement at www.cutcordsofattachment. com.

All it takes is one five-minute meditation to connect directly with any of these Divine Beings and then you can personally experience His or Her distinctive qualities.

This will enliven your experience whenever a bandage is being created. Over time, your experience of the bandage-making process may become very vivid.

Until then, if necessary, just go through the motions... and go through them with a top bandage maker at your service.

The Top 12 Bandage Makers

1. Archangel Raphael
2. Archangel Gabriel
3. Ascended Master Mother Mary
4. Ascended Master Kwan Yin
5. Ascended Master White Tara
6. Ascended Master Brigid
7. Ascended Master Lakshmi
8. Ascended Master Saraswati
9. Ascended Master Hestia
10. Ascended Master Apollo
11. Ascended Master Isis
12. Ascended Master St. Francis

Bandage making is a delightful part of the 12 Steps. Clients may surprise you with their creativity.

A Surgeon's Bandage

Cheryl was a long-term client who had done many sessions of Energy Spirituality. Working with her was altogether delightful, but my very favorite part of each session was how she would design her bandages at Step 8. Here is a typical Cheryl creation:

A six-inch opal. (Unless specified otherwise, each of the next stones in the sequence will have a circumference of three inches.)

- *Five blue sapphires.*
- *Two rubies.*
- *One garnet.*
- *Three emeralds.*
- *Twelve aquamarines.*
- *One more sapphire.*
- *For the top, a 400-carat diamond.*

Maybe the finely tuned bandage-making was due to Cheryl's professional training as a surgeon. But I'm more inclined to view it as part of her artistry in life. The woman also dressed exquisitely.

For any client, a bandage needs only to contain one big white stone; any additional stones are optional. But when a client need not pay by the ounce, let alone hire some anesthesiologist, why not splurge on something absolutely gorgeous?

After you have cut several cords of attachment, you can add this refinement. Fine-tune **duration,** how long the bandage stays with your client.

Some cords are a very big deal, energetically. Consequently the bandage needs to stay on for longer than three days.

Basic bandaging, as you have learned it, contains the necessary contingency phrase, "or better."

But to do more elegant work and grow faster as a healer, use the next technique. It is a simple variation on Questioning.

Expert Bandaging

1. After putting the bandage in place, you are holding up a hand to represent the bandage lid. Close your eyes and Get Big by thinking the name of the Divine Being who is making the bandage with you.
2. Ask "How long does this bandage need to last?"
3. Take a couple of vibe-raising breaths.
4. You will hear or see or feel your answer as a specific number of days. In my experience, the number of days could be as large as 21. That would be for recovering from an exceptionally nasty cord.
5. Whatever the time period you are given for the bandage, say it out loud, as in "Kwan Yin, have this bandage be with him for nine days or better, until the healing is complete."
6. At Step 9, make note of this time duration.
7. Refer to that number of days in Step 12, because it will be the duration for your standard going-home instructions.

BANDAGING ON PRINCIPLE

Never forget to include Step 8 when you cut cords of attachment. You are making use of an important principle. For all forms of Energy Spirituality, *replenishing must follow removal*.

There's no point to removing debris from an aura unless you immediately fill up the empty space with something positive. Otherwise, whatever you removed will soon return.

Nature abhors a vacuum, and not just when you're doing sessions of Energy Spirituality. One everyday example is the disillusioned woman who tells you that she had to break off a romance because "My ex was a nightmare." If she let him go without adding any personal growth for herself, that vacuum will soon be filled by another man who is remarkably like the last one.

Incidentally, this principle of replenishment is yet one more reason why I question how people can really expect cords to be removed permanently with just one sentence, "Archangel Michael, remove all my cords of attachment."

COLOR THERAPY

Apart from the spiritual principle to replenish after removal, you may find it helpful to think through the colorful aspect of Step 8. By asking for help with the bandage, you're informally coaching your client in **color therapy,** how to use the healing power of color to recharge his aura. Other examples of color therapy are:

- Visualizing different shades of light
- Asking your client to wear colored glasses (that you supply) during Steps 8-12
- Programming a glass of water to hold one color, chosen by the client (See more at Page 289.)
- Drinking water from a colored glass or bottle
- Even choosing a favorite color of clothing when getting dressed in the morning

You and your client can explore endless therapeutic variations on the theme of playing with color. Besides color therapy on its own, you can combine the color of your choice with healing techniques like Reiki or affirmations.

Gosh, when making a bandage, you are really combining color therapy with the 12 Steps to Cut Cords of Attachment!

Every one of your clients possesses the innate wisdom to make a fine choice about which colors will best help his aura..

At Earth School, each **color** represents a frequency of energy. Music does the same thing. Vibrations range from high notes to low, and every sound or shade corresponds to a specific quality.

- Clients who prefer hearing to seeing could sing a whole series of tones for a bandage during Step 8.
- Clients with gustatory giftedness could choose flowers or other healing fragrances.

However your client constructs that bandage, the goal is for her to enrich her aura by actively choosing the right higher-vibrational frequencies. And she will know best what is appropriate for her at that time.

Beyond the benefit to your client of the specific bandage elements, the act of choosing can be therapeutic. With your encouragement, your client is remembering to use, and trust, her own creativity.

That, as much as the bandage itself, is part of the healing process in Step 8.

Finally, supporting your client's choice at Step 8 is good practice for you as a healer. Facilitating a session of Energy Spirituality, you always co-create with a Divine Being and, also, your client.

In Step 9 you can deepen appreciation of the co-creation process, as you inwardly receive the mysterious and unexpected insights from a freshly cut cord.

Step 9.
Write the Dialogue Box

12 STEPS TO CUT CORDS OF ATTACHMENT

Step 1. Create a Sacred Space
Step 2. Make an Energy Sandwich
Step 3. Activate the Aura
Step 4. Choose Which Cord to Cut
Step 5. Locate the Cord
Step 6. Give Permission
Step 7. Remove the Cord
Step 8. Bandage to Rebalance
Step 9. Write the Dialogue Box
  Capture the Cord Dialogue
  Value Every Bit of Information
  Probe to Find Missing Persons
  Notes on Your Notes
  Prepare to Clear Sexual Abuse
  Releasing Other Abuse from the Past
  Choose a Comfortable Distance
Step 10. Discuss the Pattern
Step 11. Impact Other Relationships
Step 12. Assign Homework

LET'S GET PRACTICAL

At Step 9, you will cut your third cord of attachment. Exciting!

1. Choose another minor cord to cut.

2. Quickly do Steps 1-8, then go ahead and slowly move through your "Official Reading" of Step 9.

3. Then speed up for the remaining chapters through Step 12.

You are building skill, no doubt about it.

Which information is contained in a cord of attachment? Step 9 is loaded with techniques to find out specifically, in depth and detail, one cord at a time.

First, though, let's develop a theory base to prepare you for what to expect. Will cord contents be hugely obvious, like recognizing the proverbial elephant in the room? Or will you go scurrying after quick-moving subtleties, something more akin to hunting mice?

Already you know one thing for sure. By definition, cords won't hold the unconditional love in a relationship. That is encoded differently, as spiritual ties. Instead, cords contain energy conflicts between the people involved.

So something will dominate in a cord, but what? Nothing you can figure out based on theory alone! Cord data isn't something you can make up.

For the sake of gaining perspective, however, let's try a thought experiment. Think of one really awful relationship from your past.

Can one sentence fully summarize how that relationship affected you? How complicated need your summary be to do justice to what happened?

Innumerable events shape a relationship, triggering various emotions. Each of these emotions is encoded within you as a distinctive energy. So a huge and complex collection of energies may be stored deep within a cord of attachment.

For practical purposes, however, you will find that certain dynamics predominate. This is the amount of detail to record while doing Step 9. Goldilocks would understand: Not too much, not too little, only the amount that is just right.

CORD ARCHEOLOGY

When you report on a freshly cut cord, will you work like an archeologist at a nice new dig? Must you go through one layer at a time, starting with the most recent deposits?

Or do you expect the oldest information to be uppermost?

Neither the oldest nor the newest deposits of energy will necessarily show up in a cord. Having analyzed hundreds of cords of attachment, both major and minor, I have come to believe that cord patterns evolve over time. What dominates now may be very different from what that same cord contained years ago.

Fortunately, complete healing via Energy Spirituality only requires that you pay attention to what shows up *now* in the freshly cut cord.

This will relate to **intensity of energy.** The strongest energy pattern in the history of that relationship will dominate the cord. If Charles Darwin lived today, researching the biology of energy, here is what he might call this evolutionary process "The survival of the biggest."

- Sometimes the biggest cord patterning involves a major childhood *trauma*.

- Other times, a cord is dominated by *long-term drama*. This intense energy pattern features at least one super-intense need from either the client or the cordee.

- Occasionally, you will find patterning related to a *conflict*, comparable to a computer programming glitch. Two or more inner commands are contradictory, like a bug in a computer program. What happens then? The cord's software doesn't stop functioning. Instead, it inwardly repeats the impasse locked in the cord. Day and night, 24/7, the cord owner's subconscious mind tries (and fails) to resolve the conflict.

- Some cords contain neither trauma nor drama nor conflict. Instead, the patterning is shaped by *repetition*. Year after year, a mild but persistent relationship problem accumulates energetically, much as a simple trickle of water can, over time, wear down a stone.

WHEN A CORD ISN'T CUT

Let's pursue our thought experiment further. Whatever the energy pattern in the cord you are thinking about, what happens when you must live with it for the rest of your life?

As a rising practitioner of Energy Spirituality, you won't be having this problem in the future, but things were different in your past. So I'm sure you can remember quite vividly what it was like when the patterning from a cord replayed through your aura 24/7.

Remember what was most troubling about the relationship you have chosen for our thought experiment? What a losing proposition! No matter what you tried, that relationship made you feel lousy.

In retrospect, you can be sure that a cord of attachment was involved, a major one. Back in the day, however, all you could do was cope. Eventually, you figured out that this relationship was not working for you. What then?

Maybe a death or divorce seemed to fix the problem. Maybe you stopped speaking to the cordee. Whatever the circumstances, once you decided to let go of the painful interchange, didn't you do all you could (from your side) to break free? Which of the following did you try?

- Replaying certain scenes from your history, trying to understand what went wrong.
- Taking action in the present to change unsatisfying traditions from the past.
- Modifying your behavior with financial commitment, sex, emotional involvement, etc.
- Trying to exorcise the past through psychotherapy.
- Prayer.
- Seeking forgiveness.
- Letting time help you to heal and move on.

Any of these choices could have brought some relief. But was your aura able to let go? Probably not; an aura remembers.

Toxic components of a cord replay, even if the cordee disappears off the face of the earth. To heal your aura, you need to cut cords or else do the energetic equivalent in some other way.

Every cord of attachment contains a pattern... and a mystery. Here is what you (and any client you're helping) will learn during Step 9: Whodunit and what, exactly, was done.

DIALOGUE BOXES

Delving into cords of attachment—just the simple act of recording the data—can teach you more about the human condition than you have ever known. And remember, that's only Step 9. More insights and healing will follow all the way through to the end of Step 12.

Expect to grow enormously from doing Step 9 for yourself and any clients you choose to help. Here is one example of how I have personally grown from cutting cords.

I stopped expecting that patterns within cords would be simple. Back in 1986, I would pick up just one or two simple generalizations. With more experience, I began to record the full flow of dominant data, calling it a **Dialogue Box.**

This reads like a play between two actors, the client and the cordee. A fascinating sequence unfolds between them, every bit of it meaningful. **Cord items** is my name for each individual item of dialogue.

Steps 10-12 will draw out the implications of all the cord items you find in Step 9, bringing the most complete healing possible.

This kind of closure, however, requires that you capture that Dialogue Box information. To find precise data within a freshly cut cord, I recommend using the following variation on Touch It, Read It or See It, Read It. When experimenting with these techniques back in Step 3, it was great, no-pressure practice for now, your once-in-a-lifetime chance to diagram contents of a freshly cut cord.

Capture the Cord

1. Draw a big rectangle to contain the cord dialogue. Write your client's first name on the left, the cordee's name on the right, and leave plenty of space in the middle. (Turn the page to see an example.)

2. Get Big.

3. Set the intention to read what was in the cord you just cut.

4. Place your Hand of Preference close to your client's body, right where the cord was removed. Or, if you prefer to connect visually, aim your eyes at this location. Either way, know that you are plugged into the data. You have full access to the patterning in that cord of attachment.

5. Use Questioning to fill in the Dialogue Box. Ask inside, "What are the dynamics of this cord, step by step?"

6. Take two vibe-raising breaths. Then chug a tall glass of whiskey. (Just kidding. The breathing should be enough.)

7. Write down every bit of information you receive without censoring. Easy now, just one cord item at a time! (If you start getting excited and need to pace yourself, use extra Vibe-Raising Breaths to slow down.)

8. When finished writing down each cord item, ask if there is anything more, and repeat 2-7 as needed until you feel that the job is complete.

9. After you stop writing the final cord item, quickly review your notes. Does it all make sense? Edit while the experience of capturing dialogue is still fresh.

10. Immediately proceed to Step 10.

A BASIC DIALOGUE BOX

Joe, your client	Here is where you quickly write down the various cord items. 1. Start with the first item. 2. Number each subsequent item. 3. Finish recording and there you have it!	Jane, the cordee

PROBLEM SOLVING

Writing down Dialogue Boxes is easy once you've had some practice. But you may have some questions before getting started, so let's do some problem-solving.

Why would you feel the cord but not the bandage? You have, after all, removed the cord. You flung it into a violet flame, destroying it. Afterwards, you put on the bandage. Since it's going to be there for three days, why wouldn't that big, fat bandage be the main thing you notice?

Here's why. For a short while after any cord is cut, a trace lingers. By analogy, imagine that a woman enters the room where you are now. She is wearing way too much perfume. Even after she leaves, won't that smell linger for a while?

Well, you're reading that kind of trace, not the cord itself. Sniff out that trace. It tells the whole story.

Won't you have to concentrate really hard to pick up the information?

No extra effort is needed. One quick thought about intention will take you directly to the cord data. During all of Step 9, just be slightly more interested in the cord dialogue than anything else.

That isn't concentration, more like selectively paying attention. In other contexts, you do this often and the process is totally effortless. For instance, let's say that someone shows you a group photo. You know that you're in it. Won't you look for yourself first?

Well, it's not so terribly hard to do that, is it? You don't have to scrunch up your brain or deliberately avoid seeing the other folks in the photo. No scissors will be needed to cut them out of the picture. Attention brings to the foreground whatever interests a person most.

Expect similar ease while doing Step 9. You're pretty darned interested in finding the dialogue within that cord. Also, your previous steps of cord-cutting have trained you to know that you are in control of your mind.

Confidently know that you are in control of your mind. This simple fact helps you to steady yourself when you aim to record a Dialogue Box. Later, that same control of your mind will come in handy again, helping you to advocate on behalf of your client during Steps 10-12.

One advantage of doing sessions for clients is that many people first find the strength to become an advocate by... helping others.

Assisting a client can awaken your parental instinct, fierce caring, inspired clarity, and more. Once aroused, these same healing qualities can also be directed toward yourself.

A NEW KIND OF INFORMATION

However confident you feel now as you aim to write a Dialogue Box, just do it. Cord dialogue is a new kind of information, so you may need to cut 10 cords or more before you feel completely comfortable with the process. No biggie! The following tips will help you meanwhile.

Value Every Bit of Information

Respect yourself doing this work, whether a client is there to admire you or not. You could be the only person in your area who knows this leading-edge way to cut cords of attachment. Don't wait for any colleagues to praise you. Go forth boldly. Make yourself available to do this sacred work.

1. When you're writing down information from a cord, your only goal is to capture all the significant dialogue. Don't censor or edit. Neatness does *not* count. Scribble away.

2. Know that some cord items will come from the client, others from the cordee.

3. Don't expect a logical order. Definitely don't expect that the client and cordee will necessary alternate their dialogue.

4. Simply follow the flow of information the best you can and spontaneously write down whatever you receive.

5. Remember, you are involved in Energy Spirituality. A Divine Being is collaborating with you. No human backup could be more skillful or considerate.

Usually, cord dialogue is more symbolic than literal. In some cases, though, you may record words that were actually used by the cordee.

Why do I know this is possible? Occasionally a client will stare at me while I read out a Dialogue Box. Then she will tell me, "He used to say that all the time."

In Step 10, you will be reading the cord items out loud, which will be like showing your client a powerful play. Will there be great catchy quotes? Or will the dialogue simply be serviceable enough to move the action forward? Either way, every word will be valuable, bringing an experience of catharsis.

So long as you hold fast to your healing intention, your job at Step 9 will be simple. Just write down every word you find, using our Capture the Cord technique.

As you look over your notes, don't insist that the words read like Shakespeare. Simple contradictions or boring repetitions can become a highlight when you get to Step 10. For now, faithfully write down the play. And never bring along your Inner Drama Critic.

When "Boring" Is Good

Sometimes the dialogue you overhear in a cord might seem trivial if you didn't know better. Witnessed in a theater, the following words would make for a staggeringly dull play. Really, would you want to sit through a show with lines like this?

1. *Wyatt: I feel sad.*
2. *Mother: You can't possibly feel sad.*
3. *Wyatt: I feel neglected.*
4. *Mother: You're not neglected.*

Boring or not, dialogue like this can have great significance in the context of a cord. Why? Understand this fact: Conflicts within a cord repeat forever.

Your first reaction to Wyatt's cord items might be, "That's ridiculous." Even a 10-year old, you might think, wouldn't accept this kind of negation. Actually, many a cord's dominant patterning was put in place long before your client was 10. Without help from a healer like you, lousy dialogue like this could replay for the rest of your client's life.

FIND MISSING PERSONS

In some cases, a Dialogue Box will seem awfully one-sided. You'll scribble loads of notes about how your client pours out emotion toward the cordee, or the reverse. But, oddly, nothing seems to come from the person on the other side of the cord. Well, that silence could be golden. To use the data, just refine it a bit.

How can you turn a "nothing" into something informative? The following technique will help.

Probe to Find Missing Persons

While you are researching a Dialogue Box, sometimes you'll write down a lot of dialogue on one side of the cord only. After several such items in a row, do this special kind of Questioning:

1. If there's no input from the *cordee*, ask a question like this:
• "Where is input from the cordee?"
• "How is the cordee reacting?"
• Or simply "Where is the cordee in this picture?"
2. If input from your *client* is missing, ask a question like this:
• "Where is input from my client?"
• "How is my client reacting?"
• Or simply "Where is my client in this picture?"
3. Take a couple of Vibe-Raising Breaths.
4. Accept whatever you get. Write it down, even something abstract like "I'm as disconnected from this relationship as I could possibly be."

Sometimes a person's absence turns out to be the most important item in the entire Dialogue Box. How could a "nothing" be such a big deal? Here are a few examples. You can easily think of others:

■ A *cordee* who becomes energetically unavailable could be withdrawing purposely, manipulating your client.

■ Or the cordee may not be capable of giving love or attention. This doesn't necessarily start as anything personal. Yet, being part of a cord, it *becomes* personal. When you look at the Dialogue Box as a whole, or discuss it in Step 10, your client may have a big *aha!* "That lack of attention wasn't about anything wrong with me. I wasn't being rejected, really. I only felt rejected."

■ A power play may be involved. The most effective way for a cordee to pull energy from your client (intentionally or not) is to remain tantalizingly unavailable.

■ A *client*, being unavailable in a Dialogue Box, could be fighting for psychological survival. She might be doing her best to carve out some privacy in a relationship that would otherwise smother her.

■ Maybe your client is withdrawing as a kind of "Find me" ploy. The very next cord item could be something like, "If you really loved me, you would find me." (The rest of your client's Dialogue Box will reveal how well this strategy works.)

■ Perhaps your client is waiting for an apology that never comes.

■ Or a particular kind of support could have been requested by your client, but this never is given. What will follow this missing support? As long as that Dialogue Box replays, void and all, your client is waiting for Godot. She keeps expecting to receive the attention, the love, the whatever. So long as that dialogue pattern replays, your client's waiting will continue.

With experience, you can develop an instinct for finding the "missing items" in a cord. Really, this is no harder to find than something actively present.

For example, say that when you first write down Cord Dialogue, some of the items feel like hot water, obvious to your inner senses. As you keep exploring, you'll also touch the equivalent of cool water.

Water feels like water, whatever the temperature. Similarly, within the flow of energy in a cord of attachment, energy feels like energy, whether active or passive, pushing or pulling.

Divorced Before the Divorce

Emma had been divorced for years, yet she couldn't let go. "My ex was horrible," she told me. "Holding on to any part of this awful relationship makes no sense. Please help me to move on." Here is the pattern I wrote down in the Dialogue Box.

1. *Emma: I'll do whatever I can to please you. Just pay attention to me. I need that.*
2. *Husband: No response.*
3. *Emma: Look, I'm working really hard to please you. Isn't that great? Isn't it?*
4. *Husband: No response. (Energetically, he's as remote as he can be yet still be included in the cord pattern.)*
5. *Emma: If you don't pay attention to me, I won't have any value as a person. I'm begging you to pay attention to me.*
6. *Emma: I feel so worthless.*
7. *Husband: Interested in pornography. Keeping it hidden. "I have a right to my private life. Don't interfere."*
8. *Emma: I must have done something wrong. Until I find out what that was, I can't forgive myself. I'd better try harder and harder to make up for it, whatever it is that I've done wrong.*

Not a bad deal for Emma's ex, energetically! Whenever someone in a cord acts unavailable, he constantly draws energy from the other person. As long as Emma's cord continued, Emma was doing the equivalent of pouring her sexual energy into a leaky bucket. Sure she had trouble moving on, with limited sexual energy available for herself or to share with anyone new.

Cord items can be a shock. For the rest of your client's life, cord dialogue like Emma's will repeat, with its gives and takes, its lack of respect or downright cruelty, playing back every nuance of its ridiculous unfairness. To help end the pain, simply write down whatever you find in that Dialogue Box.

MORE PROBLEM SOLVING

Let's clear up questions that can arise when you're new to writing down cord items.

What if you don't get the words perfectly right?

So what? You're still facilitating Energy Spirituality.

Have you ever had one of those nightmares where the same weird situation replays again and again? Afterwards, you wake up and describe your dream. Maybe those words aren't perfect, either. Yet they come close enough. And, therefore, they bring relief.

Find the nearest words you can. That's good enough to release the nightmare. Healing is what matters, not perfection.

What if you feel like you're making words up?

Write down those words anyway. As you get into the feeling of a cord, translate it into the very first words that occur to you.

Making up the best language you can is perfectly acceptable. All the words or actions you find within a cord are really energy patterns. Of course, they exist beyond language. You are logging molecules of emotion.

Notes on Your Notes

Once you've written a Dialogue Box, look back over your notes. Tweak them a bit before you move on to Step 10.

1. Number every single cord item. Short or long, it counts.
2. When you read over your notes, what do you find happening with the flow? For example:
• Do you find a logical progression?
• Is there a conflict?
• Are there other patterns that might be significant?

> • Does part of the conversation repeat?
> • Do you feel a special intensity at any cord items?
> 3. Circle anything that seems significant. You'll want to emphasize this when you discuss the Dialogue Box with your client during Step 10.

In the following example, where would you find a conflict to circle? (Hint: Maybe you'll find more than one.)

Contradictions Galore

Listlessly, Wyatt walked into my session room. His voice was low as he spoke his intention. "I want to heal my throat chakra."

When asked which relationship might be most important for a cord-cutting, Wyatt didn't hesitate. His throat might have felt squeezed, but his mind worked just fine. "Mother," he said. These were the cord items:

1. *Wyatt: I feel sad.*
2. *Mother: You can't possibly feel sad.*
3. *Wyatt: I feel neglected.*
4. *Mother: You're not neglected.*
5. *Wyatt: I feel unappreciated and unwanted.*
6. *Mother: That's ridiculous. Do you have any idea how good I am to you? I buy you everything you need.*
7. *Wyatt: What's wrong with me then? I feel longings. I have ideas to share. Nobody ever is interested. You're not.*
8. *Mother: Why would anyone be interested? Your inner life doesn't matter. All I care about is having you look good and act normal.*

Congratulate yourself if you flagged the conflicts in cord items 1 and 2, then cord items 3 and 4, then cord items 5 and 6, and also cord items 7 and 8.

What might be the implications of Wyatt's repeatedly being told that he doesn't feel what he feels?

CLEARING SEXUAL ABUSE

Of all the repeating patterns that can be stuck in a client, sexual abuse may be the most toxic. Whenever there has been rape or incest, the energy replays in endless reruns. By now you know where that theater is located, right in a cord of attachment.

Prepare to Clear Sexual Abuse

No client is more grateful than one freed from sexual abuse. But in terms of your technique as a healer, clearing sexual abuse is not significantly different from cutting any other cord of attachment.

1. Even if your client has told you that a particular relationship featured rape or incest, diagram only what you find— nothing more, nothing less. When in doubt, remember this helpful hint: Assume nothing.
2. Sometimes you will find information about a sexual offense. Sometimes you won't. Don't feel pressured to find anything in particular.
3. Question without making assumptions about sexual abuse. Ask inside "What is in this cord?" not "What happened during the rape?"

Sexual misconduct is way more common than you might think before starting to work with clients. Usually, a client's memory of abuse will be all too accurate. Yet sometimes you may not find abuse where your client expects it.

For example, an innocuous incident from this life may trigger the deep memory of sexual abuse from a previous lifetime. The person who triggered the memory in this life could be considered an abuser by your client, even though the inappropriate touch happened centuries ago and was inflicted by a completely different person.

Of course, there would be no trace of abuse in your client's present-life cord of attachment. There still could be plenty worth healing in your client's cord to this person.

Alternatively, a healing practitioner may have inadvertently caused your client to construct a false memory. Again, toxic energy galore could be stuck in that cord, something very worth removing. Although the Dialogue Box won't match your client's initial idea, she will nonetheless benefit from the healing.

In general, doing Step 9, you never need to gauge the precise degree of accuracy in your client's beliefs. Nor need you know the particulars of a client's story of abuse. You'll do just fine. You'll bring wonderful healing just by going through the 12 Steps.

So don't be alarmed or doubt yourself if, recording a Dialogue Box, you don't find the specific kind of sexual abuse that you have been told to expect. If it doesn't exist in your client's cord of attachment, why would you find it?

Even when there has been abuse, that may not be the worst part of a particular cord of attachment. In that case, abuse may not be found at all as a cord item. For example, the patterning may emphasize nightmarish elements where your client screams but is never heard.

Treat all cases of abuse in the same way. Don't worry about validating your client's story. Impartially record whatever you find.

Above all, don't assume that you must act like a sportscaster, giving a blow-by-blow account of the physical drama. Even if it's a cord of attachment to "The stranger who raped me," only look for energy dynamics. You're not hunting for specific details. If a client wants that, refer her to a psychotherapist who specializes in abuse, a grief counselor, regression therapist, or other professional.

Your job is to remove the cord, write the Dialogue Box to validate this pattern, then follow through with the rest of the 12 Steps to Cut Cords of Attachment. This sequence may heal your client as nothing else has. Finally, she can let go of that old experience.

The Scream Nobody Heard

Often the victim of a rape feels trapped in a nightmare. She's screaming as hard as she can, yet nobody hears, not even (apparently) God. Julia's story was typical. Once her session started, she quickly got to the point. "I'm here to cut the cord of attachment to my father. He abused me."

Because the memories were so painful, Julia was asked to simply nod "Yes" or "No" when I read out the Dialogue Box, signaling whether she could relate to each item. Here is the sequence I recorded at Step 9, followed by her response during Step 10.

1. *Julia: Screaming in terror, yet she can't make a sound. It's like being frozen and unable to move. Inside she's yelling, "Stop doing that to me."* YES.

2. *Father: He continues using her body as if it is an object. His sexual energy moves through and around her.* YES.

3. *Julia: I recognize this sexual feeling. I don't want to feel it.* YES

4. *Father: He's satisfied. Immediately, he puts what has happened into denial. To him, it's as if nothing has happened at all.* YES.

5. *Julia: The emotional pain is crushing. She cries out for help, but nobody helps her.* YES.

6. *Father: Shut up. You're making a big deal out of nothing.* YES.

7. *Julia: I feel abandoned and helpless. I don't want to be here on earth.* YES.

8. *Julia: The only thing that keeps me going is my connection to God. I am able to connect extra strongly to God. I can do this because I must.* YES.

Starting with Step 10 of cutting cords of attachment, Julia cried hard for the rest of her session. Despite this, she listened and responded actively. It made sense to her when I pointed out logical consequences of having the cord removed.

Yes, in the future anxiety could diminish. She might finally be able to enjoy sex with a man. She might stop feeling abandoned. Also, Julia's longstanding desire to leave earth could abate.

"Yes," she told me. "For most of my life I have wanted to kill myself." Wow!

I explained that when a cord of attachment keeps sending its poison into your aura, usually the best you can do is to cope with the negative feelings. Nothing will make those feelings stop so long as the cord replays them 24/7 within your aura. But now, energetically, things can be different.

RELEASING OTHER ABUSE

You may have the privilege of facilitating healing for other types of abuse, not just sexual abuse. Congratulations! This can be a huge help to your client.

If you have never suffered abuse, you may wonder whether you are qualified to do this kind of work. Sure you are. You already have determined that your client is basically stable but just has a troublesome cord. To release it, follow the usual 12 Steps, supplemented by the following technique and your own common sense.

If you *have* been abused, you may question whether you can be impartial enough to help a client. Cutting cords to all your previous abusers will prepare you. (Just don't make those the first cords you cut. Remember? Start by honing your skills on at least 10 minor cords. And if you feel queasy about going into this scary territory alone, seek professional support.)

When your own cords to abusers are removed, you'll release any emotional charge that might otherwise distort your work. What you keep will be the wisdom.

Whether healing abuse for yourself or a client, be sure to use the technique that follows.

Validate Physical or Emotional Abuse

Maybe a client has told you about abuse before you cut the cord. Maybe not. Either way, how would you validate abuse when you do Step 9?

1. Don't expect to see the word "abuse" lit up in neon. Abuse is seldom all that you find in a cord. Instead, abuse flows through as part of a pattern. While recording the cord items, sometimes you will find particularly intense emotions directed toward your client or you will find physical violence. Should you find this, write it down as you would any other cord items.

2. Understand that abuse is encoded in a cord as emotions and energy, not literal actions. If scenes or words flash before you, write them down. But don't assume that this information is necessarily about a literal event.

3. Never make a pronouncement about the type of abuse, e.g., "She smacked you across the face a lot, didn't she?" You have been reading energy, not a cosmic transcript.

4. During Step 10, ask questions to find out what happened to the client. How were the encoded patterns expressed? For example, you could ask, "Was this rage from your ex on the level of an argument or was anything more intense involved?" A client might respond that the cordee was drunk, yelled or threw things. Sometimes intense emotion is "all" that happened. In every case, here is what matters most: The cord that contained this toxic flow of energy is gone for good.

How do you know when a situation is bad enough to technically qualify as abuse?

You don't have to. Are you Judge Judy? Or are you simply a healer who has been invited to help to remove toxic energy?

Keep it simple, Smartie. Let your client be the one to bring up the word "abuse" if he chooses.

The Perfect Wife

Who would have suspected physical abuse? Karen never mentioned it. She just asked me to cut the cord to her husband. At the time of this session, nearly 20 years ago, I knew very little about physical abuse. It never occurred to me that someone who looked so picture perfect could be involved in such misery.

But before I diagramed this cord, I'd taken the precaution of Getting Big. So my own limited experience didn't keep me from learning the truth in my first encounter with physical abuse.

1. *Karen: I'll keep up appearances, okay? Nobody needs to know what has happened between us. Let's make a new beginning, so everything can be alright from now on.*
2. *Husband: I love you for being so beautiful.*
3. *Husband: You're too beautiful. You're too nice. It drives me crazy sometimes and I want to destroy you.*
4. *Karen: What's wrong with me? What do I have to do to be good enough? Then you won't need to punish me any more.*
5. *Husband: I feel like such a sinner. I feel so guilty.*
6. *Karen: I forgive you. Let me help save you. You didn't really mean to hurt me. I know that.*

Karen gained a lot of benefit from cutting that cord. She returned for several sessions with me, releasing other cords related to abuse.

Fifteen years later, she came back, more beautiful than ever. By now, my client was divorced from the abusive husband and happily married to a new man. It was a delight to read her aura. Karen had made a wonderful recovery.

COMFORTABLE DISTANCE

A wise man once said, "It's noble to look deeper into life. Only don't look so deep that you throw up."

How deeply will you look when diagramming or discussing a cord? Your goal is to receive information, not to personally feel it.

Also, you are not in the business of analyzing where the patterns came from or applying psychological labels (not unless, as a trained therapist, you already happen to own that skill set).

Well, relax. Television has trained you well about choosing how deep to go. Viewers get used to watching a show, following a plot line. You know that you don't have to feel every blow, nor develop every disease. Depending on the show and your mood, you are always in control over the depth of your involvement.

Once you understand this concept of **comfortable distancing,** your intention for reading a cord pattern will automatically position your mind-body-spirit at just the right level.

One of the major differences between psychologically-oriented therapy and Energy Spirituality is the underlying sound quality. Eavesdrop on psychological therapy and you will hear fear or pain. A client **must** be willing to go there, making contact with the most unpleasant patterning, be it conscious, subconscious or even unconscious.

Sometimes psychological healing is the only way to remove certain patterns. (That's why, in my own practice of Energy Spirituality, I include the option of using a different skill set. Sometimes I recommend that a client work with me doing regression therapy. The form I use, learned from Dr. Coletta Long, combines psychological healing with Energy Psychology.)

Whatever the therapist's skill set for psychological healing, ideally it will be supplemented by holding a certain type of space for the client, making it safe to do work at depth.

How can a client find the strength to succeed at the tough work of psychological healing? If you listen, you'll hear it: Courage.

This is a distinctive, can-do vibration. "I am determined to heal, whatever it takes." No doubt this sound brings tears to the eyes of our guardian angels.

Where does that courage come from? Commitment can bring forth the necessary strength to do tough emotional work. Or sometimes desperation becomes mixed with persistence and becomes courage. In other cases, a client finds extra courage when she senses that one final push can remove certain problems once and for all.

Courage sounds beautiful to the deep listener. But in your sessions of Energy Spirituality, the underlying sound may move you even more than the hidden sound of courage. You'll hear a sweet silence or, even, joy.

Don't mistake that gentleness for superficiality. Case in point: The kind of healing you're learning to do with the 12 Steps for Cutting Cords of Attachment. Underlying joy in your session isn't merely some feel-good emotion, some happy-talk in which everyone pretends that everything is magically all right. Cutting cords is *real.*

So is the support of Divine Beings. They bring a deep joy to the practice of Energy Spirituality, along with a transcendent emotional security. Sometimes this is called **bliss.**

Feeling that support, deep down, will add greatly to your effectiveness as a healer. By opening up heart and soul as a listener, you'll amplify the sound of truth within.

Engaging in Energy Spirituality will protect you, not just your client. At Step 10, we'll develop even greater appreciation for the differences between the complementary approaches of psychological healing and Energy Spirituality.

Step 10.
Discuss the Pattern

12 STEPS TO CUT CORDS OF ATTACHMENT

Step 1. Create a Sacred Space
Step 2. Make an Energy Sandwich
Step 3. Activate the Aura
Step 4. Choose Which Cord to Cut
Step 5. Locate the Cord
Step 6. Give Permission
Step 7. Remove the Cord
Step 8. Bandage to Rebalance
Step 9. Write the Dialogue Box
Step 10. Discuss the Pattern
    Validate the truth
    To help clients: Define Energy Spirituality
    Productive Cord Analysis
    Reevaluate Trusted Relationships
    Smash Fantasy, Fix Reality
    Discuss Sexual Problems
    Invite New Forgiveness
Step 11. Impact Other Relationships
Step 12. Assign Homework

LET'S GET PRACTICAL

Having arrived at Step 10, you are ready to cut a fourth minor cord of attachment.

1. Quickly doing Steps 1-9, you may take your cues from our summary of the 12 Steps on the previous page. (Of course, you can always review by rereading earlier Steps.)

2. Take your time to master Step 10, slowly doing your "Official Reading" of the chapter.

3. Pick up your pace again at Steps 11-12.

See how time flies? Healing dances!

Step 10 brings the special kind of validation that comes from discovering what was involved in a cord of attachment. Be prepared for surprises, whether "the client" is someone else or yourself.

As the client, put aside knowledge of past events while you read out the Dialogue Box. Alternate being "the healer" with being "the client." You're wearing a different hat. (If it helps you to literally change millinery during Step 10, go ahead and don your gay apparel of baseball cap, bike helmet, whatever.)

If you practice by helping a friend you won't need to remove any hats. But you may need to put aside an overwhelming sense of ignorance. Usually, when you begin Step 10, all that you will know about your client's relationship to the cordee is:

- The *type* of relationship, e.g., spouse, boss, parent
- Whether the cordee is now living or dead.

Consequently, your situation as healer could be likened to the proverbial glass with 50 percent water. Will you react defensively, viewing that glass as half empty, thinking "Uh-oh, now I'm being tested"? Or will you trust that the glass is half-full, offering a unique opportunity to validate your client?

Personally, I consider it a plus when I bring dazzling ignorance about that corded relationship to Step 10. After I read out cord items, many a client has gasped in astonishment, "How could you know?"

The answer, of course, is that cords of attachment are real. Yes, they contain real information that repeats 24/7. Yes, a complete stranger can describe it.

Furthermore, when a cord's contents have been accurately described out of (seemingly) nowhere, this can really impress a client. If the cord items were encoded as energy, maybe it actually is possible that they can be removed permanently.

Go ahead. Convince your client by telling the truth.

VALIDATE THE TRUTH

Whatever ugly pattern dominated that cord, this never was who your client really was, deep down. To some extent, you have clarified that by doing the Before Picture. Another major step of progress was cutting the cord itself.

Now, at Step 10, you will remove the final layer of illusion, a "sense of cord" mistaken for a "sense of self."

If you are validating this for yourself, pretend that you're dealing with a client. This will increase your objectivity. Alternate speaking as "the healer" and responding as "the client."

Help your client, whoever that is, by reviewing cord items at Step 10.

Review Cord Items

1. Read out the sequence of cord items in your Dialogue Box.
2. Stop after each item. Can the client relate to it? Ask.
3. Listen to your client's response. Let her discharge emotions, if needed. Together, you're bringing Energy Spirituality to the level of the conscious mind.
4. Continue reading the complete sequence of cord items, discussing as you go.
5. Conclude by emphasizing anything that you find especially important. Then go straight to Step 11.

Lest this process sound abstract or intimidating, you can think of it this way. At Step 10 you have a conversation that validates your client's previous suffering. It is a conversation like any other, but more healing than most. Here is a detailed example of cord item review with a client.

An Invisible Man

Why did Danny feel like an invisible man? Read the answer in cord items from Danny's cord to his father.

I will alternate the cord items with Danny's reaction to hearing about them.

1. Danny: I'm wrong again. Nothing I do is good enough.

Was that a familiar feeling for my client when dealing with his father? Absolutely. Danny said it felt like the story of his life.

2. Father, taunting: You got that right.

Danny described this taunting as "being kicked when I was down." Even if a situation didn't start as a contest, Dad would turn it into one. Eventually Danny always expected to wind up as a loser, so why bother to talk in the first place?

3. Father: Being good means that you do what I want when I want it.

That sure was recognizable. Danny felt this cord item explained a lot about how his desire to be good alternated with an urge to rebel.

I reminded Danny that every adult has the right to do for himself what *he* wants when he wants it. While he still had the cord, however, Danny was programmed to do what his father wanted instead.

4. Father: What you do is never good enough. I'm especially annoyed that you have so many opinions and ideas. Even before I hear what you have to say, I know that you're wrong.

I asked Danny if he had always been a lot more cerebral than his father. "Well, yes." The idea that his father felt threatened was new to him, but it made sense. Ever since childhood, Danny had been called wrong for supposedly being "too smart."

5. Danny: Confronted, I become invisible. There's only room for what the other person has to say.

This may have been the very worst cord item. Danny confirmed that he often felt invisible while arguing with his father. During Step 10, we discussed this in some detail. When we moved to Step 11, we considered the implications even further. In love relationships, for instance, did Danny have a history of feeling invisible once there was conflict? "Definitely!" That pattern in all his relationships was about to change because we had removed a significant cause. This change could be an extra benefit of cutting the cord to Danny's father.

Over the years, Danny followed up with some additional sessions, a small number compared to the typical number of visits involved in conventional psychotherapy.

His life altered significantly for the better. Even the timbre of his voice changed: During this first session, he had one of those highly intellectual voices that seems disconnected from the body. Soon his voice became more vibrant, stronger, the voice of a confident man.

THE ROLE OF ENERGY SPIRITUALITY

Once a cord of attachment is cut, its toxic energy will never replay again. Why bother to do Step 10? Why would there be benefit to discussing cord items, especially if they were painful?

The answer can be summed up in two words: Energy Spirituality. This is a completely different process from other forms of inner healing.

By now you have had enough experience to fully understand the difference, so let's explore it in greater depth than we did previously. Let's compare Energy Spirituality to other types of healing.

Physical healing aims to solve problems at the level of the physical body. This approach is usually facilitated by a doctor or other medical professional. Allopathic methods of healing are standard in Western medicine, such as prescribing drugs and doing surgery.

Sometimes the healer practices so-called "alternative medicine," such as chiropractic, Reiki, homeopathy, acupuncture, Healing Touch or others. **Energy Medicine** is the 21st century name for all these forms of holistic healing. Benefits flow to the mind and spirit as well as the physical body.

Why is it called Energy Medicine, rather than Energy Psychology or Energy Spirituality? The point of entry for healing is the body, not the mind or aura.

A high proportion of my students for cutting cords of attachment have been involved in physical healing as practitioners and/or clients. Other students have done more with **Inner healing**. This can be either psychological or spiritual.

Psychological healing comes in innumerable forms. For all of them, the point of entry for healing is distress about the client's human life, the inner experience of problems. What story does the client tell herself? Which problems from the past or present afflict her now? Psychiatry, psychotherapy, grief counseling and life coaching are examples of this approach.

Energy Psychology is a holistic, 21st century approach to psychological healing, linking problems to the human energy field. For example, Gary Craig's Emotional Freedom Technique uses tapping to release emotional blockage.

Spiritual healing invites help from "the other side." Energy Spirituality brings help from the healer's team (etheric or astral) in order to alter a client's energy field.

Since you're becoming a practitioner of Energy Spirituality, it's important that you clearly understand the difference between this modality, psychic-level healing, and psychological healing.

As we explore in depth, I invite you to appreciate is how deceptive names can be. In Step 2, we distinguished the approaches of psychic and spiritual healing, and now we will go deeper, moving into a comparison of healing models.

Most inner healing today, mainstream or not, is psychological in nature. Sometimes this is obvious, as when you:

- Work with a trained psychotherapist
- Study a self-help book
- Go through a 12-step program like Alcoholics Anonymous

- Participate in a support group
- Read a self-improvement article in a magazine or online, and the article has been written by a credentialed psychologist or psychiatrist

Apart from approaches like these, psychological healing is the most common model for inner healing in America today. Most partcipants in these approaches don't yet recognize how often so-called "spiritual" approaches are really based on a psychological model.

Both are valuable. Both are different.

To distinguish psychological healing from spiritual healing you must investigate beneath the name, the claim, and (sometimes) the practitioner's fame.

For instance, psychic readings and mediumship can be extremely helpful. After the sudden death of a friend or the lingering death of a relative, what professional service can bring more comfort than this?

Many highly skilled practitioners are available today to create a kind of conference call, connecting the departed spirit and the client.

Some superstars in the psychic field charge a great deal, and special healing powers may be attributed to them. A wise consumer will care less about this than the truth value of the practitioner's work. Referals have always been helpful for finding the best practitioner for you. Now your Deeper Perception can help, too. Read your aura before and after exploring the psychic's website.

Skilled communication with beings from the Other Side can bring consolation and healing. But is this spiritual healing? Ironically, no. The psychic or medium brings information, which doesn't necessarily bring long-term healing to an aura. Instead, these channels to the spirit world often serve as counselors. Then their work fits into the model of psychological healing.

In general, don't assume that a conversation about religion, angels or spiritual growth necessarily involves spiritual healing. It's a matter of process, not content. Usually the following description will apply to the process of healing.

Psychological healing is hard work. As a client, you may do this work with skilled help, in a group or one-on-one with a trained practitioner. If you have a talent for this type of healing, you may make significant progress on your own. Whoever helps you, ultimately you must rely upon your own mind to figure out:

- How do you define the problem?
- Which are the deepest or hidden parts of that problem?
- What caused the problem?
- Once you understand the problem, how will you use your insights?

Insights unfold at their own pace, sometimes taking years. One thing is certain: Unearthing these insights takes courage. There's good reason why old problems are put into denial. It can be hard to face painful memories, hidden patterns, bad behavior from good people (including oneself).

Thus, fear and pain are involved in psychological healing. And the client needs to gain new intellectual understanding, at some level, about emotions, behavior, interpreting the past, etc.

As if all this weren't challenging enough, psychological healing demands that the client will consciously work to change patterns of behavior, one tough choice at a time. Monitoring yourself may cause you to become a detached observer of your own life. Spontaneity, innocence, and naturalness may be sacrificed. Certainly your patience and strength will be tested.

Are the results worth it? Absolutely! Sometimes psychological healing is the only way to produce results.

Sometimes, however, results are limited. Sometimes results may be lacking entirely. In the words of one burned-out therapist who became my student of Energy Spirituality, "Most of the patients who come see me don't really want to get well. They just want to satisfy themselves that they are doing *something.*"

Surely you know at least one person who has been in therapy for years, producing no noticeable results at all. The best that can be said is that the patient has gained a meaningful hobby.

It may still feel like work. One easy way to recognize psychological healing is when a client says, "I'm working on my issues."

Some of my most appreciative students (and clients) have been practicing psychologists who want to add spiritual healing to their skills. Fortunately, there is no law against supplementing psychological healing with any form of spiritual healing. These approaches can work synergistically, bringing the client great benefit.

Spiritual healing doesn't require that the client work much at all, apart from deciding to get well. Beyond that, the client only needs enough luck (or consumer smarts) to locate a practitioner like you, someone who facilitates spiritual healing.

This healer has learned how to connect with God or a Divine Being, with angels or guides, who will do the heavy lifting. The spiritual healer's job is to set up conditions where healing will happen (such as creating that Energy Sandwich you learned about earlier). Then the healer's skill set brings about results.

As a client, you tell your intention to a practitioner of Energy Spirituality, then allow him to facilitate change to your aura. Optional but helpful: The client may be guided to consciously appreciate what in his aura has changed by the end of the session. This brings closure to the session and also helps the client to become empowered, rather than possibly grow dependent on the healer.

Cutting a cord of attachment definitely counts as changing an aura. It is a fine adjunct to other forms of spiritual healing, including angelic healing, soul retrieval and Shamanic work.

(Please note, however, if you're already a spiritual healer with an existing skill set: For best results, use the full 12 Steps to Cut Cords of Attachment without modifying them. You could mostly work at an astral level to do the rest of your skill set, but for this particular part of your work it's important to make an Energy Sandwich with Divine Beings.)

All authentic spiritual healing, whether astral or etheric, is effortless. When the healer gets out of the way, the greatest results come. A client receives instant and permanent transformation.

How about the role of understanding? Consider it a *by-product* of spiritual healing, not the cause (as with psychological healing). Although included, understanding need not be time-consuming. "Aha!" goes the client. "I know that."

Understanding can come easier *after* toxic patterns in an aura have been physically removed, exactly what we do in Steps 10 and 11.

Whenever and whatever the conversation that brings inner knowing, energetic change is what frees the client from old fears or pain or behavior. Thus, spiritual healing is structured in aha!s and miracles, not hard work.

It took me years to adjust to the underlying emotion of Energy Spirituality. Having done my share of psychological healing, I was used to hard work and pain. But energy healing has the underlying emotion of joy. That's the nature of God, after all.

Does spiritual healing have to mean faith healing, like something coming from a televangelist or faith healer? Absolutely not. Innumerable types of healing belong in the category of spiritual healing. Cutting a cord of attachment doesn't demand faith any more than it requires ministerial credentials.

One of my goals with this book is to help both healers and clients understand that mainstream churches do not have the exclusive right to practice spiritual healing. This would be like saying that Good Humor ice-cream bars are the only kind of dessert.

DEEPER ENERGY, EXTRA OOMPH

Adding an energy component to healing of any kind greatly increases the results. The human energy field has always been a level of cause.

People today are switching on their Deeper Perception so that they can produce, and appreciate, results at this level of causation.

When you make a change at the surface level of life, the results are limited compared to what you can do at a deeper level.

- On the surface level, a certain amount of energy is available when you tear a sheet of paper.
- The chemical level lies deeper. If you burn the same sheet of paper, considerably more energy will be released. More power available!
- And if you could split even *one* atom from deep within that sheet of paper (not that I'm suggesting you run out and do this), even more power would become available.

Here I have given analogies about destruction. But what about healing and, specifically, what about *techniques* for healing? When you combine healing skills, a positive intention, and the power of the human energy field, healing intensifies.

- Energy Medicine has the potential to greatly increase the benefits of other forms of physical healing.
- Energy Psychology can powerfully supplement other forms of psychological healing. (Ironically, as you now can appreciate, Energy Psychology fits the model of spiritual healing, rather than psychological healing.)
- Energy Spirituality, likewise, adds greater power to the benefits of services offered in the name of spiritual healing. In practice, as we have seen, spiritual counseling and other modalities are often based on a model for psychological healing.

What can you tell a client who believes that all inner healing requires emotional release?

Agree with your client that this is true for psychological healing. Then explain you are doing something different, a form of spiritual healing. Make sure your client understands the difference. Less work! More joy!

COMBINING ALL THREE
APPROACHES

Psychological, physical, and spiritual healing can be used in combination. This, after all, is the promise of mind-body-spiritual healing. You can use Energy Spirituality as part of a holistic approach.

For instance, as a therapist you might be find a client resistant to exploring a painful area. By shifting to Energy Spirituality (e.g., cutting a cord), you could help your client to gain strength that brings more success to psychological healing.

Here's an example from my practice with clients, in which I supplement Energy Spirituality with a form of regression therapy that, as mentioned last chapter, combines psychological healing with Energy Psychology.

Healing for a Battered Wife

Ursula's first husband was violent. Not only did the crazy man beat her but, one unforgettable day, he grabbed one of their two babies and held a butcher knife to the child's throat. Ursula was frantic to protect her children and herself, and the three of them barely escaped with their lives. Other horrific incidents followed over several years.

I worked with Ursula in two different ways. First, we did a session of Energy Spirituality, where she asked me to cut the cord to her ex. I knew little about her history, but she told me about it while we were at Step 11. Except for her recounting this, our session contained very little drama. Emotional release for Ursula was minimal.

Did she still get results from that one session of Energy Spirituality? "Oh, it was like having a weight lift right off my shoulders," she told me later. "I'd been carrying that weight for more than 30 years."

A year later, Ursula requested a session of regression therapy. I used Dr. Long's techniques to permanently release frozen blocks of energy.

Although a willing patient, Ursula was difficult to help psychologically. Defenses had helped her survive nightmarish traumas. But those same de-

Although a willing patient, Ursula was difficult to help psychologically. Defenses had helped her to survive horrible traumas. Yet those very same defenses worked against her while doing therapy. It took major coaxing to move Ursula into emotional release. By the end of our three-hour session, she received some benefit but had done only moderately well.

A client like Ursula would need many painful sessions of regression therapy to achieve big results, while she gained immediate benefit from our painless one-hour session of Energy Spirituality.

As a spiritual and psychological healer, it's invaluable to me that both approaches, at the energy level, are part of my skill set. When the 12 Steps to Cut Cords of Attachment become widely known, it will be fascinating to observe the creative ways in which healers of all kinds—psychological and physical as well as spiritual—use this approach to help clients.

POSITION YOURSELF

Whatever you call your sessions, many new clients will expect psychological healing. It will be up to you to educate the client about Energy Spirituality. During all of the 12 Steps to Cut Cords of Attachment, watch carefully for signs that your client is expecting healing of a different kind, or at a different level.

Then supply the understanding that will make the difference. Often, this understanding really sinks in during Step 10, as your client wakes up to the fact that his aura has changed permanently, with important implications for practical life.

Danny, the former Invisible Man, is a good example of this. Remember when I described the cord to his father? At the start of his session, Danny had trouble setting an intention because past experiences had led him to expect psychological healing.

Ready to Change, Not Just Discuss

An exceptionally bright and articulate man, Danny had plenty of experience with psychological healing. He expected our first session to be more of the same, perhaps with a little aura-type information thrown in.

Asked to set an intention, Danny said, "I'd like to understand the problems I have with communicating. Read my aura and show me the blockage so I can have more insight."

Oh, this session was going to be good. I could smell it. Danny's aura was basically healthy, just blocked, and he really wanted to move forward. Granted, we were going to need to clarify the difference between spiritual healing vs. psychological healing.

First we did the Before Picture, so Danny would notice as much contrast as possible from the session. With Archangel Michael's help, my client was going to have his aura transformed beyond his mildest dreams.

Doing his Before Picture, how did it feel emotionally to be Danny? Uneasy. He also noticed a lump in his throat. Sense of power at the solar plexus — this he described with breathtaking accuracy as "not too much."

Back at the topic of intention, I encouraged Danny to move away from a healing model that equates discussing a problem with solving it. Here, he could aim to remove the problem directly from his aura.

This led us to discuss the difference between psychological healing and spiritual healing. A deeply thoughtful man, Danny kept repeating, "That's very interesting."

Meanwhile, with each step of understanding, his third eye continued to awaken. (It was a lot of fun for me, noticing this, as though a commentary to our conversation came straight from his aura.)

Psychological healing depends on the intellect; usually it doesn't involve a person's connection to Source. Danny had come to this session with a way out-of-proportion intellect and a closed-off third eye. Because he was so ready to grow, the balance changed immediately.

In my opinion, psychological therapy couldn't much change Danny's father-son relationship as long as his cord kept repeating its pattern 24/7. Danny would have kept on analyzing problems, not solving them.

Maybe Shakespeare's Hamlet suffered from something similar. (Please do let me know if you ever turns up a lost Shakespeare manuscript in which Hamlet's healer describes his cord items.)

PRODUCTIVE CORD ANALYSIS

Validating your client's experience is a skill that develops with practice. Since this isn't psychological healing, however, how much discussion will you really need?

Let your motto be "Enough discussion, neither too little nor too much." Elaborate discussion isn't needed. Just do your best to summarize all that you wrote in your Dialogue Box.

Often you'll find that Step 10 becomes a client's favorite part of a session because it is so helpful, having just that little bit of discussion, timed right after moving out stuck energy.

What will it take for you to develop a sense for "enough discussion"? Relax and be in the moment. I can't tell you the perfect number of minutes required. This will always depend on your conversation in the here-and-now.

Regardless of how experienced you become at Energy Spirituality, you can be guided by what you notice in the moment. Pacing is a flow.

How can you find that flow? Over the decades, with every session, there is no substitute for giving the client your undivided attention, having the intention to help, teaming up with Divine Beings, and using your common sense.

Occasionally (not obsessively), ask inside, "How is my client responding? How much more discussion is needed?"

Sometimes you will read out one cord item after another, receiving very little reaction. Other times your client will become extremely vocal. Which cord item will strike your client as especially important? There's no telling, not until your client tells *you*. If your client considers something important, it is.

But do save one point to emphasize when you conclude the validation process. This could be something you starred when reviewing your Dialogue Box back in Step 9. Or it could be any cord item that you discuss during Step 10, something that clearly carries a big emotional charge for your client.

Whichever item you emphasize at the end of Step 10, this may be what your client remembers most from the entire session.

Throughout Step 10, reassure your client as necessary. Yes, sometimes a client will become slightly alarmed during the validation process. Hearing about dynamics within a cord, perhaps she will realize that she has seemed awfully demanding. Or maybe a once-loved cordee is being shown in a new and unflattering light.

If you should sense that your client is becoming alarmed, remind her that you're simply describing a pattern from the past:

- It is not the whole story about the relationship
- or everything about your client
- or everything about your cordee
- or the unconditional love between your client and the cordee.
- Instead, these are hidden dynamics that used to repeat 24/7.

And none of these dynamics will ever hurt your client again. It's like describing a nightmare after waking up. Your client is safe now.

PROFESSIONAL RELATIONSHIPS

Sometimes the people whom we trust most are involved in the worst cords of all. I've stopped counting how many clients have come to me with hideous cords of attachment to a former healer, teacher, therapist, etc. When we feel most vulnerable and reach out for help, we want to trust. At first that trust can well deserved. But, over time, for perfectly human reasons, a trusted professional relationship may sour.

Your role in describing this can require diplomacy. Remember, your client may have a lot invested in a therapeutic relationship and feel torn about seeing it for what it really is. How can you help?

> ## Cords to Trusted Professional Relationships
>
> 1. When a therapeutic relationship is involved in a cord of attachment, read out the Dialogue Box as you normally do in Step 10.
> 2. Validate problems without turning anyone into a villain. Take care to keep the conversation balanced.
> 3. In Step 11, discuss with your client how to keep the good, release the bad.

Yes, cutting cords of attachment to a trusted professional, you can sometimes be put in a sensitive position. Let's address some of the concerns that you may have about this.

What if, as a healer yourself, you feel squeamish about cutting a client's cord of attachment to another professional?

Gossip is not your goal but healing. Here at Earth School, everyone must overcome one illusion after another. What does it take to see life clearly and accept relationships for what they are? A clear aura helps. Every time you cut a cord of attachment, you're clearing your client's aura.

But what if the psychiatrist or teacher should be right and your client is wrong?

Always assume that your client is right. Helpers are only human. Their access to intimate levels within your client can lead to problems. Some helpers keep very clear energetically, with no ego hooks, no neediness. You started exploring this back in Step 4, when you researched whether there was a cord worth cutting.

A healer's good intentions, however sincere, can be seen differently when you discuss relationship patterns within a cord.

Why Doesn't He Like Me?

Beneath his mask of professional detachment, Dr. D. wasn't an especially caring psychiatrist. So Gabrielle wasn't particularly surprised to hear about the following cord items:

1. *The Psychiatrist: I will decide if you ever become healthy enough for me to approve of you.*
2. *Gabrielle: Please like me. I want a father figure who can really understand my feelings.*
3. *The Psychiatrist: Sorry, but you don't meet my standards. You're so arrogant. I get the feeling that you question my absolute authority.*
4. *The Psychiatrist: When you act smart, I become more aloof.*
5. *Gabrielle: Please nurture me. Give to me. Care about me.*

Dr. D. might have called Gabrielle's reaction a problem of transference. But cord dynamics have meaning outside the practitioner's therapy model. Energetically, the "cure" component of this relationship may have been as bad as Gabrielle's original "disease."

My client had already released the cord of attachment to her biggest father figure, her own dad. Now she was more than willing to terminate the cord to her therapist. The insight she gained in Step 10 brought welcome clarity.

In Step 11, Gabrielle and I would discuss what needed to happen for her to recognize this pattern of power loss, since it often came up in her relationships with men. Why choose men who couldn't give to her, then blame herself? Too many men from Gabrielle's past had made their aloofness seem like her fault. Gabrielle was being inoculated against repeating this pattern.

Validation differs from fulfilling your client's fantasy. He may expect you to tell him that because he had a cord cut to his girlfriend, the cordee will now love him or will apologize for everything she did wrong. Maybe she'll suddenly pay back that $5,000 she borrowed.

Sigh! All this fantasy despite your previous explanation that cutting a cord only changes the dynamics of a relationship!

Smash Fantasy, Fix Reality

Sometimes a client needs to be reminded again, during Step 10, about the consequences of cutting a cord of attachment. So discuss ideas like these, as needed:

1. The cordee's behavior doesn't change just because a cord is cut.
2. The cordee won't be affected in any way, due to the process of Divine Homeostasis.
3. You, the client, won't necessarily become closer to this person. Nor will you automatically become distant.
4. You will simply gain freedom. Energetically, you're no longer stuck in the past.
5. In future, you can freely choose what you want for this relationship. Use the appropriate social skills. If your first experiment doesn't please you, explore other approaches until you find what does.

Does your skill set includes training as a psychotherapist? Then you can appreciate how Step 10 starts to create a link between spiritual healing and psychological healing. Your client's new freedom can be directed toward psychological growth and rebalancing.

What if you are not a trained therapist and commonsense conversation doesn't seem to help? Sometimes a client keeps slipping into fantasy, rather than accepting reality.

Or what if other aspects of the conversation during Step 10 make you wonder if your client is psychologically troubled? Consider making a referral. Many clients will benefit from therapy more than ever before, after a cord has been cut.

Can This Marriage Be Saved?

For decades, Ladies Home Journal has run a feature called "Can This Marriage Be Saved?" In each issue, a marital therapist describes a couple's problems, then reveals the impact of therapy. Every column features a fascinating new array of problems.

I believe that cutting cords of attachment can be a useful adjunct to marriage counseling. Unfortunately, the details might not make for fascinating magazine columns. Many cords about marriages are variations on the one I helped to cut for a worried wife whom I will call "Isabella."

1. Husband: I'm a forceful man. I know what I like.
2. Isabella: I'm not forceful. I'm not sure who I am. I just know that I want to please you more than anything.
3. Husband: I'll push on you to see how much I can get. You'll do anything I want, won't you?
4. Husband: How can I respect you when you constantly grovel?
5. Husband: You don't give me sex often enough.
6. Isabella: I want to be loved, not used. No sex until you recognize who I really am!
7. Isabella: I feel lonely and rejected.
8. Isabella: No matter what I do, it's never enough. I give constantly. You never give back.

In Step 12, we'll discuss homework related to cutting a cord like this. But Step 10 must be the prerequisite. It isn't unusual for a client like Isabella to think she can continue to make another person responsible for all her problems. After validating the cord dynamics, don't be too shocked to hear, "Now he'll stop being so mean to me, right?"

"Wrong," you will have to say. Sigh!

But there still is hope that this client can take more responsibility for her life, including that marriage. Go on to Steps 11 and 12.

DISCUSSING SEXUAL PROBLEMS

Cords to sexual abuse are not the only cases where your Dialogue Box will include patterns that cause, or contribute to, sexual problems.

Sometimes the cordee will be heavily involved with Internet pornography. Sometimes cord items will suggest that the cordee had an affair.

Regardless of who was to blame, any sexual dysfunction in a cord can impact your client's sex life.

But be especially tactful about discussing sexual problems related to a cord of attachment. Avoid jumping to conclusions. Cords reveal patterns of energy, not necessarily events, so the cordee's "affair" could be emotional, not physical.

Either way, what matters is freeing your client from any deceptiveness, shame, sliminess, etc. that was repeating endlessly as a result of that cord.

When discussing cord items, let your client clarify what you've found. For example, you might say, "I think there's a possibility that your ex had a problem with pornography."

Clients usually find it a relief to have their suspicions validated. Sometimes they have been painfully aware of the problem. Typically, they will give a response like, "You're asking, was there an affair? Ha! You got that right!"

INVITE NEW FORGIVENESS

Be careful how you use the F-word. More than any other word, "Forgiveness" can trigger defensiveness in a client. Use that word carelessly and you risk having the client snap back, "I've forgiven him already." Conversation over.

With Energy Spirituality, you can bring new perspective to this tender topic. Many clients have worked heroically hard at forgiveness. You'll find proof right in your client's aura, with traces at many chakras, depending on how, precisely, your client suffered, then fought really hard to forgive.

So beware innocent comments like, "Now you'll finally be able to forgive the person at the other end of this cord."

Until a cord of attachment is cut, complete forgiveness may be impossible. Occasionally someone makes a heroic leap of faith and fully surrenders the past wrong to God. Then old resentments physically leave the aura.

This degree of success seldom happens, unfortunately. Instead an aura will show signs of struggle, multiple scars that record how valiantly your client struggled, from many angles, with limited success.

What can we say, then, without using the F-word?

Praise the *effort* to forgive, when you find it in an aura. You might tell your client that his previous work on forgiveness has set the stage for today's healing.

I also recommend substituting the expression "let go" for "forgiveness." This helps clients to feel validated, rather than threatened. You can say something like "Now you'll finally be able to let go what happened in the past."

For your own benefit as a healer, note any lack of forgiveness in your own life. Think "forgiveness" whenever you find an emotion that won't go away, or when you feel the need to keep retelling a troubling story, or—as the next example illustrates—you're suffering from slow-healing physical pain that follows a disagreement with a revolting space hog sitting next to you in a transatlantic flight and —Oops, forgiveness, Rose!

Anyway, Reader, you get the practical point. Even a small incident can lead to a cord, and now you know how to remove it.

234 CUT CORDS OF ATTACHMENT

Grumbling About That Knee

If you've flown in planes often, you can relate to my tiny tale of woe. Traveling back to Virginia from Japan, I was seated to the left of Clyde, a bulky, burly man with huge territorial instincts. Either that or he lacked the muscles that a normal person can use to keep his legs together.

Settling into my aisle seat, I carefully placed my shiny new laptop under the seat in front of me. Clyde's first act, after sitting down, was to sprawl past his allotted space and place his not-so-dainty shoe directly on my computer.

When I asked him to move, Clyde seemed puzzled. When I repeated my request, he became annoyed. For the rest of our very long flight, we played territorial footsie. I kept pushing my short right leg against Clyde's long left one. "Back, back to your seat! Back! Quit the sprawling already!"

After our flight, I felt knee pain for the first time in my life. Six weeks later, I still couldn't do my usual yoga stretches. When would the pain finally stop?

Lamenting this one morning, I wondered, could a cord of attachment have been forged on that flight? Duh!

Soon as the cord was cut, I felt relief. The knee took another couple of weeks to heal completely, but inwardly, I knew that recovery started right from the moment I cut that minor but irritating cord.

Who can fathom our past-life connections to people? Perhaps Clyde and I had a stormy history dating many incarnations ago. In this lifetime, it sure was ridiculous how I couldn't let our footsie game go. On the flight, and afterwards, too, I'd tried joking, praying, forgiving, forgetting. But nothing worked until I removed the cord of attachment to my one-time seatmate.

Never underestimate the power of energy endlessly replaying its struggle within a cord. Even if you stopped at Step 10, you (or your client) would receive lifelong benefits from cutting a cord of attachment. But Step 11 will add greatly to the results of the healing you have set in motion.

Step 11.
Impact Other Relationships

LET'S GET PRACTICAL

You're at Step 11 already. And if this is your "Official Reading" of this chapter, you're also cutting your fifth minor cord. The process is becoming easier, isn't it?

1. Doing Steps 1-10, you can refresh your memory of the Steps with our summary on the previous page. (Check previous chapters if you need to supplement.)

2. Emphasize going through Step 11 slowly.

3. Step 12 will be quick and easy, given all you know now.

Behold the jewel in the crown of cord-cutting. Maybe your client brought an ambitious intention to this session, maybe not. Even if your client didn't dare hope for much, now she will receive something big. Step 11 supplies action steps for a better life.

Step 11 is when you guide a client (or yourself) to understand how cutting one cord of attachment can improve *all* her relationships. Who will describe that practical vision? Both of you—starting when you, as the facilitator, take the lead.

Of course, if you're cutting a cord for yourself, you will need objectivity. As in Step 10, switch roles between being an outside observer, "The Healer," and reacting as a person in touch with your inner truth, "The Client."

Initiate Change

Cutting a cord of attachment has cleared old patterns with the cordee. This brings freedom to change behavior. To use that freedom best, your client needs a vision of possibilities for change. So, at Step 11, move the conversation toward *action*, based on the *validation* already given during Step 10. (Of course, for your own session, you alternate the roles of Healer and Client.)

1. Listen carefully to your client's reactions during Step 10. What seems most important to him?
2. During Step 11, discuss this important issue. Then ask, "Knowing that now you are free to choose differently, what about this relationship could change for you?"
3. Add your own observations. Whatever you say, describe it in conjunction with cord items that have been released. Discuss each point in a way that empowers your client. For example, perhaps cord patterning caused your client to

> feel intimidated by his father. With this reaction over, "How might you respond now if your father starts to boss you around?"

Evolving an aura by clearing a cord—that's a big deal. New behavior becomes possible as never before. Unfortunately, most clients will squander this opportunity unless they receive encouragement at Step 11. Often a spiritual seeker will forget to balance inner change with outer action, expecting spiritual miracles to turn literal without any action on their part.

Here at Earth School, spiritual changes do eventually result in outer changes. Only they happen in the fullness of time. Well, sometimes a person gets fed up with that fullness of time.

You want results now? Take action now. Nothing can stop you except little things like confusion, inertia, or not knowing how to take responsibility in a pro-active way.

Pro-Active Responsibility

Encouragement at Step 11 can make the difference between longing for a better life and making that great life happen. The following technique will help you or a highly motivated client to become pro-active as a change agent, stop waiting and start moving. (For your own session, continue to alternate the roles of Healer and Client.)

1. Encourage your client to think pro-actively. Ask "What is your goal for this relationship now that the cord is cut?"
2. Sometimes your client will be so deeply stuck in old ways that he'll offer only a mild variation on business as usual, something like "Maybe I won't feel quite so intimidated by my dad." Challenge a client like this. Why settle for so little? Ask him, "Is that *really* the best you can aim for?"

3. Despite everything you've told your client so far, sometimes he will continue to expect the other person to change. Remind your client that he is free to seek a similar type of relationship elsewhere. You've heard of mother figures, father figures, and the like. Everyone can find Family of Choice, in contrast to Family of Blood. (Read more about this in my daybook, *Let Today Be a Holiday*).

4. If appropriate, ask your client, "Who is responsible for this person's life?" It won't be your client, not unless the cordee is under 18 and his child. Discuss how each person is his own responsibility, and that each person has a spiritual source. Help your client to question any misplaced sense of obligation. Now that the cord is cut, why would he choose to feel responsible for the cordee?

5. Since this moment is a fresh start energetically, what else would your client like to change about his life?

6. Encourage experimentation, then help your client set priorities. Cords of attachment tie a person to unproductive behavior patterns. Aurically, maybe a ton of energy was drained every day. It made your client feel and act like a loser, even though he didn't deserve that. Now your client is free to experiment with new behaviors, evaluate what happens, then try something different if necessary.

7. Help your client commit to action by asking him, "What would you like to try first?"

At Step 11, your client has new freedom to grow. You have an important freedom, too. Discuss what seems important to you. The intention for the session can provide a context for your discussion. Beyond that, trust your instincts as a healer. This will help you to grow as a practitioner of Energy Spirituality.

What Matters Most Here?

I have an assignment for you. While you read through the following Dialogue Box, consider what you would emphasize if Wayne were your client. Remember, each cord item released can bring change to all other relationships. Wayne had asked to cut the cord of attachment to his mother.

1. *Wayne: I feel so sorry for my mother. I want her to have a better life.*
2. *Wayne: By giving a lot of my energy to my mother, I can help her become more awake inside.*
3. *Mother: I constantly worry about small things. I feel frustrated, too. This keeps me from noticing how I'm cut off from my emotions.*
4. *Wayne: When I give Mom extra energy, she stops being so gloomy. But soon afterwards she falls back into dullness.*
5. *Wayne: Picking Mom up again and again is exhausting, like trying to teach a rag doll how to sit on her own.*
6. *Mother: I'm not sure whether or not I like to receive all this energy from Wayne. I only like to feel better for a short time. It feels weird, being so awake inside. So I'll resist, and quickly fall back into the kind of consciousness that is more natural to me.*
7. *Wayne: I feel exhausted. How come I never get anything back from this relationship?*

Which theme did I choose to emphasize during Step 11? **Co-dependence.** We discussed it as a widespread problem that is not unique to Wayne's relationship with his mother. Wayne was trying to fix someone who didn't believe she was broken in the first place. Codependence is a complex problem that can manifest itself in many ways, and this Dialogue Box qualified.

Although Wayne had heard of codependence, he never thought it could apply to him. But now Energy Spirituality had structurally altered Wayne's aura, so he could pursue psychological healing from a new level of clarity.

Fortunately, there are plenty of resources for releasing codependent behavior. One excellent option is support through the 12-Step program offered through CoDA World Fellowship (www.codependents.org).

However, no resource can fully succeed until a client is freed from the energy dynamics of unbalanced giving. I could reassure Wayne that, however he approached change now, he had greater freedom to succeed because the toxic energy flows from his cord of attachment had ceased.

Wayne understood. He felt hopeful about moving beyond old patterns.

Don't underestimate the impact of conversations at Step 11 in cutting cords of attachment. Energy that locked old behavior in place is gone for good.

LOGICAL CONSEQUENCES

As a practitioner of Energy Spirituality, it's important that you clearly appreciate the distinction between logical consequences and predictions. Any work you do to heal an aura can arouse fatalistic beliefs. Some popular examples are:

- "I am supposed to suffer. It's my bad karma."
- "Everything happens for a reason."
- "If I have a problem now, it is because I haven't been positive enough."

Some clients completely lose their self-authority. Because you have accurately validated a cord of attachment from the present and past, suddenly you are supposed to be an expert on predicting the future.

Instead of hearing, "Now you are free to create a new kind of relationship with your husband," a client might hear, "I predict that the two of you will reconcile. You don't need to change a thing. Your happiness (or suffering) is meant to be."

If you are a psychic, go ahead and make predictions. With a cleaned-up aura, your client will have more objectivity for evaluating your comments.

Otherwise, at any hint that your client expects a psychic reading, bring the conversation back to earth. Prod your client to think for herself: "Now that you're no longer dealing with all that anger from your ex, what might you do differently?"

Back at Step 1, when we discussed setting an intention, I raised the idea of discouraging undue emphasis on "meant to be." Step 11 is where many clients begin to recognize the power of free will. Choice becomes greater when they are healed at the level of auras, because cords of attachment can cause a person to feel helpless.

Wayne's story is an example. While attached to his mother's energy, he expected life to involve perpetual giving without receiving anything back. So long as his aura, and the cord pattern, was configured this way, whenever he looked outside himself for signs, guess what he would inevitably find?

Whether you take reality checks or look for signs—and I'll admit to doing both, on occasion—remember that the universe responds to our goals, words and actions. Step 11 speeds up this process of taking action. Energetically, your client has become capable of making choices in ways that simply weren't available before. This is what I mean by a **logical consequence.**

Invite Discussion About Consequences

Improving *all* other relationships is a common result of cutting *one* cord of attachment. Your job at Step 11 involves discussing these far-reaching consequences. The following technique helps you to present these as logical consequences, rather than predictions. (Again, for your own session, alternate the roles of Healer and Client.)

1. Ask the client if she can think of any way that her life as a whole may change as a result of cutting the cord of attachment.

2. Silently review the Dialogue Box. At every cord item, do Questioning. Ask inside how your client's other relationships may change, related to this cord item.

3. Take two vibe-raising breaths.

4. Trust what you get. Whenever you find a juicy possibility, discuss it with your client.

5. Conclude your discussion with any cord item you have circled during Step 9, when you made notes on your notes. What is your client's most important growth area for the session? Can you guide her toward taking action of some kind to accelerate this growth?

Logical consequences: This isn't necessarily an easy concept for a new client. How can you help him to understand why cutting one cord of attachment could improve his other relationships as well? Here is my favorite way to explain it:

The Drip

Have you ever seen someone in the hospital with an intravenous drip? Then surely you've noticed that clear plastic bag of fluid.

If that bag is labeled "Mother" or "Father" or "Spouse," how much does the name on the label really matter? Whatever that bag holds will become part of the patient's body.

Similarly, that old cord of attachment dripped into your entire mind-body-spirit system. It dripped away, day and night. Of course this affected your sense of self, your thoughts, feelings and actions.

Now you are no longer receiving the drip, drip, drip. So your life can really be different.

Most clients can readily understand how removing *their side* of a Dialogue Box could be life changing. But why would your client's life change by losing a pattern belonging to *the cordee's side* of that Dialogue Box?

Let's consider the energy implications of a cord of attachment. The whole show repeats, not merely words from one actor. Having a cord, you might be compared to a star from a classic movie. Ever since it was filmed, you have been influenced by constant reruns. And it was a horror movie!

Ever hear of Gestalt Therapy? It offers a fascinating approach to dream interpretation: Everything in the dream represents a part of the dreamer. In your client's dream, she could be running away from a monster. Of course, she will identify with the victim. But, according to Gestalt Therapy, the monster also represents another aspect of the dreamer.

Similarly, every part of a Dialogue Box represents an aspect of your client, replaying endlessly within her aura. Each cord item from the cordee will count, and so will removing it. The rest of this chapter will deepen your understanding about logical consequences that result from removing cord items.

FINALIZE DIVORCE

I believe in divorce. (I'd better, having been divorced twice before settling into a marriage that works.) In one way, however, I completely agree with those who don't believe marriage vows can be broken: Energetically, divorce is never simple.

Despite legally divorcing a partner, patterns from that relationship continue through a cord of attachment. Grieving can take years, as it can with the death of a loved one, adjusting to a miscarriage or abortion, or accepting that someone close to you is an alcoholic.

Sometimes, the grief never seems to end. Given all you know now about cords of attachment, doesn't that make sense? No divorce decree or death certificate will take away a cord.

So it is a great privilege to be able to *energetically* finalize a divorce like Emma's. In Step 9, we looked at the Dialogue Box related to her ex-husband. Now let's revisit those dynamics to consider logical consequences for the rest of her life.

Consequences of a No-Win Marriage

As you read the Dialogue Box, which long-term results occur to you?

1. *Emma: I'll do whatever I can to please you. Just pay attention to me. I need that.*
2. *Husband: No response.*
3. *Emma: Look, I'm working harder to please you. Isn't that great? Isn't it?*
4. *Husband: No response, he's as far away energetically as he could be, yet still be included in the cord pattern.*
5. *Emma: If you don't pay attention to me, I won't have any value as a person. I'm begging you to pay attention to me.*
6. *Emma: I feel so worthless.*
7. *Husband: Interested in pornography. Keeping it hidden. "I have a right to my private life. Don't interfere."*
8. *Emma: I must have done something wrong. Until I find out what that was, I can't forgive myself. I have to try harder and harder to make up for it, whatever "it" is that I've done wrong.*

Discussing consequences with Emma, she proposed, "It will be easier for me to let go of the relationship and date other men without feeling guilty."

So true! But that's just the start of logical consequences from cutting this cord. Listing possibilities, I'll refer to the numbered bits of cord dialogue. Notice that consequences are grouped roughly in order of the Dialogue Box, except that I saved the most important consequence for last.

1. The begging pattern (Cord item 1) can shift for all Emma's relationships. When is she lavishing time and energy on somebody who doesn't appreciate her? Now it will be easier to recognize the pattern. She has more freedom to decide, "This relationship isn't worthwhile. I'm not receiving enough in return."

246 CUT CORDS OF ATTACHMENT

2. Awareness of Emma's own value as a person (Cord item 5) might increase. Her old cord pattern contributed to a stance of desperation in life, as if Emma had no worth unless she was loved by a man. Might she now be ready to consider her life valuable, with or without male approval? (My client loved this idea.)

3. Constantly feeling worthless (Cord item 6) wasn't helping Emma's life. Yes, she might stop those perpetual battles within herself, trying to "think positive." Now Emma won't have to try so hard. She can also stop blaming her ex for "ruining her life." Sure, he made her feel bad about herself, but energetically that is finally over.

4. What about the delicate—and common—problem of a dissatisfied husband's use of pornography (Cord item 7)? The problem was easy for Emma to recognize, but she hadn't considered the long-term consequence for her own aura: "While the cord was in place, you had an energetic connection to pornography. Yes, I know you weren't the one using the porno, but it still affected you. With this gone, you may find that your sexual energy is clearer, changing what is projected through your aura, helping you to attract an appropriate man into your life."

5. Constantly blaming herself for the divorce (Cord item 8). Without that recycling self-blame, Emma might stop believing in a fantasy version of her marriage. With that relationship, and others that follow, she now has enough energetic clarity to ask the question Ann Landers made famous: "Are you better off with him or without him?"

6. Most important, Emma can regain her energy. Through the cord, she kept lavishing attention on someone who took without giving back (Cord items 2 and 4). Psychically, each person has only so much energy. I'd estimate that Emma has been surrendering as much as 10 percent

of her energy every day to that ex. Because of Divine Homeostasis, he will be okay now, while she is positively revitalized. Better able to find her own happiness, this client will become more than okay.

SEARCH FOR MISSING SOCIAL SKILLS

Could your client be missing important social skills? Cord items can warn you. As we explore this productive way to help clients, let our motto be, "Just because you didn't learn something *yet* doesn't mean that you can't ever learn it."

Here is a checklist to help you tell if a client might be missing an important social skill. Each skill is paired with the *type of comment* you might make during Step 11. (Of course, you will add new skills and comments to this list, based on a particular client's situation plus the unique wisdom that you bring to cutting cords.)

10 Essential Social Skills

1. Can your client **enjoy life on her own as an adult,** or does she feel she must always have a relationship of some kind, no matter how bad? *"Which way do you think you can attract a better quality partner: as someone with a desperate need or as someone who feels whole? How can you develop a stronger sense of self?"*

2. Check for a reasonable balance of **give and take** in relationships. *"Demand that every one of your relationships must contain a fair share of give and take. If a relationship doesn't return at least as much as you give, either change that relationship or let it go."*

3. Pursue **self-interest.** Invite your client to ask, about any relationship, *"What's in it for me?"* Energetically, your

client is repositioned to bring new common sense to old assumptions.

4. Has your client learned to **stick up for herself** during conflict? If not, *"Whose job would that be if not yours?"*

5. Exercise the right to **drop a toxic relationship.** *"What's the worst thing that could happen if you broke off contact with that person?"*

6. **Redefine** an obligatory relationship. *"If that relationship can't be dropped, how can you minimize contact?"*

7. When can **superficial relating** be good? *"During visits, what would happen if you just went through the motions, rather than staying deeply involved?"*

8. Actively **make new friends**, rather than expecting them to appear by magic. *"Now that you're free inside, are you interested in making new friends? How could you do that?"*

9. Recognize that each adult is his **own responsibility,** not your client's job to fix. *"What needs to happen for you to allow a Higher Power to take care of this person instead of you?"*

10. **Set goals,** then follow up with daily action. It isn't enough, just thinking a goal. *"Now you can stop reacting and start acting. What is one goal you could set for yourself? Name one action that you can take to bring that goal closer."*

How can you tell for sure if your client lacks a social skill from this list?

Who says you must know for sure? All you really need is a hunch. Observe your client's reactions as the two of you discuss how life might change. If you suspect that a particular skill might be missing, gently ask a question about it.

Depending on how a person was raised, or how the relationship in a cord was defined, even an otherwise super-sophisticated client could lack a basic social skill. How can he proceed to develop that skill? He could:

- Identify other troubling relationships related to the missing skill, and make these relationships the focus of future sessions with you.
- Make developing this skill a new priority in life. (Once your client starts paying attention, he may develop the skill on his own really easily.)
- Work with a friend to practice the skill.
- Join a formal support group.
- Meet with a psychotherapist, social worker, spiritual counselor or life coach. (Make a referral.)

Note that only the first of these options would necessarily be done with your help. Other resources will work better now, because your client has been freed from the cord. Because you helped to heal your client's aura, he can progress faster psychologically. As an example, let's go back to Wayne and his relationship with his mother.

Missing: One Social Skill

Near the start of Wayne's session, he mentioned that he still lived at home. The man was 35 years old, successful in his career, and unmarried.

During Step 11, I asked him, "Why do you still live with your mother?"

He said, "I keep hoping to make her life better."

Soon as the words came out of his mouth, Wayne did a double take. Fresh from removing that cord of attachment, he could reevaluate his old assumption. Before, the pattern of trying to fix his mother kept repeating 24/7. Now Wayne could think more objectively about how he chose to live.

*Remember Social skill #1 from our list? It involves whether your client has learned to **enjoy life on his own as an adult.** Usually this comes up in sessions with clients who jump from one bad love relationship to the next. But sometimes a client hasn't become a fully fledged adult. He has never figured out how to separate from his parents.*

Teenage rebellion serves a purpose. Wayne didn't need much reminding to get the point. The habit of being a good little boy no longer served him. Actually, changing that habit could be fun.

ENCOURAGE ASSERTIVENESS

Assertiveness means advocating for yourself without being unduly aggressive. Most of your clients will have heard of it. Not many know how to do it.

How can they, so long as a cord of attachment endlessly exerts its push-pull? Depending on the nature of a particular cord, your client may feel doomed to failure no matter how hard he tries to stick up for herself. With Step 11, that can finally change.

Use the Assertiveness Formula

Once a cord of attachment is gone, your client can stand up for herself in ways that had previously been unavailable. Ask if she is familiar with this simple formula for assertiveness; if not, teach it to her:

1. When you do X,
2. I feel Y.
3. I need you to do Z.

You can teach this Assertiveness Formula quickly, based on what was in the cord of attachment. Let your client play with it like a game during Step 11. For example, Wayne could tell his mother:

- When you complain about how I vacuum the house,
- I feel unappreciated.
- I'd like you to do the vacuuming next time.

How can a client have missed out on such a basic social skill as speaking up for himself?

Your client may be a loving person like Wayne, well trained to serve others but discouraged from sticking up for himself. Or your client may know the social skill in theory but be unable to practice it, prevented by dynamics in a past cord of attachment.

Once the cord is cut, a simple reminder from you during Step 11 can make all the difference. Even if assertiveness never developed before, a willing adult can catch up fast.

Why, Why, Why?

Some clients turn wistful during Step 11. Often, they'll agree that some very basic aspect of life has been missing. For example, a grown woman may realize that she never received the basic nurturing she needed.

I will tell such a client a variation on the following—not just to make her feel better, but because I believe it to be the truth:

If things in your life had gone smoothly, this piece of your development would have happened automatically. By the time you were five, you would have had absorbed this basic kind of nurturing.

But consider the possibility that all major events in a lifetime, up to age 21, are part of a person's **life contract.**

This is a design you made for your life before incarnating here at Earth School. After age 21, basics of the contract remain in place but much more about life is negotiable. Depending on how you have responded to that early script, using your free will, you set in motion new consequences. That's how everyone learns here at Earth School.

Why would you write such a painful lack of nurturing into your life contract? If all had gone smoothly, you would have been nurtured. Still, you wouldn't have learned much about the process. Instead, consider what is going to happen now:

As an adult, you will be able to fill in that gap, bit by bit. Consciously, you will start to choose relationships that nurture you. Consciously, you will develop wisdom about how to recognize them. Consciously, you can discover what it means to trust someone who really cares about you.

All of this amounts to a deep kind of learning. After you gain the knowledge consciously, you can teach others to do the same thing. Painful though the process may be, it can become a means for your soul to gain deep wisdom that couldn't be acquired by any other means.

NEW STORIES

To skeptics, cords of attachment seem unreal.

Not only are cords real, but their presence can influence people to believe plenty of other things that aren't real at all. How ironic is that?

Cords re-circulate false ideas about the self. Then these illusions become **self-fulfilling prophecies.** When people subconsciously believe limiting stories about who they are, they act in such a way as to make the false stories come true. So long as a cord re-circulates its toxic energy patterns, no amount of psychological inquiry can completely eliminate self-fulfilling prophecies.

Another popular term for destructive inner programming is **negative self-talk,** where people constantly berate themselves inwardly. Sure, it absolutely makes sense to change that inner conversation, and many mental health professionals help their clients to change destructive self-talk.

But how successful will a client be as long as that chronic badmouthing repeats endlessly through a cord?

- In Step 7, you have used Energy Spirituality to initiate permanent change.
- At Step 9, you wrote the Dialogue Box, providing evidence of destructive self-talk.
- As you expand your client's understanding in Steps 10 and 11, you help the client to overcome illusions contributing to self-fulfilling prophecies.

Cutting a cord can really change a negative inner script.

Separate Strengths from Illusions

Many cord items give rise to illusions. Each time you encounter one, here's what you can do at Step 11:

1. Discuss the illusion involved in a cord item. It may have
given your client a false sense of being weak, unlovable or
otherwise defective. Be specific.
2. Invite your client to question whether the old accusations
or criticisms were warranted.
3. Ask your client how she thinks the cord item might have
distorted her sense of self.
4. Explain the concepts of self-talk and self-fulfilling prophecies. Now that the cord is gone, how does the client think
her self-talk might change, with no effort needed?
5. Encourage your client to start acting outwardly as the
strong person she always was, deep down.

At Step 12, you can follow up by assigning homework related to
positive, truthful self-talk.

Awakening from the Enchantment

June looked exhausted. Even before she spoke, I saw such fatigue in her eyes
that it was as if her soul was numb. "Please cut the cord to my mother," she
asked.

Removing the cord from June's high heart chakra, I felt the fatigue go all
the way down to her bones. "You're exhausted, aren't you?" I asked. She nod-
ded.

We talked about physiological depression. Of course, I recommended that
she get a checkup, and June agreed. By the end of the session, however, I had a
hunch that June's depression was already ending, a fairy-tale awakening for
which she had been waiting a very long while. Here is the pattern I reported
from the cord, which she verified down to the finest detail:

1. *June: Criticism is constant. It's heard. It's felt.*
2. *Mom: I try so hard to be good to my daughter, but my anger and rage leak out. When that happens I feel guilty.*
3. *June: I feel her guilt as though it is my own.*
4. *June: I feel shamed, disapproved of.*
5. *June: What's the point in my trying anything? Whatever I do turns out wrong.*
6. *Mom: I feel threatened by June's exuberance. Ever since she was a baby I've been embarrassed by her, from toilet training onward.*
7. *June: I will stay in this numbing enchantment until she, or the universe, releases me.*

Perhaps when making her life contract, June's mother hoped that she would be able to learn from the joyous soul who would incarnate as her daughter. But sometimes we fall short of the ambitious goals in a life contract.

Was June's mother too proud to learn from her own child? Too stressed? Whatever the cause, this mother felt threatened by her daughter's natural joy. Ironically, this caused the mother to live with something at least as difficult, her daughter's resulting depression. Since June felt too bad to work, she still lived at home, dependent and sad.

Initially, the mother had trapped her daughter. Then the mother became trapped in turn. Perhaps this sad enchantment could finally end for them both.

NO-WIN RELATIONSHIPS

Sometimes your client will be attracted to a kind of relationship that can never bring happiness. Online forums are buzzing about narcissists, sex addicts, abusers and other troubled souls who cause misery for their loved ones.

Intellectually, your client might know better than to choose one of these no-win relationships. Yet, somehow, she might find herself drawn to the same no-win pattern again and again.

Marionettes, it turns out, aren't the only ones pulled by strings. Cutting cords of attachment helps to loosen the attraction of no-win relationships.

Don't people have something to learn from every relationship? Sure. But sometimes the Cosmic Lesson is simply learning how to wave goodbye.

What is a **no-win relationship?** I define it as being involved with someone who has such a serious personality disorder that, by definition, he will always blame others rather than being willing to change himself.

Your client may keep giving her no-win relationship just one more chance—until she understands that some relationships can never be set right. Superman couldn't do it. Even God couldn't do it, not without that person's consent.

How can you tell if a cordee qualifies as a no-win relationship? Any one of the following characteristics would constitute a Keep Out sign to the wise:

- Verbally abusive
- Physically violent
- Sexually demanding, yet incapable of intimacy
- A pathological liar
- Jealous for no reason
- Addicted to sexual promiscuity or pornography
- An alcoholic or drug addict who refuses treatment
- Emotionally draining, yet never satisfied
- Always the center of attention, deeply uninterested in others, spoiled or selfish
- Narcissistic
- A sociopath or psychopath

Lotto for Grownups

As a child, you played Lotto, didn't you? Picture recognition games are fun for a kid, matching a lion with a lion, a lamb with a lamb. When you facilitate a session of Energy Spirituality, you can help clients play a version that relates to emotional intelligence: Lotto for Grownups.

The stakes are higher that with a kid's game. You are helping your client learn to distinguish between relationships with fulfillment potential versus dreadful no-win relationships.

1. After you look over the Dialogue Box at the end of Step 9, does the cordee seem like a really difficult person? You're only reading about the relationship energy from a cord, not necessarily behavior. Still, does any cord item from the cordee sound a warning bell that this could be a no-win relationship?
2. When discussing the relationship pattern at Step 10, does this still sound like a no-win relationship?
3. If the cordee appears to have serious problems, discuss the meaning of no-win relationships. It's a kind of psychological Lotto for Grownups. Let your client decide what to call the cordee's emotional ailment; you don't have to supply the diagnosis. What matters is recognition that the cordee has a serious problem which your client never caused... and can never change.

Usually, a no-win relationship is recognized by Step 10, when the client finally recognizes the negative side of being close to the cordee. Even more exciting, in Step 11, the two of you can go to the next phase, recognizing similar relationships.

Sometimes complete healing for your client will require that he cut a whole series of cords to no-win relationships. (If you know how to cut cords for yourself, you'll certainly want to do this.) But for some clients, it's enough to do the following.

Release Other No-Win Relationships

Here's how to help your client recognize and avoid other versions of a no-win relationship:

1. After identifying the no-win relationship from a cut cord, discuss what made it no-win from your client's perspective. Encourage him to stop feeling guilty about the old pattern. Teach him that he will never be able to fix this problem (nor would doing so be his job in life, anyway).

2. Ask your client if he can recognize a similar pattern in any *other* relationship.

3. Awaken your client's ability to become an advocate for his own happiness. Explain how one-way relationships, encoded in auras, can become addictive. Be specific, for example, "Emotionally, this cord has kept you stuck trying to fix something that's impossible to fix. Is that fair?"

4. Extend the understanding, e.g., "It's common for a person in this kind of relationship to seek out, consciously or not, a similar relationship because he hopes to succeed this time. But he won't succeed with that new relationship, either. It's a game he can't win."

5. Discuss the logical consequence of changing that no-win pattern in your client's aura. What will happen with the cord of attachment gone? Let your client realize that, from now on, he may find it easier to recognize this kind of game and then refuse to play.

6. Ask your client, "Do you choose to let go of this pattern permanently with *everyone?*" Continue to discuss until your client gets the point.

7. Conclude on a note of celebration. Before, with the cord of attachment in place, your client couldn't stop this pattern. Now he can. All that one-way giving is history. Starting now, he can choose relationships that balance give and take.

8. At Step 12, give homework to reprogram your client's subconscious mind.

Many a client has wondered if she could ever be helped. And many a therapist has wondered the same. Cutting cords of attachment can change patterning that seems to go hopelessly deep. As a client with a history of toxic relationships removes her cords to them, the inner change could be likened to releasing a chemical addiction. Stinking thinking can be recognized, then rejected. With a clearer mind-body-spirit system, new clarity becomes available, so let freedom ring.

An Impossible Test

Mother-in-law jokes are common. But sometimes a mother-in-law isn't just funny. She's toxic. This was the case for Phyllis, who scheduled a session because of a problem with an especially scary mother-in-law. Can you find the no-win pattern?

1. *Phyllis: I'd really like to please you.*
2. *Mother-in-law: I think you're crazy, but maybe you're not. I'm going to give you a little test. Act the way I want you to. Do it in front of the family.*
3. *Mother-in-law: Oops, too bad, you flunked again. Now I have the right to badmouth you behind your back.*
4. *Phyllis: Give me another chance, please.*

5. *Mother-in-law: If you would just do what I say, I could approve of you.*
6. *Phyllis: Whenever I'm with you, I freeze up.*
7. *Mother-in-law: You'll never be normal. Prove to me that you aren't crazy.*
8. *Phyllis: Why do you always have to criticize me?*
9. *Mother-in-law: I can't explain yet. Keep pouring your energy into me until I'm satisfied. Then I'll stop criticizing you.*

Actually, the tough thing here would be to find a cord item that wasn't no-win. Kept busy placating her mother-in-law, poor Phyllis had no extra energy to question the no-win pattern.

During Step 11, I suggested that Phyllis walk away from any relationship about pleasing somebody else. Why stay involved with someone who demanded that Phyllis work that hard? She had been pouring energy into someone else's aura and receiving what in return? Her big reward was nothing but disdain.

Ending a no-win relationship sounds good, right? But how can a client cut off communication with a family member ?

Limiting communication can be a matter of degree. During Step 11, you can help clients like Phyllis to consider their options.

Before, Phyllis didn't have much choice. The energy drain continued 24/7. Even if she never saw her mother-in-law again, Phyllis would be fighting that losing battle until the last day of her life.

Now freed up energetically, Phyllis could begin some creative problem-solving.

Have fun with your client whenever the two of you brainstorm possibilities during Step 11. How can your client stop fighting a losing battle?

Practical options for Phyllis might include:

- Enlisting active support from her husband.
- Telling the mother-in-law that Phyllis and her husband will no longer tolerate rudeness in front of the family.

- Making an Agreement with her husband, then with the family, e.g., Criticizing Phyllis is no longer acceptable behavior during family visits. If any family member criticizes Phyllis, one warning will be given. If it is ignored, Phyllis and her husband will leave.
- Following through on any Agreements, being consistent, e.g., If any criticism is given after a warning, Phyllis and her husband will immediately leave, no explanations necessary.
- Limiting the number of family visits.
- Changing the location where family visits take place.
- Keeping each family visit very short.

Besides brainstorming ideas like these, you can discuss other relationship patterns that could be similar.Given what you are discussion in the context of this cord, might your client go through the same kind of pain or frustration in other relationships?

With Phyllis, for instance, can she think of someone besides this mother-in-law who requires constant begging for approval?

Encourage your client to change such a pattern. No, you can't promise that cutting one cord will instantly solve all relationship problems. But what *has* been accomplished? It could be a big deal.

Your client has gained a new degree of balance within her aura. She can think more clearly and, therefore, some old distress patterns may stop getting in her way.

With each cord cut, a client like Phyllis can move forward *more quickly*. Encourage her to move forward in both directions: Future sessions of Energy Spirituality (spiritual healing) and a referral to her choice of psychotherapist or life coach (psycholoical healing).

HEAL YOUR OWN RELATIONSHIPS WITH DIFFICULT CLIENTS

Unappreciative clients are rare, especially if you are cutting your own cords of attachment. Read the following only if you plan to help others... and if you have a strong stomach!

Assuming that you give hundreds of sessions of Energy Spirituality, which I hope you will, you are bound to encounter occasional problems. I'd like to offer you the benefit of my experience.

Service with a Smile, Regardless of Outcome

Every client has an agenda. A client's negative desires may surprise you because they are so thoroughly unlike how you, personally, would approach a session of Energy Spirituality.

Strange as it may seem, occasionally a client may not really come to be healed. Help yourself do the best possible, under the circumstances.

1. Never quiz a client about how much healing he is willing to accept. Treat each client equally, as someone ready and willing to heal.

2. Define your job as fulfilling your client's stated intention the best you can. As a healer, don't expect immediate results.

3. If necessary, remember this: A client's choice is never the healer's responsibility.

Why would someone go to the trouble of scheduling a session if not to be healed?

- Some clients come to vent their frustration. They're gathering new material to complain about.
- Others bring completely unrealistic expectations. They want you to magically fix all their problems.
- A highly skeptical client might disguise her negativity, all the better to find fault with you.
- Some clients come to test you (whether you know it or not). When such a client catches you in any seeming mistake or inadequacy, she imagines that she has won the game.
- Reluctant clients may come to you at the insistence of a spouse or friend. They have no desire to heal or change; instead, the agenda is to tell whoever sent them, "I followed your advice. You were wrong. This nonsense doesn't help."
- Or a client's game may be to find new reasons to feel sorry for herself. If she judges the session a failure, she can later whine, "My problems are too big and important to be fixed."

You get the idea. There are endless, interesting variations on the theme of "Client Not Ready to Heal."

Accept Negativity Gracefully

Even when a client is committed to getting results from his session, he may not always agree with you. How can you best handle that?

Let's use the example where a client doesn't relate to your description of a cord, during Step 10. He may validate certain details, disagree with others. But when a client completely disowns every single one of your findings, don't be too quick to blame yourself. Instead:

1. Listen to your client's feedback with interest. Even if unexpected or negative, maybe it can teach you something.
2. Present further information without becoming defensive.
3. If a client becomes angry, stop immediately. Nothing more will be heard.
4. Keep in mind Shakespeare's great line from *Hamlet*, "The lady doth protest too much, methinks." Allow a client's lengthy protestations to stand as the last word for him, a private question for you.
5. Never apologize for ideas that you have raised in a session. They will continue to be processed by your client's subconscious mind long after the session is over. If wrong, your ideas will be dismissed. If right, you will have planted a seed for future growth.
6. Find a positive way to conclude your session. Step 12 should help you to do this. For instance, you can sum up what you did during the session and the homework that your client can use. The After Picture will probably show improvement.
7. Sometimes your client simply needs to express herself. You'll help by listening with interest and paying attention. Maybe no one has ever really listened to him before.
8. You have done your best with this client. Never count any session as a failure, because you can't gauge long-term benefits by a client's immediate reaction.

A client may surprise you with his reactions during Step 11. Sometimes he may cry. Sometimes he will repeat your language and be dazzled by *his* insight. Other times he will reconsider something he disagreed with during the session and get back to you with a big fat YES. Occasionally, a client may try to manipulate you, consciously or otherwise, based on a self-centered agenda.

For example, when you're new to doing sessions of Energy Spirituality, a client may try to take advantage in order to receive extra help, extra time, etc.

How can you protect yourself from manipulative clients? Set a policy right now, in advance. Decide how you will handle special demands.

- How long are you willing to talk with clients before they commit to a session?

- Some people will demand "free samples" before committing to a session. Are you willing to do this? If so, why?

- What is your response to those who believe that anything spiritual should be free?

- When a client complains about his financial situation, does that obligate you to give him a session?

- Will you gently but firmly insist that your sessions end on time?

- What can you tell a client who ends a session by bringing up new questions or projects? (You might want to practice saying, "Bring that up at the start of your *next* session, okay?)"

- Will you choose to manage your time based on a client's needs rather than your own? Think through the consequences of letting a session last indefinitely. Is it in your client's interest to continue until she says that she is satisfied? (Maybe sometime next week.)

- Follow-up questions may arise. A client may assume you are available to answer unlimited follow-up questions after a session is over. How do you like that idea?

- Do your sessions come with a free lifetime warranty of unlimited phone calls and e-mails? Otherwise, how can you break the news to your client?

- When a prospective client has an emergency, does that become *your* emergency?

Vaguely Discontented

Iris was a talker. During her session, she talked incessantly. So maybe I shouldn't have been surprised when, days after the session, she started complaining. There were many phone messages, then a lengthy email:

"I don't feel satisfied. I don't know exactly what I was expecting, but what you did wasn't it.

"I don't feel like you answered all my questions. And I feel like you rushed me. And I didn't get all the information I needed. And I didn't feel heard. And oh, I don't know. I think you should give me a refund."

How you handle such a client is up to you. Personally, I set a fee based on the time spent with a client. In the rare instance when a session doesn't work out, this will become obvious within minutes, so I'll end the session immediately and there's no question of asking for payment. When a session goes all the way to the end, however, I expect to be paid for my time.

If you feel reluctant to do this for your own sake, consider it a service on behalf of your colleagues. Someone like Iris is likely to play the same game with many healers.

Assume that every client is satisfied. If she has a problem, she will let you know. More often, praise goes unexpressed.

Clients expect to be helped from their session; they also expect you to be secure enough to know your own worth. Take it as a compliment if a client is so busy sorting out all that has happened that she doesn't thank you.

Thank you emails, gifts and cards from appreciative clients-- sometimes they come, too. A completely unexpected surprise can just make your day.

I would like to share one example, a belated thank you. When you turn the page, imagine that this message has been sent personally to you. If you like, consider the words as a place-holder message to *you* from future clients. Eventually, if you do sessions for others, you will have many clients like Kaori, and some of them will take the time to send you a great big, bold thank you.

Gratitude Revisited

Months after I did a session with Kaori, this Japanese client sent me a thank you by e-mail. Although she apologized for her English, I felt that the awkwardness of her words made them all the more beautiful:

> You cut a cord of attachment among me and my mother. After session, the situation does not change, as you said. However, myself changed surely. I can start to live in the life of my own.
>
> Though I lived for years, it is the first sense.
>
> I can feel that myself and mother live in the different life. I am very calm. But I am not yet used to feel that feeling.
>
> Actually, this week was my birthday. I have a feeling that at last it was reached my birthday of the truth. I thank you very, very, very much!!!

Step 12. Assign Homework

12 STEPS TO CUT CORDS OF ATTACHMENT

Step 1. Create a Sacred Space
Step 2. Make an Energy Sandwich
Step 3. Activate the Aura
Step 4. Choose Which Cord to Cut
Step 5. Locate the Cord
Step 6. Give Permission
Step 7. Remove the Cord
Step 8. Bandage to Rebalance
Step 9. Write the Dialogue Box
Step 10. Discuss the Pattern
Step 11. Impact Other Relationships
Step 12. Assign Homework
  Assign Creative Homework
  Assign Decision-Making Homework
  Assign Active Homework
  Assign Voluntary Agreements
  Winning Affirmations
  Give the Going-Home Instructions
  Program Water for Healing
  Do the After Picture
  Officially End the Session

LET'S GET PRACTICAL

Cutting your sixth minor cord at Step 12 is a great way to celebrate all you have accomplished so far.

1. Remember, practice your skills by cutting at least 10 minor cords before you cut any major ones.

2. When you do your "Official Reading" of this chapter, read it as if for the very first time.

3. Step 12 will officially complete your learning this method to cut cords of attachment. Afterwards you will own the skill set for Energy Spirituality.

Be proud of yourself; I sure am!

What is a **teachable moment**? At every major stage of growth and learning, there comes a time when everything clicks.

Remember when you first learned to read? No matter how hard you had worked previously, wrestling with phonics or whatever method was popular back in the day, suddenly you could read and it was effortless.

With any major learning in life, one special moment will click it into place. Once everything comes together, for a short time afterwards you become ready to learn at a faster pace than normal. Enthusiastically, you can gobble up huge amounts of information and draw in all the nutrients. This is a teachable moment.

One of them occurs at the end of Step 11. Removing a cord of attachment and understanding its implications, your client has fully released a major limitation in life. How fortunate if the healer recognizes this teachable moment! It can be used to accelerate further learning.

In the next chapter, I'll supply a context to give you a deeper understanding about your involvement in teachable moments. For practical purposes now, it's enough to understand this: Major shifts to an *aura* have been set in motion. Now your client can quickly integrate the results by doing a simple homework assignment. This will hasten benefits of cord cutting for *physical reality*.

Of course, both levels of life can affect each other. Step 12 works powerfully, right at a teachable moment, because of the reciprocal relationship between auras and physical reality.

Are Those Flowers Really So Gorgeous?

Let's say you find a beautiful bouquet of roses for sale. In the store, they're so gorgeous, you can't resist buying them.

Alas, after you bring them home, the poor dears start drooping. By the next day, the flowers are no longer beautiful. In fact, they're obviously dead. Sighing, you fling your bad purchase into the trash.

Half-dead flowers, darn! Why didn't it show?

Actually, it did. A smart consumer will always reads flowers' auras before buying. You know, humans aren't the only ones to have a personal energy field crammed with bits and bytes of information. Right in the store, while shopping for flowers, you can use See It, Read It. Or you can use my favorite, Feel It, Read It.

When flowers display a lively aura, their vitality will produce physical consequences. The flowers will continue to look good for about a week after purchase.

What about flowers with a puny, sad aura? That will soon show physically, too. Sooner or later, the truth of an aura always works its way out to the level of physical reality.

Thank goodness you're no cut flower, having only one chance to blossom. A human being can go through many cycles of blooming and wilting, life and death, all within one lifetime. Based on choice, or prayer, or innumerable other factors, you and your aura can be born again. These days, I think of this as **virtual reincarnation,** a very 21st century opportunity to move through many lifetimes within one earth life.

By cutting a client's cord of attachment, you help him to experience a kind of rebirth into a more evolved lifetime. Well chosen homework hastens this, causing results from your session to display sooner, rather than later.

So go ahead, take advantage of your client's teachable moment and assign some homework.

Introduce Homework

Assigning homework could become your favorite part of a session. Why? Receiving homework is fun. It's a way for you or a client to help yourself. Right now! Free! At this teachable moment!

1. Explain to your client that now is the best time to receive a small homework assignment. It will be easy for him, and take no more than 10 minutes. But the impact can be enormous. Why? His whole mind-body-spirit is adjusting to the cord being gone for good. If your client will do a simple bit of homework just once during the next 24 hours, he will gain huge benefit. Who wouldn't want that?

2. Choose a unique homework assignment. (Specific ideas will follow.)

3. Explain the assignment to your client.

4. Answer questions, then finish Step 12.

Reassure your client that even if he doesn't do the homework, his cord is gone for good. You may be surprised at how eagerly clients are to supplement their sessions. Ten minutes of homework, at just the right time, is a fabulous investment.

If you are a life coach, you will find it tremendously helpful to synchronize assignments with Step 12. If you do not have this skill set, you can do a piece of it at Step 12 by explaining to clients the value of setting goals, then giving your clients homework, and otherwise encouraging them to aim for practical results.

ABUNDANT POSSIBILITIES

Finding homework is fun because you have so many choices. Let's use the example of Isabella to illustrate the many ways you might turn cord items into homework assignments.

Remember Isabella, the unhappy wife from Step 10? Here is the Dialogue Box from cutting her cord of attachment to her husband.

1. Husband: I'm a forceful man. I know what I like.
2. Isabella: I'm not forceful. I'm not sure who I am. I just know that I want to please you more than anything.
3. Husband: I'll push on you to see how much I can get. You'll do anything I want, won't you?
4. Husband: How can I respect you when you constantly grovel?
5. Husband: You don't give me sex often enough.
6. Isabella: I want to be loved, not used. No sex until you recognize who I really am!
7. Isabella: I feel lonely and rejected.
8. Isabella: No matter what I do, it's never enough. I give constantly. You never give back.

Thinking expansively, you may find many possible themes for homework. Here is my short list. (I'll put in parentheses the cord item related to each.)

- Learn how to recognize when her husband acts too demanding. (Cord item 1)
- Focus on anticipating her needs rather than her husband's. (Cord item 2)
- Stop agreeing to things that she doesn't really want to do. (Cord item 3)
- Develop enough social skills to be able to *ask* that her husband show her respect. (Cord item 4)
- Consider whether her husband is *capable* of showing her respect! (Cord item 4)
- Stop working so hard to please someone who doesn't reciprocate. (Cord item 8)
- Develop the social skills to build self-respect in other relationships. (Cord item 8)
- Grow more independent socially, financially and emotionally. (Cord item 8)

Although each Dialogue Box is unique, you'll typically find many growth areas as a possible basis for homework. So how do you choose? That's an important part of your training to do Step 12.

If you are cutting cords of attachment for yourself, resist the temptation to skimp on Step 12. Put on your special cord-cutter's beanie, or whatever hat you wear while healing yourself. Then treat yourself with as much respect as you would any client, doing a great job at homework selection for that very loyal, long-term client who deserves the very best work you have to offer.

Assigning homework for yourself or another client isn't hard once you decide which type of homework is needed *most*. Sometimes that choice will be obvious. But what happens when many life themes come up in the Dialogue Box and subsequent discussion?

Use your full skill set to decide. That includes plain old common sense, training at counseling or healing, your inner guidance, and that advanced non-academic degree you have earned at Earth School. Of course, what else has been part of your skill set, ever since Step 2? Questioning!

Find the Best Homework Topic

You've done Questioning before. Do it now to make an inspired choice of homework assignment.

1. Get Big. Once again, think the name of the Divine Being helping you.
2. Set the intention to find the most appropriate homework for your client.
3. Ask inside, "Which homework topic would help my client most?"
4. Release the question with two Vibe-Raising Breaths.
5. Accept whatever you get, and use that as a basis for choosing the homework.

What if you're not sure you have the wisdom to choose the best homework? Could you just ask the client?

Sure, only do it in such a way that you empower the client, rather than disparage yourself. I'll warn you, though. Guess what will usually happen if you give your client the option to choose his own homework?

About 99 percent of the time, the client will prefer for the healer to do it. Remember, however inept or discouraged you feel sometimes as a spiritual healer, chances are that your client feels worse.

Several different homework options follow. Given all that you have learned about your client during Steps 1-11, you can use one of the following types, to be described in detail:

- Creative Homework
- Decision-Making Homework
- Active Homework Related to Lifestyle
- Voluntary Agreements
- Winning Affirmations

BOGGART REMOVAL

You don't have to be accepted at Hogwarts to follow some sage advice courtesy of J. K. Rolling. In the Harry Potter books and movies, **boggarts** are frightening magical creatures who take the form of a person's worst fear. To remove them, witches and wizards must harness their creativity. They imagine something funny related to the fear, as when timid Neville Longbottom pretends that his grandmother's clothes are being worn by sinister Professor Snape.

Then follows the magic word: *Riddikulus!*

Your client needs no magic word or magic wand to remove old fears. Creativity can work impressively all on its own, especially for healing the subconscious mind.

Creative Homework

Ever since childhood, playing has been good for us: Pretending, acting goofy, flowing creatively. So guess what? Creative play is often the best way to try out new behavior. Assign creative homework to help your client change an old pattern, transform a troubling relationship or practice ending a no-win relationship. How can you find a creative assignment?

1. Discussions with your client in Steps 10 and 11 will alert you to a client's keenest desire for change.

2. During Step 11, invite your client to choose one first step for moving forward, This can become a homework topic for Step 12.

3. Assign a two-part project related to that theme. Ask your client which type of creativity she prefers, such as drawing a picture, writing a poem or letter, doing a dance, singing a song or improvising on a musical instrument.

4. Explain that this creativity will be used for a ceremony to reprogram her subconscious mind. Right from the start, she will say aloud, "Subconscious mind, pay attention, because this is going to be a reprogramming ceremony."

5. Your client creates something related to the *old* pattern. Then she says, "Out with this old pattern."

6. Your client creates something about the *new* pattern. Then she says, "In with this new pattern."

7. A reprogramming ceremony needs to be done just once, preferably within the next 24 hours. It need not be fancy. Actually, it will probably take under 10 minutes. Remind your client. "This homework will speed up results from your session, with the potential to move you ahead by the equivalent of several months."

Exchanging 90 days for 10 minutes just by doing this homework during a teachable moment—not a bad return on your client's investment, is it?

Encouraging Independence

For Isabella's homework I selected the theme of independence. With the cord to her husband gone, she would find it easier to be her own person.

What could help Isabella to figure out what she liked (or felt, or enjoyed) on her own? Creativity can jump-start independence. So, let Isabella's creativity time begin!

Which kind of creativity did she prefer? When I asked, she told me drawing, so I assigned two quick self-portraits:

Part One: Who did she used to be? Small? Holding out her hands and waiting?

Part Two: Who is she now? Isabella can draw herself as she would like to be: Confident, able to protect herself, happy even when alone, and definitely independent.

At a teachable moment, even the simplest creative actions can powerfully reprogram subconscious patterns.

ACTIVATE WILL (AND WON'T) POWER

Taking action in the objective world can be hugely important for improving your client's life. Yet sometimes a cord of attachment has made it virtually impossible for that action to take place. Until you facilitated Steps 1 – 11, your client wasn't clear enough inside to know what she really wanted.

Deciding this is especially important when a cord of attachment relates to a present relationship. (Remember, many cords don't.)

Decision-Making Homework

Now that your client has been set free energetically, use that momentum to make life better. Don't shy away from assigning decision-related homework.

1. Discussions with your client in Steps 10 and 11 will alert you to a client's need for decision about a life choice, such as whether to remain in a particular relationship.
2. Still in Step 11, discuss one decision that your client can make. This need not be final, never to change, but simply the best choice for now.
3. After your client agrees to make this decision, move over to homework creation in Step 12. Ask your client to make a commitment. Will or won't he actively start the decision-making process? To take advantage of the teachable moment, request that this happen within 24 hours of the session.

GENERATING NEW AGREEMENTS

An **Agreement** is a personal commitment to take a particular kind of action or to become a particular kind of person. Once stated aloud, a voluntary Agreement generates immense spiritual power.

One Helpless Victim Finds Gumption

Ruth came in like such a victim that I felt a flicker of doubt I could help her. Sometimes people fall into such a pit of self-loathing and helplessness that they can't summon the strength to get out. Here's a typical sample of Ruth's Before Picture: "What do you feel in your ribcage about personal power?"

"Nothing."

She got that right! Still, Ruth surprised me. She was motivated to change, big time. Here was the pattern in the cord to her husband:

1. *Husband: Angry at life, angry about lots of things having nothing to do with Ruth, but taking it out on her.*
2. *Ruth: What did I do wrong?*
3. *Ruth: Since he's angry at me and I can't fix it, I feel like my whole world is crumbling.*
4. *Ruth: If I can't be a good wife, I have no reason for living.*
5. *Ruth: I must indulge his every whim, begging and appeasing.*
6. *Husband: Not responding to her efforts, except for contempt that she is groveling.*
7. *Ruth: I don't know what else to do to make my marriage a success. Miserable!*
8. *Ruth: What am I SUPPOSED to do? If I can't make him happy, maybe I should kill myself.*

Ruth recognized all the cord items. After discussing them with me, we agreed that Items 2-7 weren't particularly productive or, even, rational. Sure, they were understandable while she had the cord, but now she would have a lot more choice.

Ruth seemed torn about what to do with this relationship. Was the security of her marriage worth the price? To help her decide, I might have given her decision-making homework in which she could make a two-column list.

She could head one column "Staying with My Husband." What were the benefits of staying? What could she reasonably expect to change? How could she lower her expectations?

The other column on Ruth's list would be "Leaving My Husband." Would she be better off? What actions would she take if she made that choice?

Actually, I gave Ruth lifestyle homework instead, as you'll soon see described. When a client is in a vulnerable state, decision-making may not be appropriate. When it is, however, Step 12 is an ideal time to assign it.

ENCOURAGE LIFESTYLE CHANGE

Lifestyle change may seem like the most obvious way to make your client's life better. Except maybe the possibility isn't obvious – not to your client, not at all. Maybe he was so bound up in a relationship that he couldn't begin consider the possibility of real change. Maybe your client tried changing his lifestyle long before coming to you but couldn't act freely because of a cord of attachment. Once freed from this cord, his life can finally improve. A simple homework assignment could encourage such a client to take effective, constructive action.

Active Homework

Remember, you've just done a powerful procedure, so pushing will not be needed. Active homework is most effective when assigned with finesse; collaborate with your client, rather than giving advice. The following method can help you to find the right balance.

1. Ask questions that start your client thinking, such as:
• "Now that you've released this cord of attachment, are you interested in changing the relationship?"
• "With the cord cut, you're freed up energetically. What action can you take, knowing that action will be much easier now?"
2. Brainstorm to find one simple action that your client can take. Discuss this as possible homework.
3. Keep discussing until you and the client can agree on a specific, but not-too-big, homework assignment.
4. Also encourage your client to take action beyond that first 10 minutes of homework. Express interest in what he will choose to do, but don't complicate matters. Next session, your client won't be shy about reporting additional self-assigned projects, and how well they worked.

Lose That Groveling Lifestyle

Which homework did I wind up assigning Ruth, the unhappy wife? Remember her cord item #5? It was, "Husband: Not responding to her efforts, except for contempt that she is groveling."

During Step 10, Ruth didn't understand the concept of groveling. She asked for an example. I described a mother with a spoiled little boy who won't eat lunch, so Mommy follows him around, offering chocolate bars, begging him to do her the favor of eating them. When Ruth's eyes lit up, I knew she she understood.

For homework, Ruth was asked to imagine three different scenes where she would refuse to grovel. Instead of begging she would walk away, or insist on discussing the problem, or make her husband buy his own chocolate bars, etc.

Why did I choose the easier assignment? Ruth needed to make a decision about this relationship, didn't she? So why did I settle for lifestyle homework?

Homework that involves lifestyle decisions or major Agreements must be timed sensitively.

Beware. Sometimes a client will start her session by saying her goal is to make a decision. If a client is receiving physical abuse, urge her to make that decision. But otherwise she might need to develop more strength before she can make a wise decision (or is able to handle the consequences).

When she came for her session, Ruth was fragile. Cutting the cord to her husband would strengthen her. So would some relatively simple homework related to lifestyle. With more strength, Ruth would be in a better position to decide whether or not to stay in her marriage.

PAIRED ASSIGNMENTS

Can one simple session really instigate major lifestyle changes?

I've seen it happen. Removing a cord of attachment can make a huge difference, even if a client has felt stuck for years. For a really ambitious client, you might pair a simple piece of homework with a bigger long-term project. Here are some examples.

Lifestyle Situation: Alcoholic father
- Immediate homework: Find the nearest Al-Anon meeting.
- Long-term lifestyle change: Attend meetings until you have established healthy new behaviors for coping with your father.

Lifestyle Situation: Ex not leaving
- Immediate homework: Act out a short ceremony where you officially say goodbye to that ex-lover.
- Long-term lifestyle change: Find a way to get rid of the suitcases he left in your bedroom. Together, decide on a specific date for him to pick them up. Make it clear that if he misses that date, you will throw his belongings into the trash. Be prepared to do so.

Lifestyle Situation: Bossy spouse
- Immediate homework: Imagine a conversation with a bossy spouse where you manage to stick up for yourself.
- Long-term lifestyle change: In real life, when the spouse acts up, try out that new behavior. Develop consistency with acting this way.

GOAL SETTING AND BEYOND

Maybe your client has set goals before, unaware that a cord of attachment limited his ability to succeed. Now that his aura has healed old limitations, goal setting can work more effectively. You may even be able to help your client go beyond setting goals or making plans. For the most long-lasting results, forge an "official," aligned, and very conscious Agreement.

Voluntary Agreements

Think New Year's Eve. Think birthday. Everyone believes that certain times can be auspicious for a new start. Let your session of Energy Spirituality count as one of these times.

1. Choose whatever seems important as a topic for homework.
2. Remind your client that aura transformation creates a new beginning. Then assign your client to sit down and brainstorm about that new start, making a wish list of new **goals.**
3. Offer a choice of ways to make that wish list:
• Writing down ideas, point by point.
• Drawing cartoons, symbols or meaningful doodles to fill up a page.
• Speaking into a recording device, e.g., CD recorder.
4. Optional: An enthusiastic client can add **plans.** What might she say or do to bring about that goal? Plans can follow each goal, for instance:
• Jamil's *goal* is to stick up for himself when with his bossy boss.
• His *plan* is to write down words he could use at work—different ways that he might speak up for himself.

> 5. Ask your client to *commit* to doing this Agreement-setting homework. Which method would he prefer to use? When can he find the 10 minutes within the next 24 hours?
>
> 6. Once he states his choices out loud, he has begun to forge a new Agreement with every level of himself. Help your client to appreciate the significance of doing this.

Agreements are always made in a context. If your client were simply working from the conscious mind, results would flow only that far. But the 12 Steps to Cut Cords of Attachment bring in the power of the subconscious mind and the Higher Self. And because you are working with your client's choice of Divine Being, any Agreement will be supported by spiritual Source.

This approach is radically different (and far more empowering) than the popular alternative: Passively wait for life events to reveal "what is meant to be."

For a spiritually motivated client, you can explain the technical name for what he is doing by making a new Agreement, then doing related action. He is **co-creating with spiritual Source.**

As appropriate, you can also encourage your client to supplement action by keep track of results and reporting back to you at the next session. (Use this option only when you feel reasonably sure that you will *have* a follow-up session.) Remind your client that every bit of inner healing empowers him to make real changes in life.

Action in the world can be needed to bring a life into balance. Yet sometimes a person can't take the action he desires until his inner balance alters, just what happens with the release of a cord. If a client is willing to schedule at least one more session with you, together, the two of you can start building cumulative results.

Goodbye, Turtle. Hello, Tiger.

Frank told me, "I have the biggest library you've ever seen of metaphysical books." Alas, they weren't helping him to have much of a life. At the time of our first session, Frank was the kind of person who fades into the woodwork.

He asked me to cut a cord of attachment to Andrew, a coworker. Cord dynamics went like this:

1. Frank: Just leave me alone to go about my business.
2. Andrew: What matters around here is that I'm the important one. You'd better act like I'm important. I want you defer to me in every possible way. Nothing is too petty for me to demand your obedience. Unless you help me feel important, I'll slap you down.
3. Frank: How about MY value? You have no idea what I can do. You don't see me.
4. Frank: I'd rather die than be a show-off like you.
5. Frank: How dare you make me seem so small? I'm furious at you.
6. Frank: And I'm even angrier at myself, because I don't let my own light shine.

Discussing the cord, Frank sighed with relief. The healer had pegged it perfectly. Now he could sit back and have the healer (me) announce that all of Frank's anger would magically disappear.

As if! I did say, "You 'go turtle' a lot, don't you?"

The pattern pervaded his aura, so I went on to describe what showed in several different chakras. Whenever someone seemed to belittle Frank, he would go into hiding, just like a turtle crawling into its shell.

Frank admitted this was true. Together we explored goals to change this, and we found one: Speaking up for himself right in the moment when he felt he had something to say. Frank would find this easier to do without the cord that set off the pattern of "going turtle."

For his homework, Frank was asked to write small-sized plans to implement his overall goal of speaking up for himself. What were some situations where he could speak up for himself more? What might he say? What Agreement might Frank make to help himself leave that turtle shell behind?

AURA-APPROPRIATE AFFIRMATIONS

Affirmations are positive statements, carefully chosen to reprogram the subconscious mind. Effective though they can be, affirmations usually take a lot of time to produce results. Can you appreciate why that would be, given what you now know about cords?

Here's an example of a common problem related to affirmations. Tom tries using affirmations for anger management. Every day he repeats his perfectly good affirmation: "I am peaceful."

When temper flares up, Tom berates himself for not having enough faith. "If only I believed," he thinks, "I would get results."

What doesn't Tom know? Every day, he receives a ton of anger through the cord of attachment to his first girlfriend.

In life, there's a natural order for making things work. If you put the cart before the horse, how can you expect the horse to pull it? Affirmations can't work productively while contracted by a much stronger force of negativity that comes from a cord of attachment.

Now that the cord is gone, a client like Tom will receive much better results from using affirmations.

During this special teachable moment, however, don't assign just *any* affirmation. Find out what really resonates with your client's subconscious mind.

HOLISTIC AFFIRMATIONS

Combine physical awareness with affirmations for a winning combination.

1. Find 1-3 major themes from the discussion with your client during Step 11.
2. Construct one affirmation at a time. Make a sentence that is:

- Personal
- Present tense
- Positive
- Believable
- Simple

3. Ask your client to notice how she feels in her body.
4. Have her open her eyes and speak the affirmation three times out loud.
5. Ask your client to notice how she feels now, physically.
6. Repeat 2-5, trying out different affirmations until you can find one that causes your client to feel something significant. This is a winning affirmation.

Assign up to three winning affirmations for homework.

I Feel Passion Now

Naomi asked me to cut the cord of attachment to her father. By Step 12, I understood the wisdom of her choice. In her Before Picture, Naomi noted that she felt tired, confused and struggling. At the end, she checked in with her feelings, then said in a voice filled with surprise, "I feel passion now." Here's what had been in the cord:

1. *Naomi: Helpless, that's how I feel.*
2. *Dad: Everything in our relationship is about what I want.*
3. *Dad: I am effective. You are not. Nor will you ever be.*
4. *Dad: I am MALE and, therefore, superior to any female.*
5. *Dad: I will give you little tests. We'll just see if you ever pass any of them. (I doubt it.)*
6. *Naomi: Whenever I try to make him happy, I fail.*
7. *Naomi: My actions are useless.*
8. *Naomi: My willpower is fading away. This goes beyond merely not feeling confident. I'm losing the ability to even try things. Why bother? No matter how hard I try, I'm going to fail.*

To help Naomi reprogram her subconscious mind, I gave her two affirmations. Alone, they might not have done much. But after releasing the cord, Naomi was wonderfully ready to build her self-confidence:

- I can succeed.
- My choice is always a good choice.

COMFORTABLE CLOSURE

As a facilitator of Energy Spirituality, you have just done psychic-level surgery. Therefore, it is your responsibility to give going-home instructions. It's just as necessary as if you had done surgery at a physical level. Inwardly, your client needs closure.

Even simple self-care after an operation can make a huge difference for smoothing a client's experiences. Repeat instructions like these during Step 12 for every session of Energy Spirituality where you cut a cord of attachment:

Going-Home Instructions

1. Explain that the following going-home instructions will help your client to have the smoothest results possible. Do the following for the next three days.

2. Water—if your client doesn't already drink lots of water, invite him to drink more than usual during the next three days.

3. Sleep—your client may need more than usual during the next three days.

3. Emotions—sometimes strong emotions arise due to re-balancing. In this way, Energy Spirituality resembles any other form of holistic healing. Explain that "If you experience any emotional releasing after your session, don't take it seriously. Just get extra rest. The roughness will pass."

> 4. Optional: If you made a sound recording of your session, recommend that your client listen within 24 hours. This will activate healing energy from the session while your client's subconscious mind is at its most receptive.

Give your client a chance to discuss these going-home instructions. The part about emotions is most apt to need clarification.

Pins and Needles

My favorite analogy about post-session emotions comes from that universal experience of having your foot fall asleep. Ask your client what she does after her foot falls asleep. (Actually, the answers I've heard are quite fascinating.) Steer your client toward remembering that eventually she moves her foot around. Then ask:

"What happens next? Do you feel better instantly?"

Any client who says "Yes" is either in denial or not human. Remind your client about that tricky transition time of shooting pains, sometimes called "pins and needles."

If you didn't know better, you might have thoughts like, "Now I've ruined everything. My foot will hurt forever." Actually, you know the pain is temporary, a transition while circulation returns to your foot.

To conclude, tell your client, "If, and I do mean IF, you should have intense emotions after this session, while waking or sleeping or dreaming, remember the pins and needles. Don't be overly concerned, because the emotional discomfort is just as temporary."

Why would holistic healing cause emotional discomfort, even temporarily?

Allopathic healing, the kind done by a physician, suppresses symptoms. But **holistic healing** rebalances the mind-body-spirit system toward greater wholeness. These side effects can happen after sessions of meditation, Reiki, angelic healing, acupuncture, chiropractic, aromatherapy, etc.

Emotional rebalancing can also occur after the jet-propelled holistic technologies of the 21st century, Energy Medicine, Energy Psychology, and Energy Spirituality.

Temporary moods, physical sensations, even brief pains or twitches can develop as part of the releasing process. These side effects of natural healing are far more benign than the side effects of prescription drugs. The following technique can help.

Program Water for Healing

Water is one of the easiest substances on earth to transform energetically. (To learn about this in depth, see *The Hidden Messages in Water* and other books by Dr. Masaru Emoto.) Here is a co-creation technique I developed to bring results quickly and easily.

1. Hold the cup or bottle of water between your hands.
2. Invite a Divine Being to bless the water. One simple sentence will do it, like, "Tara, please help me to bless this water."
3. Request a particular program, such as "I am strong."

There you have it, a magic potion, brewed instantly! Maybe you will drink a toast to your client right before doing the After Picture.

DO THE AFTER PICTURE

Thank goodness for that Before-and-After Picture. Your sessions don't necessarily involve great drama. Remembering her time with you, a client may be interested by some of the ideas you exchanged, even amazed at how accurately you described her cord items. But the paired "photos" can provide a truly memorable contrast.

Incidentally, when you do sessions for yourself, don't rush past this part of Step 12. It will bring home the personal benefits of working with that awesome healer, you.

Record the Results

Recording results from a session is simple. For an After Picture, you'll repeat what you did for the Before Picture.

1. Use whatever technique you used in Step 3 to read your client's three databanks, e.g., The Call It, Read It technique.
2. Explore the very same three databanks that you researched at the start of your session.
3. Write down each result next to your client's experience with the Before picture.
4. Usually a client will be extremely impressed by the contrast. If not, remind her what changed. Or do some interpreting, as in the second example that follows.

Typically, After Pictures show significant improvement.

A BEFORE-AND-AFTER PICTURE, COMPLETED

Chakra Databank	Before Picture	After Picture
Root: Connection to physical reality	Painful.	Fine. (Client surprised.)
Solar Plexus: Solving conflict in important relationships	Burning.	Burning is almost completely gone.
Heart: How it feels to be YOU right now	A bit cold.	Fine!

A contrast like this speaks for itself, with no comment needed from the healer. Sometimes a little clarification is needed, as in the next example, where results seem more mixed.

If She Did Have Power, Could She Recognize It?

Remember Jessica from our Preview? She had broken up with Mel, her boyfriend of eight years. Good riddance! (That was her attitude, mingled with grief.)
Everything about the session seemed to please this client until we got to her After Picture. Commenting on an after picture is a delicate business. One doesn't want to overstate results. But it isn't fair, either, to let a client's experience of new strength be dismissed as "I feel confused." Jessica welcomed discussion.

Chakra Databank	Before Picture	After Picture
Root: How you relate to the world	Heavy, tense.	Soft. Good. Cushiony.
Solar Plexus: Having power when you are on your own, not in a love relationship	Like a hole.	A little something is there, but I don't know what.
Heart: How it feels to be YOU right now	Confused.	Better, except I still feel confused.

Contrast at Jessica's root chakra was clearly an improvement. What a great symbol about the world feeling safe, as though Jessica's body had turned into a cushion! But she was puzzled by the second part of her Before-and-After picture, the power dynamic.
Jessica asked, "What's the good of having a little something?"
I said, "Could that little something be the start of your power returning?"
Jessica got it. Previously, there had been such a lack of power, she couldn't recognize how power would feel if she had some.
As for the emotional confusion, I encouraged Jessica that it would soon be gone. "Bandage is on for three days, remember? Check back with yourself then."

SAYING GOODBYE TO AN AURA

During the session, you've been reading your client's aura. You have done surgery on it. Bits of your client's aura may be sticking to you, and vice versa. So it's only a matter of spiritual hygiene that, before saying goodbye, you must separate energetically. Easily done.

Aura Seal

Here is a quick but effective way to energetically separate from your client at the end of a session.

1. Request permission to put your hands on your client's shoulders, e.g., "I'm going to seal off your aura, so you can leave as *you* and I can leave as *me*, without our auras being connected."

2. Wait for your client to say yes. (No client of mine has ever refused.)

3. Stand up and lightly place each hand, palm down, on your client's shoulders.

4. Inwardly ask the Divine Being you're working with to help you separate both your auras. Through your hands, feel them separate completely or wait two minutes, whichever comes first.

5. Return to your chair.

What if you don't feel a whole lot happening? Will the aura seal still work?

Yes! And, with practice, you'll become more sensitive about feeling what happens during this simple technique. Meanwhile, trust the Divine Being working with you to fulfill your intention and get the job done.

INVITE FINAL QUESTIONS

A few minutes before a session ends, ask your client, "Any questions before we're done?"

Don't be shocked if, before leaving, your client needs you to repeat things that were previously said in the session. Here are my most popular last-minute requests from clients, along with my quick, end-of-session answers.

- Q. What if the cordee contacts me?
  A. Decide how you want to handle it. You will have more freedom now.
- Q. Will the cord come back?
  A. No, this is a permanent healing.
- Q. Must I stop talking to the cordee?
  A. No. What has changed is that you have been released from an old pattern of energy connection. Talk or not, as you see fit.

Officially End the Session

Everyone needs closure, both clients and healers. So design a simple routine to conclude each session. Here's mine.

Claim Your Happy Ending

1. Out loud, thank the Divine Being(s) invited by your client.
2. Say "This session is ended."
3. Offer your client the choice of a handshake or hug. (If you have been doing the session of Energy Spirituality for yourself, congratulate yourself.)

You can now consider your session complete, whether for yourself or a friend, whether for practice or to change the life of a paying client.

Yes, you have gone through the full sequence of 12 Steps to Cut Cords of Attachment. Still, don't miss our final chapter. It will complete your basic instruction in the 12 Steps to Cut Cords of Attachment.

Review and Overview

The 12 Steps to Cut Cords of Attachment, as you have learned to do them, can help you (and clients) to rebalance life emotionally, physically, spiritually, sexually and socially. No longer need toxic flows of energy endlessly repeat within you, controlling your life without your conscious consent. Let your life as a marionette be over and full freedom begin!

This freedom won't instantly solve all your problems. But every cord properly cut helps supplementary healing methods to work more effectively. Psychotherapy, for instance, can stop repackaging distress from a cord. Meditation will bring more bliss, Reiki healings hold better. Emotional Freedom Technique, good though it is, will not be needed nearly so often.

Having given yourself first aid by cutting cords (and, perhaps, helped a cord-cutting friend), you know that your new skill set has healing potential. In this final chapter, I aim to deepen your perspective about those skills.

Remember The Three Worlds, those human, psychic and spiritual levels that you can access? Given what you know now about using all 12 Steps to Cut Cords of Attachment, which level is most important for bringing results?

The short answer is: *All three.*

And you are learning to dance between them.

296 CUT CORDS OF ATTACHMENT

For the sake of quality control, you took the time to go through all 12 Steps. Now you're poised to appreciate the secret mechanics hidden behind what you have done. To put it bluntly, you deserve to know.

DANCING BETWEEN THREE WORLDS

Never underestimate your power of consciousness. Consider it a big deal that you can move from one spiritual world to another. By now, you know that you can do this easily, quick as a wish. So you might be tempted to take your super-flexible innermost self and its travels for granted.

Don't.

In our metaphysical geography lesson from Step 2, we went through a working definition of The Three Worlds. Now let's seek to understand their significance more deeply. What does it mean that you can, as I put it, **dance between three worlds?**

With just one tiny intention or wish you can shift, in consciousness, from one world to another. Okay, this dance doesn't involve your physical body. Yet all the other qualities of dance can be present: Grace, rhythm, wholeness, presence, expressiveness, movement and joy.

And what do these three worlds, or dance floors, mean energetically?

The Human World is where physical reality seems to be all that counts. Sure, we encounter infinite variety, but that entire infinity is carved out of earthly material. Flesh and bones; blood, sweat and tears; labor and achievement; friends and foes—all of this bears the distinctive quality of life on earth, The First World.

The Psychic World is home to angels, guides, and ghosts. This Second World is also the realm of spirits (plural), in contrast to The World of Pure Spirit, a.k.a., The Spiritual World, the Third World.

What kind of bodies, what substance, do you encounter in The Second World? It is astral material, with varying degrees of fineness and purity.

Reading auras, most (but not all) of the information is located here at the astral level. And, of course, cords of attachment also exist at this level.

Technical point of clarification: Some practitioners refer to cords of attachment as etheric, rather than astral. Yet the more experience you have as a healer, the more obvious it will become to you that the etheric realm is God's world, a realm of perfection. Problems, dangers, fears, pulls and tugs, will either be physical or astral. Cords of attachment, clearly, belong to the latter category.

In **The Spiritual World,** God is experienced with the greatest directness and clarity. Why? The Third World belongs exclusively to Spirit.

As for embodied beings, all the ones here are made of etheric light. Here, for instance, you find the Ascended Masters, Divine Beings who serve humanity. Other Divine Beings are Archangels, those executives among angels.

Besides Archangels and Ascended Masters, The Spiritual World holds information about a person's soul qualities, vibrating at the highest frequencies of the human aura.

A record for each human soul exists here as well. **The Akashic Record,** like the rest of the Spiritual World, is made of etheric material, also known as akasha.

Earlier, we discussed popular ideas about cutting cords. I called your attention to problems of quality control. Without using the 12 Steps to Cut Cords of Attachment, people commonly find that cords of attachment cannot be cut without a struggle, or else that the cords return. Now can you fully understand the most obvious reason why. There is no Energy Sandwich.

Unsuccessful attempts to cut cords are typically done from either the human level or with the help of an astral being. Although spirit guides and angels are the best collaborators for many kinds of holistic work, they exist in the Psychic World. Therefore, these helpers move at a vibration similar to that of the cord itself.

When making an Energy Sandwich, right from Step 2, you request help from a higher vibration than any cord of attachment. Combining *human* and *spiritual* energy, you facilitate cutting cords at the *psychic* frequency in between.

Making this Energy Sandwich is comparable to what professionals do in the construction trade. What if an old, damaged building needs to be demolished? A sturdy construction worker, hard hat and all, could stand well over six feet tall, but he's still way smaller than a 100-foot building.

In terms of our analogy, here is a healer from The Human World trying to make a change at the higher level of the Psychic World.

What if our construction worker gets a big ladder, climbs all the way to the top, and from this vantage point tries to demolish the skyscraper? A really fancy electric ladder could make the man 10 feet higher and provide very stable footing. Even by increasing his reach in this way, however, our construction worker would be pulling sideways on the building. This is not an ideal way to remove a structure at his level or higher.

In terms of our analogy, our healer has teamed up with an astral guide. Being on the same level as a cord of attachment, he has improved his ability to *describe* the problem. Information can flow abundantly. But making a real change is different from giving a good description, and moving something out from its own level will be slow going indeed.

To become successful, a modern construction worker would, obviously, hail a passing spaceship. Just kidding. He's more likely to use a very large tool that can reach down from a higher level than the building itself. Such a tool won't move sideways but down and away. So instead of a fine, sturdy, 10-foot ladder, our construction worker might avail himself of an 89-ton Caterpillar forklift with a reach of 108 feet.

This, of course, is the part of our analogy about demolishing a cord where help comes from a higher source. For cutting cords, you're teaming up with a Divine Being. The higher frequency helps to bring results. Perspective from above, combined with instructions from below, creates change in the middle.

My construction analogy can give you a sense of the scale involved in moving between The Three Worlds. Of course, it is far more graceful to do a dance of healing than to smash concrete and plaster. For cutting cords of attachment, you lift yourself up with consciousness rather than ladders or forklifts. Isn't it ironic? The very people who fear physical heights in The Human World may absolutely adore whizzing upward into The Spiritual World.

Whether you move between The Three Worlds with confidence or trepidation, at least you now know that you are capable of doing this kind of work. You have proven this to yourself by practicing the 12 Steps to Cut Cords of Attachment. Does making an Energy Sandwich feel as though you are dancing yet? With more practice, it will.

DANCING TOO FAST

Certain quality control problems happen when people try to cut cords by using the method popularly described as "Just ask Archangel Michael to cut all your cords." At this point, I'll share with you the name that I privately (until now!) use for this method. I call it the **"Celestial Quickie."**

One quick, simple request—it sounds so appealing. And sometimes a person will add a meaningful prayer or improvise a beautiful visualization. Even a total novice to energy work is likely to love the Celestial Quickie. It can *feel* like a dance.

But this unskilled approach isn't a dance between words, just a leap into faith. Someone who asks for the Quickie may not even be positioning her consciousness at a high enough vibration. Instead, she's doing wishful thinking in The Human World.

Therefore, little may happen except for a temporary mood.

Alternatively, depending on the practitioner's training and level of consciousness, she might succeed at moving into The Psychic World or The Spiritual World. A request for the Celestial Quickie will then bring more powerful results than asking from The Human World. Even so, a quick request for cord cutting won't produce the same results as taking the time and care to do the job thoroughly.

By contrast, what happens with the method you have just learned? Steps 1 through 6 create a strong connection between all Three Worlds, automatically shifting consciousness for both client and healer. The two of you (or just you, if you are cutting your own cords) will inwardly become as wide awake as you are capable of being. You will really start dancing between the Three Worlds, waking up humanly, psychically, and spiritually.

In his Spiritual World, if requested to do a Celestial Quickie, Archangel Michael could certainly cut *all* of your cords of attachment in 10 minutes. But a healing like that would have very limited value in The Human World. In the absence of Steps 9-12, within 24 hours those very same cords (or their equivalent) are likely to return.

What, doesn't a Divine Being care enough to do a thorough job? That's not the problem.

An etheric-level being like Archangel Michael lives in bliss. As you may have noticed, human life involves more than bliss. To us, relationship problems, survival needs, fear, pain and all the rest seem very real. You can't expect a Divine Being to instantly provide precisely the human insights we require to heal fully.

Remember the saying, "Heaven helps those who help themselves"? It helps to co-create with the Divine, even when we receive miracles. Teaming up, we supplement Divine grace with human wisdom. A Divine Being gets to live in bliss; humans get to evolve. And, thus, reality at Earth School teaches us important lessons. No wonder your cord to Aunt Matilda is different from your cord to Uncle Sam. The special qualities of pain or fear, etc., don't seem trivial while you're in the throes of suffering.

Therefore, for results to be real here in The Human World, a client must be consciously and humanly present before cords are cut. And the healer needs to be inwardly awake, to the greatest extent possible, holding a space in all Three Worlds.

To receive real results in The Human World, we must focus on healing one cord at a time. When you follow the full sequence of all 12 Steps, both the healer and client will benefit from doing the complete process—yes, all 12 Steps every time. It isn't enough to theoretically know what the sequence will be.

Completing Steps 9-12 matters just as much as the physical cord cutting. Actually, that final Step 12, the homework, may matter most of all. Here's why.

The surgery itself, Steps 7-8, is done at the *astral* level, not the lower-vibrational *human* level. Whenever an aura improves, results eventually trickle down to the human level; it's the spiritual equivalent of "trickle-down economics." The technical term for this is **out-picturing.**

For instance, what if you help a married client to release sexual problems by cutting a cord of attachment? Although a good start on a better sex life, still it is only a start. Your client will need to reach out and touch his partner before results can occur physically. Whenever the potential for better sex produces a real-life "Wow!", that will be an example of out-picturing.

Without homework, out-picturing will happen eventually. But it might take years.

At Steps 10 and 11, you have helped the client to *preview* the likely out-picturing, Because a particular cord has been cut, there will be certain "logical consequences."

Just having this conversation can accelerate the process of manifestation. Results can out-picture faster because a client has consciously appreciated what could change.

At Step 12, you hasten the out-picturing even more. Your homework assignment will use the power of your client's free will to bring results faster.

Your timing for this homework assignment is perfect when you do it at Step 12. This is your client's teachable moment.

Incidentally, what would happen if you gave the very same homework assignment *before*, rather than *after*, cutting a cord?

That would about as efficient as washing the dinner dishes before you serve any food, just to save time.

By assigning homework as the last Step of healing, you add the missing piece, and maybe even some missing peace.

GRADUATION CELEBRATION

So you are ready to graduate, you intrepid spiritual healer. You have cut at least six minor cords. At the rate you're going, soon you will have cut 10 minor cords, the minimum recommended before you begin to cut major cords.

Your practice so far combines direct experience of the 12 Steps with a theoretical understanding that spans all Three Worlds. To honor your graduation, let's celebrate! Here comes a review of all 12 Steps to Cut Cords of Attachment with a sample session.

For this concluding example, I've chosen an average session. Sure, I have facilitated many sessions that were more dramatic, cord-cuttings that released rape or incest or physical abuse, that dismantled intricate patterns of hatred, jealousy or lies.

If you do many sessions of Energy Spirituality, the law of averages will supply you with plenty of clients who have intense problems like these. But you won't find major drama in most of the cords that you cut (including those cords of attachment you cut for yourself).

What will you accomplish during a typical session of Energy Spirituality? You'll facilitate the removal of somebody's fear or pain, the not terribly dramatic everyday stuff that robs days and nights of their joy. In the following sample, you can follow the flow of all 12 Steps.

Would you take the same approach as I did? Maybe not. That's not bad. You are becoming an awesome healer in your own right. With this new, reliable skill set, you can do healing *your* way.

To add depth to the following example of cutting cords of attachment, I will stop the narrative periodically to pose some common questions. If you wish, answer them before I do. And, as you read the following, imagine that you are here, right by my side, with this teacher who is so proud of you.

The Real Monster

These days, we hear plenty of tales about "Failure to Launch," where an adult child will extend adolescence by living at home. Bonnie could have launched, but instead she stayed home to help her mother. A successful professional, Bonnie was beautiful inside and out. She kept thinking that she shouldn't leave home until she could help her unhappy mother feel better.

But this mother was far from grateful. She complained constantly. Supposedly, Bonnie was selfish and self-centered, with a negative attitude that repulsed everyone. Could the constant accusations be true?

Nothing about this problem was mentioned initially. Instead, here is what Bonnie told me about her intention:

"Everywhere I go, strangers tell me I look like an understanding person. Read my aura. Tell me if they are right. Is it true that I'm a good person?"

Bonnie chose to Get Big with Jesus. She did a nice job with her Before Picture—seemingly surprised that I asked her to do some of the work, and yet *fascinated that she could read her own aura so well with the Call It, Read It technique. As we discussed her aura further, my new client trusted our session more. She felt safe to be herself, no hiding needed.*

Soon she was ready to refine her intention for her session. I was glad. Surely Bonnie deserved more from Energy Spirituality than to confirm the opinions of strangers.

Which Steps have been done so far? If you answered 1-3, you're right. Even an average session won't necessarily go in apple-pie order, however. Soon I went back to refine Bonnie's intention. But let's pause here. Any questions?

Since she wanted to find out if she was a good person, did you check her aura right away and tell her what you got?

No matter what a client requests, your job is never telling someone whether she is "good" or "bad." Obviously, this client needed encouragement, so I gave it extra generously. But flattery, just to make her feel good for five minutes? Not from this healer!

I'm not coordinated enough to simultaneously read an aura and do other things, like the different steps of cord cutting. Should I stop from time to time? Won't it sound weird if tell my client, "Excuse me. I need to slow down and take another peek at your aura"?

Work at your own comfortable rhythm, and ask whatever you need to ask. Usually it's only important to check out an aura in Steps 3, 5 and 7. As for sounding weird, no matter what you say, with this kind of work somebody is bound to consider you weird. So what?

What did you learn about Bonnie's aura?

First, I discovered that her sexuality was under siege, with lots of old pain, confusion and frustration.

Her second most important growth area was communication, at her throat chakra.

Besides that, Bonnie had a fabulous root chakra, plus significant strength at her third eye.

At the heart chakra, I found wonderful qualities, but noted extreme turbulence at the present time. Was she stable? Definitely.

These first impressions were all I needed in order to facilitate her session.

With an initial aura reading, surely you don't take all day going into huge detail. Or do you?

Not unless your client has booked an all day session! A quick glimpse will tell you whether your client is basically stable, which will help you decide whether it is appropriate to cut a cord of attachment.

What would you do if the client hadn't been stable? What if she was a walking, talking wreck?

I'd read her aura in detail, emphasizing gifts of her soul. Then I'd use techniques from the rest of my skill set. Somehow, I would find a way to honor her intention, slipping in techniques that would help her to have some improvement.

When you did Bonnie's Before Picture, did you start with her area of greatest pain?

Never start there. Instead, begin with an area where your client has a moderate degree of pain or releasing. That way, the Before Picture won't horrify your client, yet there will still be plenty of room for improvement at the After Picture.

With this client, you say that sexuality was her biggest issue. What if it were only a moderately important issue? Would you include it in her Before Picture?

Guess which is the big taboo subject to avoid mentioning at all unless your client brings it up first? Unless your client's intention involves sexuality, don't include it *anywhere* in the Before Picture.

Clients feel exposed enough as is. Besides, you're not obligated to tell a client all that you notice.

Intention, Refined

Refining Bonnie's intention was easy once I had gained her trust by reading her aura. I asked, "Why does it matter what other people think about you?"

Turned out, Bonnie was looking for something to give her confidence until her life started "working better. "

> *And what about her life wasn't working? "Oh, my relationship with my mother, for one thing."*

Here was my opportunity to explain about cutting cords of attachment. Bonnie seemed to wake up within her eyes, and she began nodding her approval. Now that our session had some real juice, we were ready to change Bonnie's official intention for the session.

Restated, Bonnie's intention was, "To help me release unnecessary conflict with my mother, plus whatever else will make my life work better for me."

Thus, after a quick zip back to Step 1, we were ready for Step 4. So let's pause for more questions.

Why would you presume that a client's intention isn't good enough, and decide that you must change it?

While it's clearly important to honor a client's goals, you want your session to have depth. Question any far-from-self, way-too-general intention like this one. Think about it. Why would your client *need* reassurance that she's a good person?

What other intentions would you flag?

"Meant to be" intentions are questionable, such as "I want to find out if I am on the right path" or "I want to know who is my soul mate." Research your client's aura to learn what makes a general intention seem so urgent. Or ask her directly: "What is happening in your life right now that makes you care so much about your path?" Aim to uncover the present problem.

Maybe a client will choose something general because she feels like a hopeless case. What if she has oodles of problems?

No matter how bad things are, your client knows which problems seem most pressing. Usually she will bring out a biggie right after your conversation turns specific. Other times she will give a whole list, where an item or two jumps out more than the rest. One way or another, you will be able to choose an appropriate intention for the session.

For instance, let's say that your client gives you a list of five problems. While mentioning one of them, her eyes narrow, her posture stiffens, rage shoots out of her aura and you feel a 7.9 earthquake on your inner Richter scale. Bingo!

The Biggie

Bonnie listed several areas where her life might improve. Her understated language was endearing, especially when she said, "Oh, my relationship with my mother, for one thing."

Despite the casualness of her words, Bonnie's body language and aura revealed that this was a serious topic.

What happened when I researched whether there was a cord of attachment worth cutting? Whoa! The cord impact was huge. And we definitely had permission to cut this particular cord.

To locate it, I used Questioning. The cord walloped me at my own solar plexus. So I looked at this part of her aura and, sure enough, saw a huge cord right there.

Ready through Step 5 now, let's answer more questions.

Could you use more than one method to locate the cord? Should you?

Should you? No. Testing and retesting yourself will only slow down your development as a spiritual healer.

But sometimes extra information will simply come to you. It's as if you were picking ripe cherries off a tree. You aim for one, but several extra cherries just tumble into your hand. This is like what happened to me. Besides receiving information from Questioning, I spontaneously felt it and saw the cord.

Wait, you're going to do surgery to somebody's aura. Don't you need to make sure that your location for the cord is ultra-precise?

Remember, this kind of surgery is co-created with a Divine Being who will do any fine tuning necessary. Unlike physical surgery, cords are cut as part of an easy flow. So you're better off staying in that flow, rather than worrying about precision. As soon as you start double-checking, you risk disrespecting yourself and the information that you've been given.

Permission Fully Given

When we started the Permission Statement, Step 6, Bonnie began to look worried. First she said, "I now give permission." Then she stopped. She blurted out, "What will happen to my mother?"

Although this had been covered before, Bonnie needed extra reassurance that cord cutting wasn't going to hurt her mother in any way. We spent about five minutes discussing what would and wouldn't change. Then Bonnie was ready to finish her Permission Statement.

The cord moved out easily. What was noteworthy about Step 7? The cord was enormous, extending all the way from Bonnie's waistline to right below her breasts.

For her bandage, she chose diamonds, emeralds and a great big crystal. Making room for her gigantic bandage, soon I was standing right against the wall. I asked, "Do you mind if your bandage isn't any bigger than this?"

Bonnie laughed. She needed to laugh. This was a serious healing for her, as became obvious when I diagrammed what was in this cord of attachment.

Steps 6-8 were now complete. Surgery accomplished! And, just as in a regular session, let's immediately diagram the relevant Dialogue Box. Save any questions or conversation for later.

Conflict Within Cords

What was in that cord? Here was the pattern I diagrammed from Bonnie's cord to her mother at Step 9:

1. *Bonnie: I feel alone, emotionally abandoned.*
2. *Mother: You should care more about me. You should fix all my problems.*
3. *Mother: You should meet all my needs.*
4. *Mother: My life is so hard. I've sacrificed too much already. You owe me.*

5. *Mother: Anger comes out toward you. Or sometimes I send you self-pity. The assorted emotions I send your way may seem completely random.*
6. *Bonnie: I'm scared to feel my feelings. If I pay close attention to myself, maybe I'll find out that I'm as messed up as she is. Pleasing others is safer.*
7. *Mother: You're not satisfying me. Do more for me.*
8. *Bonnie: Guilt that I'm not "successful" at making my mother happy.*

Okay, let the questions flow.

When you're going into detail like you did here at Step 9, do you ever feel scared? What if you're completely, totally wrong?

Being wrong with cord items is highly unlikely. In other aspects of life, I have my share of insecurities. Not here. The Steps just work.

As a newbie, if you have moments of self-doubt, blow them away. Literally! Take some extra Vibe-Raising Breaths.

Bonnie's mother sounds a lot like my mother. Could I be dealing with my own unfinished business when I diagram someone else's cord?

Should the same pattern comes up again and again, or you have several clients who don't agree with your description of what's in *their* cords, then it's time to consider help for your own healing.

Otherwise, know that you will often attract clients whose experiences have been similar to yours. Why *wouldn't* you attract these very clients? You have the perfect background to help them. And now, Step 9 is complete, so on to the next steps in the sequence.

What Might Change?

In the cord, Bonnie had received anger on a random basis (Cord item 5). That was over. Sure, her mother might still throw tantrums, which Bonnie would deal with as best she could. What changed was having anger pour endlessly, and unchecked, into Bonnie's own aura.

To help a client like Bonnie understand this change, you could ask her to imagine a big fire hose aimed at her. Whether she meant to or not, Mom used to squirt globs of ugly orange paint through the hose, and they would always reach Bonnie right in the gut. Well, the fire hose wasn't squirting any more. Could this make for an easier life?

One of the themes flowing through that hose was that Bonnie couldn't do enough to satisfy her mother (Cord item 7). Energetically, that was over now. Would her mother suddenly become grateful?

Don't count on it. Bonnie was the one who had decided to change. Now she was free to consider whether it would be worth her while, constantly trying to lift up someone who didn't want to be lifted.

Bonnie was a sensible woman. Apart from the cord, her aura showed plenty of strength. How long, now, would she persist at the thankless—and, frankly, impossible—task of pleasing her mother?

Discussing cord items at Step 10 can bring out a lot of questions from clients. Maybe you have some questions, too.

Did you ever ask Bonnie what was going on with her mother in everyday life?

Definitely. The healer is always allowed to ask questions, and I chose to do this during Step 10. After Bonnie recognized all the cord items, I did ask her to describe the relationship.

She explained that she still lived at home. She stayed home despite being in her thirties, despite having a successful career, and despite her mother's financial independence.

So why did your client choose to stay?

I asked her this, too. Bonnie said she kept hoping that she would be able to help her mother become happy.

If this were an investment, surely it would qualify as throwing good money after bad. In this relationship, Bonnie received no dividends. Instead she was given exactly the opposite, constant criticism. This included the absurd assertion that she was a bad person.

Discussing Bonnie's choices with the cordee gracefully brought us to a more general discussion about logical consequences. Removing one cord pattern can affect all of a client's relationships. What logical consequences would we find in Step 11?

Important Logical Consequences

Cord items 1, 6, and 8 had all kept Bonnie feeling bad about herself. Distant from her own feelings and waiting for others to offer approval—wasn't that exactly how she had come to this session? Finally that could start to change.

At the gut level, Bonnie's deep sense of self had been poisoned by the cord to her mother. Without this poison, Bonnie could grow more confident, and perhaps she might now have incentive to choose friends who reciprocated her caring ways.

Step 11 is a delight to do with a client. It brings an opening into possibility. Once you get into the flow of this conversation, nothing is easier. If you're new to the process, however, you may have questions. Let's hear some.

What would keep Bonnie from immediately forming a cord to another relationship with another taker, somebody else who would be as bad as her mother?

While she had that cord of attachment to her mother, Bonnie accepted a way of life in which she constantly gave to an ungrateful recipient. Without the full procedure for cutting cords of attachment, Bonnie *would* most likely create a similar situation with somebody else.

Further sessions would could enhance her prospects for a better life—whether additional sessions of Energy Spirituality or a referral for psychotherapy, regression therapy, etc. But within the context of what can be accomplished in just one session of healing work, the results for Bonnie were huge.

Basically, Steps 8-12 of Cutting Cords of Attachment guard against recurrence of a client's original problem. In particular, Steps 10 and 11 are done at a critical time of transition, where your client's aura has moved out of toxic patterns.

Right after removing a cord, a client's conscious mind is ready to question old assumptions. Equally important, her subconscious mind is primed for change.

In terms of The Three Worlds, change and repair are occurring at the psychic level. Meanwhile, your client continues to be irradiated with spiritual energy from the Divine Being in charge of the surgery. And you, as the healer, hold the space that I call an Energy Sandwich, which is present both humanly and spiritually.

This is the *energetic context* for Steps 10 and 11. Conversation during these steps is expressly designed to safeguard against backsliding. Admittedly, the words are just conversation, with no guarantee that life will improve. Can any healing work guarantee that?

My discussion with Bonnie during Step 11 helped her to ask questions like these:

- What was her sense of herself as a person? Did this have to depend on the opinion of someone who would never be satisfied?
- What did Bonnie expect from a close relationship, anyway?
- Could she recognize the signs of one-way giving?
- Was Bonnie ready to choose relationships that would be 50-50? If she wasn't ready yet, what would it take?

So, those are questions I might ask a client. What questions do you have to ask me as a healer?

Just one: Did you spend a year of therapy discussing all these issues?

Okay, our session lasted just an hour, with an open door for Bonnie to return. What mattered was that Bonnie began to ask these questions. In her own way, she would be able to work out a solution that satisfied her.

I do encourage all clients to consider follow-up sessions of Energy Spirituality. That represents a **time commitment** about halfway between having the occasional psychic reading and long-term psychological counseling.

Here is what I gave Bonnie as homework at Step 12.

Bonnie's Homework

Seldom does homework from a session need to take more than 10 minutes. Given at Step 12, a client's homework is custom designed to take advantage of the teachable moment occurring right after cutting a cord of attachment and discussing the logical consequences.

To assign homework, I used the Questioning technique. (Yes, I really do use exactly the same techniques I have shared with you in this book.) Then I assigned Bonnie to make a list with two columns:

*Heading 1: What I **can** expect from my relationship with my mother.*

*Heading 2: What I **can't** expect from my relationship with my mother.*

By considering this relationship objectively, and with the toxic Mother-cord now gone, Bonnie might surprise herself.

What I **didn't** tell Bonnie is something that you can appreciate, since you are a healer rather than a client. The very act of questioning and evaluating a relationship was what mattered most about this homework assignment.

Like a muscle that has started to atrophy, Bonnie's self-authority circuits needed a good workout. This assignment was a way to help Bonnie start flexing those muscles.

During our conversation at Step 11, Bonnie began to question why she still lived at home at all. Living with her mother, Bonnie's self-esteem was constantly under attack. Before our session, she used to believe that if only she worked hard enough, she would eventually be able to make her mother happy.

Not especially rational, this expectation made complete sense given what was in her cord of attachment. Recycling 24/7, that cord had kept Bonnie trying.

Now, however, she had no compelling reason to keep living at home, other than force of habit. It takes self-authority to overcome inertia. Bonnie was assigned to ask questions that could motivate her to take action.

And now, what about you and *your* healer's questions?

People make lists all the time, but what does that really accomplish? How do you know Bonnie won't just be in a good mood temporarily, make a list for 10 minutes, and never change a thing, really?

Bonnie's homework was given in the context of major change to her aura. Therefore, a short list can have the greatest possible impact.

When people find themselves stuck in life, being influenced by toxic cords 24/7, how easy is change? It can require monumental willpower, decisive action, or even an intervention. Making a list seems inconsequential by comparison.

For perspective, however, let's bring back our earlier analogy about the fire hose. While her cord dumped the equivalent of orange paint onto Bonnie, gallons of paint every minute, some little list on a piece of paper would be drenched along with everything else.

Without the energy flow from the cord, however, her list could remain readable.

Experience will prove to you that the 12 Steps to Cut Cords of Attachment really do change lives. A client's relationship to the cordee will feel (and be) different energetically. Given this energetic freedom, other relationships can change, too. All changes are in the direction of your client becoming the kind of person he or she has always wanted to be.

What about your dreams for what you have always wanted to be? Maybe those dreams didn't originally include working in the 21st century field of Energy Spirituality.

Well, you can bring healing now, for yourself and others. And maybe this skill set will add scope to your earlier dreams. Working as a pioneer, you can use your lifelong gifts to help people change for the better. You can explore to your heart's content, learning and serving as part of the world's growing community of spiritual healers.

Isn't it exciting to know that you now own all 12 Steps to Cut Cords of Attachment? May this skill empower you for the rest of your life!

Your Stories

I welcome your stories of personal healing and descriptions of your successes with clients. Email them to my current email address (at this writing, RoseRosetree@Verizon.net) or write to Rose Rosetree, 116 Hillsdale Drive, Sterling, VA 20164-1201.

I look forward to reading about what you, personally, discover when cutting cords of attachment.

If you have questions, I invite you reserve a session of Personal Mentoring, in person or by phone. To arrange this, email rose@rose-rosetree.com or call 703-450-9514. It would be my delight to spend quality time with you, coaching you and helping you to apply your gift set to the skills involved in sessions of Energy Spirituality.

A personal session is the appropriate time to discuss your questions at length. Otherwise, unfortunately, I am not available to answer questions by phone or email. As a healer yourself, you may be in a position to understand why. If not yet, I hope you will soon!

Further Training and Healing

If you are interested in the fullest possible training at 12 Steps to Cut Cords of Attachment™, this book has given you a solid foundation. To refine your skills, I offer Intensives which can move your work forward by several months or, even, years. For an up-to-date schedule, see www.rose-rosetree.com.

What if you would prefer to bring me to your area to give an Intensive? Invite me (preferably by email) and we'll discuss how to make it happen.

Telephone sessions of Personal Mentoring are also available. For information:

- Visit www.rose-rosetree.com
- Email to rose@rose-rosetree.com
- Call 703-404-4357
- Or send your written request (with a stamped, self-addressed envelope, please) to:

Further Training with Rose Rosetree
Rose Rosetree, LLC
116 Hillsdale Drive
Sterling, VA 20164-1201

How does skill at cutting cords develop? In my experience, there are two directions for growth.

■ One involves *knowledge*, such as becoming comfortable with your personal gift set.

■ The other involves bringing clarity to the *knower*. To what degree are you now using gifts of the soul that show in your aura? How much stuff is in the way? Whenever you remove "stuff" you will enhance the quality of every skill you possess.

This book has helped you with knowledge, the first way to develop skill at Energy Spirituality.

Using this knowledge to heal yourself, or by trading sessions with a buddy, you will also develop as a knower. In addition, other healing modalities and practitioners can become important resources.

One of those resources might be the one-on-one sessions I do with clients. (Yes, I call them sessions of "Energy Spirituality.") And they do include my facilitating the 12 Steps to Cut Cords of Attachment.

Besides removing cords, your telephone session with me could include reading your face and/or aura. Regression Therapy is another option. You will find FAQs galore at www.rose-rosetree.com. Use information on the previous page to set up an appointment.

Annotated Bibliography

Our bibliography for cutting cords would not be complete without links to websites and blogs. You'll find these at the Online Supplement to this book, at www.cutcordsofattachment.com. Here follow my strongest recommendations for the best books to prepare you for a career in Energy Spirituality.

FOR ALL HEALERS

Bill Bauman, Ph.D. *OZ Power.* St. George: Center for Soulful Living. 2005. www.billbauman.net
Here Bill shares what he has learned from decades as a practitioner of Energy Medicine, Energy Psychology and Energy Spirituality.

Winn Claybaugh. *Be Nice (Or Else!) And What's in It for You.* Laguna Beach: Von Curtis Publishing. 2004. www.beniceorelse.com
People skills for the healer—so many books have been written on this topic, but I've never seen one better than Winn's.

ENERGY MEDICINE

Donna Eden and David Feinstein. *Energy Medicine.* New York: Jeremy P. Tarcher/Putnam. 1998. www.innersource.net

A complete education between covers, here is the classic work in the emerging field of Energy Medicine. Donna's wisdom, creativity and stubbornness shine through the pages. If you are willing to do your part, she can help you heal.

Mona Lisa Schulz, M.D. Ph.D. *Awakening Intuition: Using Your Mind-Body Network for Insight and Healing.* New York: Three Rivers Press. 1999. www.drmonalisa.com
What is the role of a medical intuitive? Might you have talent in this specialty? Consult the neuropsychiatrist.

ENERGY PSYCHOLOGY

Gary H. Craig. *The EFT Course on DVD.* Coulterville: World Center for EFT. www.emofree.com
The founder of Emotional Freedom Technique gives you permission to make and distribute up to 100 free copies of this 13-hour course in his easy-to-learn, yet powerful, healing technique.

David Feinstein, Gary Craig, and Donna Eden. *The Promise of Energy Psychology: Revolutionary Tools for Dramatic Personal Change.* www.innersource.net
Energy pathways in the body are in constant motion with other energies. This book explains how to shift these energies to improve mental and physical health.

Martha Beck. *Leaving the Saints: How I Lost the Mormons and Found My Faith.* New York: Three Rivers Press. 2006. www.liveyournorthstar.com
Brilliant and beguiling, Martha is an extraordinary writer. In this autobiographical work, the life coach recounts her struggles to overcome sexual abuse. This is also a masterwork about exiting a cult.

Thus, Martha's book will inform you about two major themes that can show up when you work with a variety of clients. Besides that, Beck models qualities that could serve any practitioner of Energy Psychology.

ENERGY SPIRITUALITY

Tantra Maat. *Embodying Your Truth s Daily Reality (Audiobook).* 2007. Sacramento: Metapoints. www.metapoints.com
Listening to this CD set, you'll hear a gentle but passionate, heart-centered voice. One of the world's great masters of Energy Spirituality, Tantra can move you far out of your current paradigm and into your future.

Katrina Raphaell. *Crystals and New Age #1: Crystal Enlightenment: the Transforming Properties of Crystals and Healing Stones.* Santa Fe: Aurora Press. 1995. webcrystalacademy.com
Are you interested in crystals as a component of Energy Spirituality? Then you owe it to yourself to read Katrina's entire trilogy. Read her aura from photos in the book and you will find that she really does have the standing to write about "Crystal Enlightenment."

James Hillman. *The Soul's Code: In Search of Character and Calling.* New York: Warner Books. 1997.
Let the visionary psychologist inform your approach to spirituality. Add Deeper Perception. Stir. Serve to humanity!

Thomas Moore. *Care of the Soul: Guide for Cultivating Depth and Sacredness in Everyday Life.* New York: Harper Perennial. 1994. www.careofthesoul.net
Moore is an outstanding exponent of spirituality, as well as a thought-provoking writer.

Chrissie Blaze. *Workout for the Soul: Eight Steps to Inner Fitness.*
Fairfield: Aslan Publishing. 2001. www.chrissieblaze.com
    Blaze helps to enliven the deep energy connection needed for
Energy Spirituality.
    So many paths are available, with related books and websites.
But you'll seldom find a writer with the grace and purity of this
particular teacher.

MORE BOOKS BY ROSE ROSETREE

Let Today Be a Holiday: 365 Ways to Co-Create with God
Published the year before *Cut Cords of Attachment,* this how-to
can greatly add to your skill set with Energy Spirituality. Featuring
over 450 techniques, *Holiday* is a daybook. But you can also browse
at will, strengthening your Gift Set for helping clients.

Aura Reading Through All Your Senses
Here Rose pioneers her easy-to-learn method of Aura Reading
Through All Your Senses®. This book shows how aura reading can
improve relationships, health, even your choices as a consumer. The
how-to includes over 100 techniques.

Empowered by Empathy
Rosetree's book was the first to show how to use spiritual awareness
to turn inborn gifts OFF or ON at will. This contrasts with more
common approaches, behavior based, such as "strengthen your
boundaries." Energy Spirituality uses the power of consciousness to
bring empaths cumulative empowerment and true peace of mind.
(Both Print and Audiobook Editions are available.)

The Roar of the Huntids (A Novel for Empaths)
This spiritual thriller is a coming-of-age story about Energy Spirituality. Set in the year 2020, the story is spiced with social and po-

litical satire, plus a fast-moving plot, romance, and quirky characters (some of whom are empaths and some who are definitely not).

The Power of Face Reading
Rosetree has been called "The mother of American physiognomy." Her system of Face Reading Secrets (R) brings you soulful interpretations of physical face data, with nuanced but highly accurate readings about personal style—an easy, useful addition to your skill set for doing Energy Spirituality.

Wrinkles Are God's Makeup: How You Can Find Meaning in Your Evolving Face
In the 5,000-year history of reading faces for character, this is the first to explore how faces change over time. Using comparison photos, you learn to become a spiritual talent scout.

Many of Rose Rosetree's titles are available in foreign editions. For links, see the publisher's website, www.womensintuitionworldwide.com.

In the U.S. and Canada, order Rose's books 24/7 with this toll-free number: 800-345-6665.

WEBSITE RESOURCES

Whatever your strongest interests with deeper perception, you can find the latest developments at one of these websites:

- www.cutcordsofattachment.com
- www.aurareadingmadepractical.com
- www.co-createwithGod.com
- www.empoweredempath.com
- www.facereadingsecrets.com

Index

Rose Rosetree is the founder of Energy Spirituality. Her academic education includes degrees from the United Nations International School and Brandeis University; graduate study in social work and education.

Rose's how-to books (including a national bestseller in Germany) are available through her website, www.rose-rosetree.com.

Over the past 37 years, she has given more than 750 media interviews, with her work praised in publications as varied as *The Los Angeles Times*, *The Washington Post*, *The Washington Times*, and *The Catholic Standard*.

About You

In this age of information, we're tempted to leap from one book to the next, one technique or project to the next. Let me invite you to stop for a moment and look before you leap.

What has this book taught you about YOU?

What did you learn about your personal gift set?

How do the skills you have claimed through this book complement the rest of your personal skill set?

Cutting cords of attachment, what results have you gained so far?

Have you had the privilege, yet, of facilitating this kind of healing for somebody else? What did that experience teach you?

Now that you have gone through the whole book, your personal goals for cutting cords may have changed. What is your latest thinking? How would you like to use what you've learned? You can make such a difference by cutting cords of attachment. What is one worthy goal, something to aim for right now?

ONE FINAL QUIZ

Are cords of attachment one of the major causes of human confusion and suffering? YES

To remove a cord permanently, does it take more than a quick request? YES

Do cords contain useful information for reprogramming the subconscious mind? YES

Can I really succeed at using the 12 Steps to Cut Cords of Attachment™? YES

Is aura reading required to cut cords with quality control? YES

Is aura reading also a survival skill for the 21st century? YES

Do I have a complete, even glorious, gift set for reading auras? YES

Using it, can I read 50 databanks of information in any chakra I choose to explore? YES

Does cutting cords in this way produce both short-term and long-term benefits? YES

Can I help others as well as myself by removing cords of attachment? YES

Will this skill set complement my other skills for psychological, physical, and/or spiritual healing? YES

Learning the 12 Steps to Cut Cords of Attachment, can I serve humanity as part of an informal community of healers in the emerging field of Energy Spirituality? YES

It has been my delight to teach you.
If you have enjoyed what you read,
please invite others to buy this book
and learn this "cutting-edge" skill.
—*With best wishes from Rose*